INTRODUCTION

Last school year, you probably completed your very first state standardized test. The key to taking tests is developing good study habits and test taking skills. This book will teach you and your Guide strategies that will help you be an excellent learner. You will learn about rubrics and how they are used to write great answers to essay (open-ended) questions. This year, you will not only continue building skills to be an independent learner, but you will also learn how to be a successful test taker.

3, 2, 1 Blast Off! is a workbook of activities that was created for your fourth grade year. In fourth grade, you will be required to take several state standardized tests that will have you writing more than ever. You will not only have to answer questions, but you will also have to "explain your brain." That means you will have to write about how you know an answer is correct. Don't worry if you don't fully understand what "explain your brain" means. This book will teach you the vocabulary of test taking. You will also review tips for time management, setting goals, and study skills. Learning how to be a great test taker will help you be a successful student now and in the future.

ICON / CHARACTER KEY

lesson title

lesson number

approximate time in
minutes needed to
complete each lesson

lesson body
(quoted information
represented in blue)

section heading

tabbed lesson
grouping
(groups of 20)

lesson continued on
back of page

page number

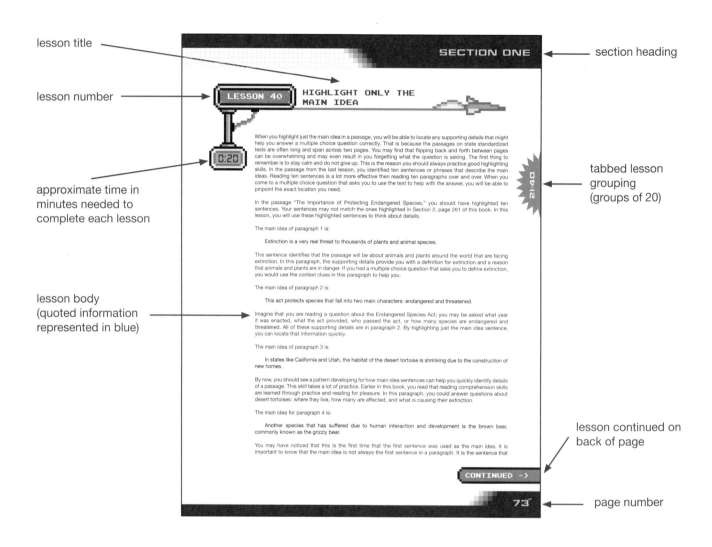

SECTION ONE

LESSON 40

**HIGHLIGHT ONLY THE
MAIN IDEA**

`0:20`

When you highlight just the main idea in a passage, you will be able to locate any supporting details that might help you answer a multiple choice question correctly. That is because the passages on state standardized tests are often long and span across two pages. You may find that flipping back and forth between pages can be overwhelming and may even result in you forgetting what the question is asking. The first thing to remember is to stay calm and do not give up. This is the reason you should always practice good highlighting skills. In the passage from the last lesson, you identified ten sentences or phrases that describe the main ideas. Reading ten sentences is a lot more effective then reading ten paragraphs over and over. When you come to a multiple choice question that asks you to use the text to help with the answer, you will be able to pinpoint the exact location you need.

In the passage "The Importance of Protecting Endangered Species," you should have highlighted ten sentences. Your sentences may not match the ones highlighted in Section 2, page 261 of this book. In this lesson, you will use these highlighted sentences to think about details.

The main idea of paragraph 1 is:

Extinction is a very real threat to thousands of plants and animal species.

This sentence identifies that the passage will be about animals and plants around the world that are facing extinction. In this paragraph, the supporting details provide you with a definition for extinction and a reason that animals and plants are in danger. If you had a multiple choice question that asks you to define extinction, you would use the context clues in this paragraph to help you.

The main idea of paragraph 2 is:

This act protects species that fall into two main characters: endangered and threatened.

Imagine that you are reading a question about the Endangered Species Act; you may be asked what year it was enacted, what the act provided, who passed the act, or how many species are endangered and threatened. All of these supporting details are in paragraph 2. By highlighting just the main idea sentence, you can locate that information quickly.

The main idea of paragraph 3 is:

In states like California and Utah, the habitat of the desert tortoise is shrinking due to the construction of new homes.

By now, you should see a pattern developing for how main idea sentences can help you quickly identify details of a passage. This skill takes a lot of practice. Earlier in this book, you read that reading comprehension skills are learned through practice and reading for pleasure. In this paragraph, you could answer questions about desert tortoises: where they live, how many are affected, and what is causing their extinction.

The main idea for paragraph 4 is:

Another species that has suffered due to human interaction and development is the brown bear, commonly known as the grizzly bear.

You may have noticed that this is the first time that the first sentence was used as the main idea. It is important to know that the main idea is not always the first sentence in a paragraph. It is the sentence that

CONTINUED ->

`21:40`

ZACK

DATA

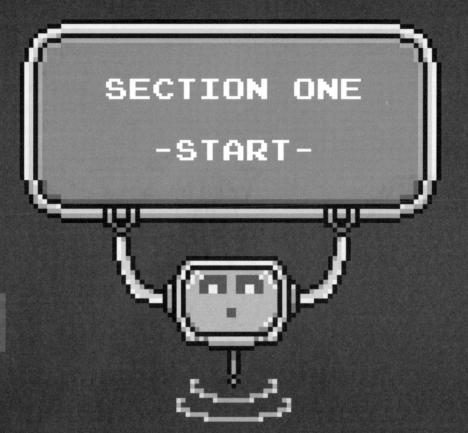

SECTION ONE

-START-

1-20

BEEP
GREETINGS HUMAN!
ARE YOU READY
TO BEGIN?
BEEP

HI! I'M ZACK
AND THIS IS
DATA! WE'RE
HERE TO HELP
YOU ALONG THE
WAY! GOOD LUCK
AND HAVE FUN!

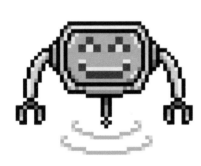

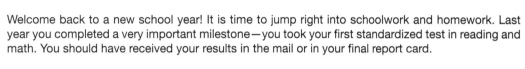

LESSON 1

WELCOME TO FOURTH GRADE!

1-20

Welcome back to a new school year! It is time to jump right into schoolwork and homework. Last year you completed a very important milestone—you took your first standardized test in reading and math. You should have received your results in the mail or in your final report card.

It is important to review your accomplishments and set new goals for this year's standardized assessments. In fourth grade, you will once again complete standardized tests for math and reading, and you will also complete one for science. As you can see, you have a lot of school responsibilities and studying to work into your daily schedule. The most important thing to remember is to make time for everything you have to do in a day, week, and month. Planning a schedule should include everything from tests you will take and projects you need to complete to after-school clubs, sports, and bedtime. A regular routine is a very important part of being a good learner. Are you ready? Let's get started with some basic activities that you will need to plan for.

Complete these questions:

1. What day of the week will you have a regular spelling test?

   _____

2. What time do you go to bed every night?

   _____

3. What day of the week do you participate in an extracurricular activity (sports, clubs, tutoring, and so on)?

   _____

4. What time have you set aside to complete all school work regularly? (For example: 3:30 p.m. – 4:30 p.m. on Monday – Thursday)

   _____

```
*BEEP*
EACH DAILY LESSON
IS AN OPPORTUNITY
FOR YOU AND YOUR
GUIDE TO READ
TOGETHER AND SHARE
YOUR THINKING.
*BEEP*
```

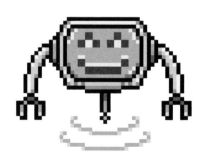

LESSON 2　MANAGING YOUR TIME

0:20

A good learner is prepared to follow a regular routine and make time for all his activities. It is your responsibility to find a regular time and regular place to study every day. It is important to prepare a study area with all the school supplies you need. You can keep them on a desk or in a container for you to easily access. It is important to keep your supplies up-to-date and organized.

Each day, you and your Guide will explore new lessons in reading, writing, math, science, and social studies. You will have regular Scan it! activities and formal assessments to complete with your Guide and, sometimes, on your own. Each week, you and your Guide should fill out a weekly calendar schedule of all the important activities that need to be completed.

Here is an example of a well-prepared weekly schedule:

Tyler's Weekly Schedule

Time	Monday	Tuesday	Wednesday	Thursday	Friday
8:00 a.m.	Breakfast	Breakfast	Breakfast	Breakfast	Breakfast
9:00 a.m.	Language Arts	Language Arts	Language Arts	Language Arts	Language Arts
10:00 a.m.	Language Arts	Math	Language Arts	Math	Language Arts
11:00 a.m.	Math	Math	Math	Math	Math
Noon	Lunch	Lunch	Lunch	Lunch	Lunch
1:00 p.m.	Social Studies	Science	Social Studies	Science	Social Studies
2:00 p.m.	Science	Social Studies	Science	Social Studies	Science
3:00 p.m.	Free time	Free time	Free time	Free time	Free time
4:00 p.m.	Homework	Homework	Homework	Homework	Homework
5:00 p.m.	Sports	Club	Free time	Sports	Club
6:00 p.m.	Dinner	Dinner	Dinner	Dinner	Dinner
7:00 p.m.	Free time	Free time	Free time	Free time	Free time
8:00 p.m.	Reading time	Reading time	Reading time	Reading time	Reading time
9:00 p.m.	Bedtime	Bedtime	Bedtime	Bedtime	Bedtime

You can also keep a monthly schedule that helps you remember important dates coming up in the month that may change your weekly schedule. This allows you to plan for days in which you have to change your study time and homework time.

Here is a good example of a monthly schedule:

JANUARY 20XX

SUNDAY	MONDAY	TUESDAY	WEDNESDAY	THURSDAY	FRIDAY	SATURDAY
1	2 Holiday	3	4 Math Test	5	6 Spelling Test	7
8	9	10 Science Test	11	12	13 Spelling Test	14
15	16 Holiday	17	18 Math Test	19 Club	20 Spelling Test	21
22	23	24 Social Studies Test	25	26 Game	27 Spelling Test Vacation	28
29	30 Vacation	31 Vacation				

The next two pages are blank schedules that your Guide can make copies of each week and month. You and your Guide should set a regular time each week to plan out your schedule for the upcoming week. At the end of every month, you and your Guide should plan out your monthly schedule and use it to help remember events that will need to be worked into your weekly schedule. If you make this a regular habit, you will see positive results in your schoolwork. Good luck!

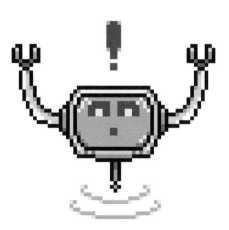

BEEP
WHENEVER YOU SEE
THIS ICON, THE
LESSON CONTINUES ON
THE BACK!
BEEP

CONTINUED ->

1-20

MONTH:

	SUNDAY	MONDAY	TUESDAY	WEDNESDAY	THURSDAY	FRIDAY	SATURDAY

Mon: _____

| 8 | 9 | 10 | 11 | 12 | 1 | 2 | 3 | 4 | 5 | 6 | Evening |

Tue: _____

| 8 | 9 | 10 | 11 | 12 | 1 | 2 | 3 | 4 | 5 | 6 | Evening |

Wed: _____

| 8 | 9 | 10 | 11 | 12 | 1 | 2 | 3 | 4 | 5 | 6 | Evening |

Thur: _____

| 8 | 9 | 10 | 11 | 12 | 1 | 2 | 3 | 4 | 5 | 6 | Evening |

Fri: _____

| 8 | 9 | 10 | 11 | 12 | 1 | 2 | 3 | 4 | 5 | 6 | Evening |

LESSON 3   WORDS ARE TOOLS

0:20

One of the most important strategies you will learn in Language Arts is how to build your vocabulary. But vocabulary is also learned in science, math, and social studies. You and your Guide will use this book to build your knowledge of assessment vocabulary. You are probably thinking, "Assessment vocabulary, what's that?" Assessment vocabulary is made up of performance verbs. These are all the words that appear in questions you will be asked on a test. For example, **describe** the strategies you used to answer the word problem, **make a prediction** about the character in the story, or **evaluate** whether the main character made a good decision. Words like *describe*, *evaluate*, and *predict* are often used in extended response questions on tests you will take. Extended response questions ask you to "explain your brain," so the teacher can see how well you comprehended what you read.

Building your vocabulary means you are able to read more difficult words and understand how they are used to communicate your learning. You and your Guide will review new vocabulary words almost every day, so it is important for the both of you to have quality discussions about the new words. Assessment words are the most important ones to know because you will not have your Guide's help when you take a test. The next six lessons will review all the ways that assessment questions try to figure out if you really learned about a topic. This strategy is not used to confuse or trick you—it is so that you can see that there are many ways to ask the same question. It is a good strategy to review these lessons before your formal assessments and standardized test so that you can practice using the strategies that will help you become an excellent test taker. Good luck!

Let's begin by reviewing some important words. Use what you know to answer the questions. Don't worry if you can't answer them right now. These words will be part of your vocabulary in fourth grade.

Answer these questions:

1. What is an analysis?

   _____

2. What is an evaluation?

   _____

3. What is an inference?

   _____

4. What is compare/contrast?

   _____

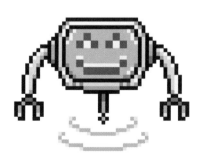

BEEP
REMEMBER THAT YOUR
GUIDE CAN HELP YOU
THINK THROUGH THESE
TYPES OF QUESTIONS!
BEEP

LESSON 4   PERFORMANCE VERBS

`0:20`

You took your first standardized test last year. Standardized tests let you know how well you learned in school. These tests also help teachers identify skills in which you might need extra help. Standardized tests are taken to help you be the best student possible.

Extended response questions are part of every state's standardized assessments. They require you to write about how you understand information. Every time you read an extended response question on an assessment, you will need to pay attention to the performance verbs. These help you understand exactly what you need to do to perform well on your test. A good first strategy to use before you even answer the question is to read the question carefully out loud in your head. That means you should read the question in your head and listen to the words carefully. Then, you should highlight performance verbs in the question so you know the exact answer you will need to provide. Last, you should look back in the reading selection or math problem and highlight the text that you can use in your answer.

Here is a chart of the top twenty performance verbs used on standardized tests. You and your Guide should review these words each week so you can practice what you will need to do when you read a test question with one of these words.

Skill	Definition
analyze	to examine parts (of a story or a math problem) and see how they fit together
compare	to look at similarities and differences of parts
conclude	to reach an opinion or decision
contrast	to look at differences of two or more parts
construct	to make or create something out of parts
describe	to show/express in words what something is like
evaluate	to make a decision or judgment using your own words
explain	to make the correct answer clear by giving reasons (how and why)
formulate	to develop a new idea based on information already given
identify	to name or list using evidence from text
infer	to draw a conclusion beyond what is stated
interpret	to explain the meaning of
plan *	to organize your answer
predict	to tell what could happen next
restate *	to use your own words to state the question
review *	to read your answer again out loud in your head to make sure it is well written
revise *	to make changes to your answer to correct any grammar or spelling errors
summarize	to briefly state only the main points
support	to give facts or examples to justify your answer
trace	to describe a path or sequence

Skills with an asterisk (*) are strategies you will need to write great answers. They may not appear in test questions.

LESSON 5   TOP TWENTY COUNTDOWN

1-20

0:20

You will take a lot of tests in fourth grade before your standardized state assessment. You and your Guide will have a lot of practice looking for the performance verbs in a question and analyzing what you need to do to answer an extended response question correctly. The Top Twenty Performance Verbs will help you understand all the strategies that you will need to read an assessment question. You and your Guide should review these words before every formal assessment you will take this year. This way you will have a lot of practice understanding the language used on tests. The performance verbs are not used to trick or confuse you; in fact, the state standardized assessment is taken to make sure you have learned everything you are supposed to learn for fifth grade.

These examples will show you what each word means when you answer an extended response question. You and your Guide should spend a few minutes on each one to make sure you understand the strategy or task you will need to perform. There will be times that a performance verb doesn't appear in the question but the strategy that you need to use will be a performance verb. You will begin to use these strategies right now, so don't forget to review them often. Good luck!

You will need to decide which choices will best answer the question.

This is your total sum.

analyze: to examine parts of a question to see how they all fit together

Your favorite aunt gave you a gift certificate for $50.00. You decide to spend the entire amount. Your choices are movie tickets: $7.00, amusement park tickets: $30.00, skating rink tickets: $22.00, or arcade center tickets: $17.00. What can you buy to come as close as possible to spending all of your $50.00?

These are your addends.

This is the question you have to answer.

1. What do you need to do to get an answer to this question?

_____

_____

1-20

Usually when you compare two things, you also contrast. Often these two words appear in questions together.

Since there are two subjects, a Venn Diagram would be a great tool to use on scratch paper.

contrast: to look at differences of two or more parts

compare: to look at similarities and differences of parts

Sam and Alan are friends at school. Sam eats peanut butter and jelly sandwiches and plays kickball. Sam also likes to read and wear different color socks. He also plays the trumpet. Alan skateboards while wearing his new orange helmet. Alan likes to read and write short stories. Alan plays hockey and goes for pizza after practice. Sam and Alan both love language arts. Compare Sam and Alan to answer the questions below.

This was a lot of information to read before you found out the questions. Don't forget to read each question all the way through all the time.

Highlighting or circling the important information will help you complete your diagram.

2. Name another type of diagram you could use to help organize your information.

_____

_____

Since you will only need to list similarities, a T-chart is a great tool to use to make a list of similarities.

The text is only about orca whales. You should only use information from the reading passage to write about whales.

conclude: to reach a decision or make an opinion about what you have read

How is a family of whales similar to a human family? Use information from the text passage and your own ideas and conclusions to support your answer.

Drawing conclusions is the same as the word *conclude*. The question gives you a clue about what the word means; use your own idea. That means you will have to look at all the information you took from the text about whales and decide what makes them similar to your family.

3. A good strategy is to look at the list of characteristics of an orca whale family and see how they are similar to your family. What else could you do to answer this question?

_____

_____

LESSON 6 **FOUR MORE ACES**

1-20

0:20

An important strategy you will learn in this book is ACE. ACE will help you to properly answer an extended response question. ACE is an acronym for *Answer*, *Cite*, and *Explain*. Once you have reviewed all of the Top Twenty Performance Verbs with your Guide, you will begin to understand how to use the ACE strategy to write the best answers for extended response questions.

In a state standardized assessment, every constructed response is scored by a rubric. A rubric is a scoring guide. Rubrics will help your Guide know what a quality answer should look like and help you know what information is needed to fully answer a question. We will discuss rubrics later in this book.

As you read each of the examples for the performance verbs, make sure you and your Guide have a discussion about strategies. You should plan on reviewing these important performance verbs often.

Usually, when you are asked to make something from parts, you will be asked to expain the steps you took to get an answer.

construct: to make or create something out of parts
explain: to make the answer clear by giving the reasons "why" and "how"
Mrs. Fisher wants to tile the foyer of her house. She is planning on using 3 different colors of tiles for her design. She wants ½ of the tiles to be green, ¼ of the tiles to be brown, and ¼ of the tiles to be blue. Construct a floor plan using the grid below. Label each tile with the first letter of the tile color. Show all your work. Explain in words how you found your answer. Tell why you took the steps you did to solve the problem.

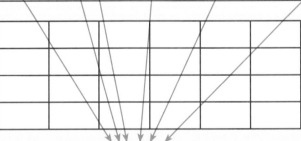

Make sure you highlight all the verbs in a question. In this example, you are given the context clues "why" and "how" to help you remember what the performance verb *explain* requires for an answer.

---

1. What could you do to help you answer a question with a lot of steps?

_____

_____

> **describe:** to express (show) in words what something is like
>
> What word or phrase could describe both Ella and Latasha? Use at least one example from the passage to support your response.
>
> **A good strategy is to read the passage again. Then you can highlight or make a list of all the examples that show how the characters are alike. You will need to write your answer in a sentence.**

2. When you give your answer, a good strategy to use is to restate the question. How would you begin your sentence for this answer?

_____

_____

> **evaluate:** make a decision or judgment using your own words
>
> In the story, the author describes the process of starting her own business. Evaluate what a young person can learn from the steps the author completed to organize her business and overcome her worries. Use information from the story and your own observations and conclusions to support your answer.
>
> **Your answer will need to cite information from the text.**
>
> **In this example, you are given the context clue "your own observations and conclusions" to help you remember what the performance verb *evaluate* means.**
>
> **Read the passage again and highlight the information you learned about starting a business and overcoming worries.**

3. Have a brief discussion with your Guide. How can a T-chart help you evaluate information from a text or passage?

_____

_____

LESSON 7 — ANSWER FOUR MORE

The most important skill to learn when completing an extended response question is answering the question properly. You and your Guide will complete many Scan it! activities this year that will allow you to practice answering extended response questions. Restating a question, the first step in the ACE (Answer, Cite, and Explain) strategy, will help you make sure that the question is answered first.

When you read an extended response question on a test, a good strategy to use is to underline the question. After you underline the question, you can begin your sentence by restating the question to help guide you to a good answer. It is also an important skill to use every day. If your Guide asked you, "Why is it important to do your homework every day?" you could answer, "It is important to do my homework every day so I can practice what I learned in school." By restating the question, you are demonstrating good listening and comprehension skills. Restating the question will help you focus on exactly the right answer.

You will have a lot of time to practice answering extended response questions with your Guide. You and your Guide will need to practice what you will do before you write an answer. First you will need to read the question carefully. Then you should underline the question and think about the answer. Ask yourself what the question is asking and where to find the information in the text. Restating the question becomes your topic sentence and **citing** examples from the text will help you **explain** your topic. You will be able to use the ACE strategy without even thinking about it!

plan: organize your answer
restate: use your own words to state the question
review: read your answer again to make sure it is well written
revise: make changes to your answer to correct any grammar or spelling errors
These performance verbs don't normally appear in extended response questions. They are really strategies that you will need to use when answering questions. You and your Guide can practice answering questions every day using these strategies. Before you know it, you will naturally remember these steps.

Restate the following question: Why is it important for you to become a good test taker?

_____

_____

LESSON 8 — CITING FROM THE TEXT

0:20

1·20

Reading comprehension is what allows you to relate with the text. When you read, do you picture what is happening in the story or text in your head? That means you are interacting with the text and using what you know to understand what you are reading. This is a very important skill to practice because without comprehension you are just reading words. It is important for you to read for pleasure so that you can practice sounding out new words, learn words in context, and practice reading aloud in your head. Reading aloud in your head means that you are concentrating on what you are reading.

Another skill you will learn is how to use evidence from the text to explain your answer in an extended response question. The E of ACE stands for "explain." That means you have to learn to **e**xtend your answer using **e**vidence from the text to **e**xplain how you know your answer is correct. Just saying "because I knew" or "because the story said" is not enough; you have to use your own words and evidence from the text to **e**xplain your brain. The following performance verbs are very important because they require you to cite evidence from the text to support your answer. When you see these words, make sure you reread the text before you answer the extended response question.

---

identify: to name or list using evidence from the text

On the lines below, identify **TWO** ways in which Latasha helped her mother. Use information from the story to support your answer.

Use your own words to restate what a character said or did in the passage.

Reread the text to identify sentences that support your answers.

---

1. Discuss with your Guide: What is the most important word to identify in the question?

   _____

   _____

CONTINUED ->

interpret: to explain the meaning of

Twenty-one fourth graders were surveyed to find out what their favorite subject was at school. Using the data from the pie graph, determine the total number of students that chose math and language arts. Show all your work. Explain in words how you found your answer. Tell why you took the steps to solve the problem.

As you can see, the word *interpret* does not appear in the question at all. However, *interpreting* is another word for explaining. Remember that explaining means to give reasons why and how you found an answer.

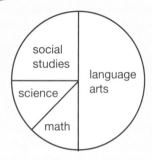

social studies

language arts

science

math

2. Discuss with your Guide: How will you know when the performance verb *interpret* needs to be used? (Hint: math and science)

---

summarize: to briefly state the main points of the text or passage

After Latasha's mother gets a new job, things change for Latasha. In the box below, summarize three things that change during the day that make Latasha worry.

Usually when you are asked to summarize, you are also given the number of examples that you need to provide. Don't forget to reread the text passage to cite evidence from the text.

3. How will you begin the answer to this question? (Hint: restate)

support: to give facts or examples to justify your answers

What word or phrase could describe both Ella and Latasha? Use at least one example from the passage to support your response.

Make sure you give evidence from the text to explain how and why you got your answer.

4. Discuss with your Guide: If the extended response question only asks you to give one example, why should you give two or more examples?

_____

_____

YOU MAY WANT TO VISIT THE PAGES WITH PERFORMANCE VERB EXPLANATIONS REGULARLY WITH YOUR GUIDE.

LESSON 9

TOP TWENTY COUNTED DOWN

1-20

0:20

Today you will review the final four performance verbs. All of these performance verbs either appear in questions or are strategies you will need to practice to be a great test taker. Last year, you completed your first state standardized assessment. This year, you will not only take your reading and math standardized test, but you will probably also take a science standardized test. It doesn't matter what the subject is—you will see these performance verbs on all of them. You will also use all the performance verb strategies that you have read about.

You and your Guide will have plenty of opportunities to practice being a great test taker. You can and should review these strategies as often as possible, especially before formal assessments. The best strategy for test taking is to comprehend what test words mean and what you need to know to give a great answer. When you plan your weekly schedule, you and your Guide can assign one study day to reviewing the Top Twenty Performance Verbs. Remember, practice is the only way to improve your skills. You will soon see that every time you get to an extended response question on a formal assessment, you will know exactly what you need to do.

---

formulate: to develop a new idea based on information already given

Latasha made a plan to keep Ella from bothering Mrs. Okocho. In your opinion, was Latasha's plan successful? Use evidence from the text and your own opinion to formulate a plan that you think may work better for Latasha. Use as much detail as possible to describe your plan.

These two phrases are context clues to help you identify what the word *formulate* means in this sentence.

The performance verb *formulate* means you take information from the text or passage and combine it with what you know or think and explain new information.

---

1. Discuss with your Guide: Which strategy or graphic organizer would you use to formulate a plan, idea, or problem?

_____

_____

predict: to tell what will happen next
infer: to draw a conclusion beyond what is stated
The words *predict* and *infer* are closely related words. When you make a **prediction,** you must infer what is happening in a text or passage and tell what may happen next. There is one major difference. When you infer, you are using evidence from the text and your knowledge about a topic to make an **inference** that is close to the truth or close to being possible. When you predict, you are using evidence from the text to guess what could happen next even if it is not possible.

2. Discuss with your Guide: When you make predictions about a story or passage, you will be proven right or wrong by the end of the story. When you infer, you may or may not know the answer to what happened by the end of the story. Can you think of one example of each?

_____

_____

trace: to describe a path or sequence
Explain what a quadrilateral shape is, then trace over one of your pattern blocks that is NOT a quadrilateral. Explain your choice using what you know about shapes to support your answer.

The performance verb *trace* has two different meanings. In this example, you are asked to use a shape to copy its outline on a paper. That is one definition.

Sometimes you may have to describe the steps that were taken to solve a problem or answer a question. In this type of problem, you can use words like *first*, *next*, *then*, and *last*. These allow you to show a sequence of events.

3. Discuss with your Guide: Trace back all the things you did today. Use the words *first*, *next*, and *last* to describe your day with your Guide.

_____

_____

LESSON 10   MATH VOCABULARY

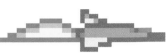

1-20

0:15

Every subject that you take in school has its own vocabulary words. Mathematicians, writers, scientists, and historians all use their own special vocabulary to communicate. In fourth grade, you will work on math problems that ask the same question in a lot of different ways.

Look at this simple math problem:

$$17 + 3 = 20$$

Example 1:

Debbie had seventeen pencils in her desk. Joe had three pencils in his desk. How many pencils did they have altogether? Show all your work.

Example 2:

Find the sum of the addends 17 and 3. Show all your work.

These examples ask you the same question. The only part that has changed is the vocabulary they used. When you take a state standardized assessment, you will be asked to find the sum of, combine, total, and tally numbers. All of these words are asking you to solve the math problem you see written in numbers. The important thing to remember about being a good test taker is to understand what you are being asked to perform in each question. Performance verbs will help you understand what you need to do to answer extended response questions; however, you also need to understand the vocabulary that is unique to the subject matter of your test. Don't worry, though; you have an entire year to learn vocabulary for a subject matter. Don't try to learn everything in one day. Keep a log, a journal, or a word wall of new vocabulary words so you can review and practice them during your regularly scheduled study time.

Discuss with your Guide: How many more ways can you think of to describe the word *addition*?

_____

_____

LESSON 11

INTERPRETING MATH QUESTIONS

1-20

In fourth grade, you will use all the multiplication skills you learned in third grade to multiply two-, three-, and four-digit numbers. You will learn how to find a missing addend in addition problems, and you will learn how to find a missing subtrahend in subtraction problems. Most importantly, you will learn how to read math word problems and figure out what mathematic skill you need to apply to answer the question. Over the next few weeks, you will complete sample standardized assessments questions and refer to Section 2 for answers and explanations. You and your Guide should take time to review each question and discuss the answers. Even if you got the answer correct the first time, practice the E (**E**xplain) of ACE by describing to your Guide how you solved the problem. Make sure you use math terms to explain your solution to your Guide. Look at this sample conversation to help you.

Example:

○ $57.00   ● $38.00

○ $43.00   ○ $28.00

Mark your answer.

Terry bought 3 pizzas and 1 sandwich. The price of each pizza is $11.00 and the price of the sandwich is $5.00. What is the total price?

After you solve the problem, you and your Guide may have the following discussion.

I.   Restate
     A.   To get a total price I knew I had to add numbers because the word *total* also means sum.
II. First Step
     A.   First I had to add $11.00 three times for the pizza and get the total of $33.00; or
     B.   First I had to skip count by $11.00 three times to get $33.00 for the pizza.
III. Next Step
     A.   Then I had to add the total pizza price of $33.00 to the $5.00 for the sandwich to get the total of $38.00.

What other way could you explain the first step?

_____

_____

LESSON 12 ADD IT UP

0:20

It doesn't matter what language you speak; everyone in every country knows how to speak math language. One of the most important math skills you can practice is being able to write and speak about math using proper math vocabulary. In fourth grade, you will learn how numbers, sets, and functions are used to add, subtract, multiply, and divide. You will use words to identify symbols; for example, > means greater than and + means to add. Most importantly, you will know what all the symbols mean and how they work with numbers.

Math is important to many professional careers. For example, scientists use math to conduct experiments and chefs use math to measure ingredients. The five examples that you will work on in this lesson will use the same skill but present it in different formats. You will see how formal assessments and state standardized assessments test the same math skill using different vocabulary. You and your Guide can find the answers to the questions below in Section 2, page 235. Good luck!

1. What property does the following number sentence show?

    $$450 + 250 = 250 + 450$$

    ○ the distributive property   ○ the commutative property of addition

    ○ the property of zero for addition   ○ the associative property of addition

2. What is the sum of 53,370 and 19,656?

    ○ 46,326   ○ 73,026

    ○ 82,409   ○ 61,291

3. What is 9,236 in expanded form?

    ○ 9,000 + 200 + 36   ○ 9,000 + 200 + 360

    ○ 9,000 + 200 + 30 + 6   ○ 9,000 + 200 + 300 + 6

4. Allison bought 2 comic books for $5.36 each and a bookmark for $1.59. What is the total amount of money she paid?

    ○ $8.54   ○ $6.95

    ○ $8.95   ○ $12.31

5. Casey, Tyler, and Nicole each put $8.00 into a jar to start their car washing business. On Saturday, they washed 2 cars. They collected $6.00 for each car washed. On Sunday, they washed just one car and collected $10.00. How much money was in the jar at the end of the weekend? Show all your work. Explain your answer using words.

Discuss all your answers with your Guide.

THIS IS YOUR TIME TO PRACTICE SKILLS AND STRATEGIES WITH YOUR GUIDE. DON'T FORGET TO CHECK YOUR ANSWERS IN SECTION 2 OF THIS BOOK.

1·20

LESSON 13 TAKE AWAY

0:05

In Lesson 12, you learned many ways that addition questions can be used in an assessment. Today you will review the vocabulary words that describe subtraction before you review your answers with your Guide. When you read questions that ask you to perform subtraction, you will see terms such as *take away*, *less than*, *minus*, *subtract*, *how many are left*, *remove*, and *difference*. A subtraction sentence in words is: *minuend – subtrahend = difference*. You won't really have to worry about knowing the vocabulary for the numbers in a subtraction sentence, though. The key is to know how many ways an assessment question can ask you to subtract. The trick to getting subtraction questions correct is to make sure to check your work. Addition is a very important way to check your work in subtraction problems.

Go back to Lesson 12 and spend some time discussing how you came to a solution for each sample problem. Don't forget to schedule some time in your weekly planner to review study strategies, performance verbs, and vocabulary. Before long, all these skills that you practice will become part of your thinking process and you can schedule time to study other skills and strategies.

LESSON 14

ADDITION CHECKS SUBTRACTION

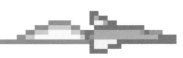

0:20

One of the biggest mistakes that you can make on a formal assessment or state standardized test is not checking your work after you answer a question. Reviewing and revising your work takes practice and skill. In math, subtraction and division can be checked using addition and multiplication. It is one of the reasons you learned about fact families. Fact families are three numbers that are related in a number sentence.

Here is an example:

Addition Fact Family	
3 + 5 = 8	8 - 3 = 5
5 + 3 = 8	8 - 5 = 3

Multiplication Fact Family	
3 x 5 = 15	15 ÷ 3 = 5
5 x 3 = 15	15 ÷ 5 = 3

When you work on subtraction and division questions, take the time to check your answers to make sure you did the math correctly. Spend some time during your weekly study time and math homework to practice checking your work. Today you will work on practicing subtraction and division word problems. Make sure you show all of your work and practice using what you know about fact families to check your work. You and your Guide can find the answers to the questions below in Section 2, page 237.

1. Find the difference between 37,829 and 18,007.

    ○ 19,822   ○ 9,202

    ○ 21,822   ○ 27,082

2. Find the quotient if the divisor is 8 and the dividend is 96.

    ○ 13   ○ 14

    ○ 12   ○ 15

CONTINUED ->

3. Mr. Ford wrote these number problems on the board:

$$11 \square 1 = \underline{\hspace{1cm}}$$

$$11 \square 1 = \underline{\hspace{1cm}}$$

Write a different sign (+, −, x, ÷) in each box above that would give the same answer for both number problems. Then write the answers to the problems on the lines. Use your knowledge of properties of math to support your answer.

4. There are 117 donuts in the display case at Todd's Bakery. The bakery sells powdered, glazed, and jelly donuts. If there are 26 powdered donuts and 38 glazed donuts in the display case, how many *jelly* donuts are in the display case?

5. Casey and Holli have been saving pennies. Casey has 433 pennies, and Holli has 142 pennies. How many more pennies does Casey have than Holli? Show all your work.

6. Adam wants to give 27 baseball cards to 3 of his friends. He gives the same number of baseball cards to each friend. How many baseball cards does Adam give to each friend? Show all your work.

LESSON 15

SAY IT ANY WAY YOU WANT

1-20

Don't forget to set a schedule on your weekly planner. It is important that you set aside time every day to review strategies and skills that will help you become a great test taker. Math vocabulary is important to know and understand because you will see questions asking you to solve the same types of problems using different vocabulary words. One strategy you can use is to keep a notebook with sections for each subject. Write new vocabulary words and their definitions and also write an example that can help you remember how the word is used in context. Once you know the word without having to look back in your book, you can cross it off so you can concentrate on studying the words you don't know.

For example:

Division: breaking a number into small groups of equal quantities

Division vocabulary to know: *quotient*, *divisor*, *dividend*, *equal parts*, *divided*, *equivalent*, *how many to each*, *multiples*, *divisibility*, *common divisor*, *break apart*, *sets*, *repeated subtraction*

Addition: uniting two or more numbers into a sum; counting the total

Addition vocabulary to know: *addends*, *add*, *sum*, *total*, *altogether*, *how many more*, *more than*, *commutative property*, *associative property*, *grouping property*

LESSON 16

EXPLORE THE WORLD AROUND YOU

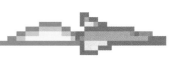

0:20

From the time you could speak, you've probably been asking the question "Why?" That is one of the reasons you study science in school. When you understand the language of science, you can learn to think and solve problems. You are able to ask why the world around you is a certain way, and seek answers or solutions to your questions. The scientific method helps you organize the process you use to discover the real world.

This year you will continue to build upon the knowledge you gained in third grade. Most fourth graders complete a state standardized assessment for science. Just like in math, science has its own language and vocabulary. That is why it is important to always schedule study time to review and practice all the new material you learned. Usually when you study science, you will be asked to keep a science journal of all your experiments. A good strategy to use during your study time is to review all of your experiments and highlight vocabulary words that you need to study a bit more. On the chart below, use your own words to explain what you know about each vocabulary word. Try to do this activity without a dictionary to test how much you know about each topic. This will help you identify the areas of science that you need to practice this year. You and your Guide can find the definitions to these words in Section 2, page 240. Good luck!

biome	
energy	
matter	
organism	
producer	
consumer	
herbivore	
carnivore	
omnivore	
decomposer	
food web	
food chain	
ecosystem	
biotic	
abiotic	

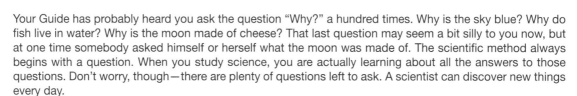

LESSON 17

THE ANSWER STARTS WITH A GUESS

0:20

1-20

Your Guide has probably heard you ask the question "Why?" a hundred times. Why is the sky blue? Why do fish live in water? Why is the moon made of cheese? That last question may seem a bit silly to you now, but at one time somebody asked himself or herself what the moon was made of. The scientific method always begins with a question. When you study science, you are actually learning about all the answers to those questions. Don't worry, though—there are plenty of questions left to ask. A scientist can discover new things every day.

Your state standardized test will challenge you to demonstrate what you learned about the world around you, on such subjects as food chains, weather, simple machines, plants, animals, measurements, and more. A good strategy to use when you complete your lab experiments is to write your final statement with as much detail as possible. Make sure you include a diagram or drawing, all the vocabulary words that you can review during your study time, and any observations you made that were not part of the experiment. Making notes will help you answer extended response questions in science. Complete the following questions and think about how your science journal notes can be improved to help you study these question types. You and your Guide can find the answers to the problems below in Section 2, page 241.

Base your answers to questions 1 through 3 on the water cycle diagram and on your knowledge of science. Letters A, B, and C represent three processes in the water cycle.

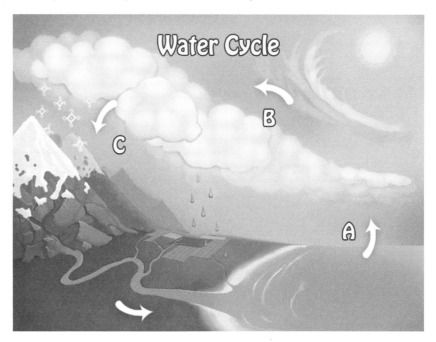

1. Identify process A. _____

2. Identify process B. _____

3. Identify two forms of precipitation that return water to the earth's surface in process C.

    _____ and _____

CONTINUED ->

Base your answers to questions 4 and 5 on the diagram of a food chain shown below.

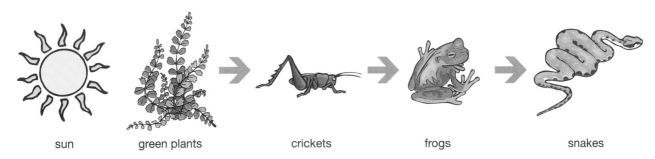

| sun | green plants | crickets | frogs | snakes |

(Organisms not drawn to scale)

4. Identify a predator in this food chain. _____

5. Explain why the population of crickets might **decrease** if the number of frogs increases.

_____

_____

_____

LESSON 18

STUDY SHEET STRATEGIES

0:20

1-20

Making a study sheet is an important step in developing good study skills. A study sheet is a shorter version of all the notes you have taken about a particular unit. Study sheets may include important facts that you know, but they need to focus on ideas that you don't know so well. Focusing on ideas that you don't know will help you to learn those ideas better through repetition. As you are pulling out the most important ideas of your notes, you are rewriting those ideas a second time. Make sure your study sheet is no longer than one page and it is organized by units. Decide on the type of format you want your study sheet to follow. It is important to complete your study sheet three to five days before your exam. This will ensure that you have enough time to prepare for your exam.

One way to format your study sheet is to list a key idea and briefly describe that idea. These notes will allow you to remember the most important dates, names, and facts learned in the unit.

What would you and your Guide put in a study sheet?

_____

_____

LESSON 19 — STUDY TIME

Creating study sheets that help you learn about a subject is a great strategy to focus your attention on one topic. You and your Guide will make many study sheets to help you practice difficult concepts during study time. Study sheets are used only for the period of time you need to learn something that is still not clear in your head. Once you fully understand the topic or the information, you can set aside the study sheet in a folder and only review the material if you need to. This way your study time is not spent reviewing all the sheets you create, just the important ones.

One way to format your study sheet is to list a key idea and briefly describe that idea. These notes will allow you to remember the most important dates, names, and facts learned in the unit. For example, your notes may explain that the sun is 93 million miles away from Earth, which is called 1 Astronomical Unit. You can shorten this information on your study sheet this way: Sun = 93 million miles or 1 AU.

A second way to format your study sheet is by completing a word list. A word list will describe on what page or what date a certain idea was taught. For example, *Astronomy (pages 100 – 105)* will tell us what page in our textbook explains astronomy. Another way is to write the word and the date the word was taught. For example, *Astronomy (12/12/11)* will tell us that on 12/12/11 you learned about astronomy and you should refer to those dated notes.

There are many other ways to format study sheets, such as outlining chapters, creating flashcards, and making definition lists. These are just a few examples of study sheets that can be used. If you haven't already made your own type of study sheet, try to think of a type of study sheet that best works for you.

Think about the different courses you are learning about. Language arts, math, science, and social studies will be easier to understand with the creation of study sheets. As you go through these courses, you may see that different study sheets are used more often depending on the course. What types of study sheets will help you in the different subjects you are taking? What subjects would you use flashcards in more often? Would it make more sense to make a definition list for math or science? What type of study sheet would more likely be used in social studies? Understanding these questions will better prepare you as you begin to create study sheets. Use the following example to help you and your Guide begin planning a study sheet that works best for you.

Study Guide Topic: _____ Subject: _____ Text Pages: _____

What I know:

How can I explain the topic in my own words?

What I need to know:

Vocabulary:

Where can I practice talking about this?

For example: When it rains, I can talk about the water cycle.

or

When I'm with my friends outside, we can talk about the ecosystem in our community.

What I need help understanding:

LESSON 20

WHAT ARE THE FACTS?

0:20

As you prepare your weekly schedule, you need to focus on the amount of time you set aside for homework practice and study time. Your study sheets are an important tool because they can focus your attention on what you really need to study, so you don't waste time trying to locate information in notes and textbooks. State standardized assessment questions are not all extended response questions; there are a lot of multiple choice questions that test vocabulary and facts. That is why it is important for you and your Guide to create study sheets. You will be able to focus on learning quick facts and information over the course of your fourth grade school year. You and your Guide can find the answers to these questions in Section 2, page 243. After you and your Guide answer the questions, don't forget to set up your weekly schedule. Also, think about how these questions could be part of a study sheet.

1. You would need _____ energy to cut a piece of wood into smaller pieces with a saw.

   O light
   O heat

   O sound
   O mechanical

2. To conduct electricity, the best material to use is _____.

   O metal
   O wood

   O glass
   O plastic

3. Which energy transformation occurs when a person hits a xylophone with a mallet?

   O electrical to light
   O sound to electrical

   O light to mechanical
   O mechanical to sound

4. John went out on a cold winter day and rubbed his hands together. The heat that warmed his hands was produced by _____.

   O friction
   O light

   O gravity
   O magnetism

5. A magnet and a metal object will have the strongest magnetic attraction when the distance between them is _____.

   O 5 centimeters
   O 15 centimeters

   O 10 centimeters
   O 20 centimeters

LESSON 21   STUDY HABITS

`0:20`

21-40

When you create study sheets, you can reduce the amount of time you spend studying. This is because you are studying while you decide what information you want to learn. While you are writing it out, you are learning because you will read what you are writing in your head. There are many types of study sheets, such as outlines, flash cards, and word lists. Learning how to create and learn from these study sheets, will better prepare you for formal assessments. When you prepare to write out notes, you will decide which type of study sheet should be used with the different courses you are taking. You can use any type of study sheet for any subject, but it may make more sense to use one rather than another depending on the subject.

You and your Guide will discuss and decide which study sheets should be used for the listed subjects. Choose from the different types of study sheets below and place them with the subject they can be best used for. You can choose more than one study sheet for a subject.

1. Language Arts	a. Key Idea and Description
2. Math	b. Word List and Date Taught
3. Science	c. Outline
4. Social Studies	d. Flash Cards
	e. Definition List

LESSON 22 — HOW YOU LEARN BEST

`0:20`

21:40

As you and your Guide prepare your study sheets, make sure you discuss the ways in which you learn best. If using a vocabulary list is not the best way for you to learn, then you should think of other strategies that are similar and are more effective for you. For example, you can replace vocabulary lists with flash cards. In social studies, you may decide that outlines of lessons are the best way to create a study sheet. Look at the study sheet and answer the questions. The study sheet will not give you the answers to the questions, but it may be enough information to remind you of what you have already learned. You and your Guide can find the answers to the questions below in Section 2, page 245.

BEEP
WHERE IS THE
STUDY SHEET?
BEEP

ON THE NEXT PAGE! SOMETIMES IMAGES AND CHARTS ARE TOO BIG FOR JUST ONE PAGE!

Study Guide Topic: <u>Themes of Geography</u>   Subject: <u>Social Studies</u>   Text Pages: <u>XX - XX</u>

What I know:

seasons in my community and state

equator, North Pole, South Pole,

longitude and latitude

How can I explain the topic in my own words?

Earth is a planet in our solar system. It is made up of different spheres.

Earth can be studied based on its geography, physical features, and human features. Earth's geography allows us to study different human environments which influence natural resources and the way people live.

The themes of geography are made up of location, places, human environment interaction, movement, and regions.

What I need to know:

Layers of the earth: lithosphere, hydrosphere, atmosphere, biosphere

prime meridian, Tropic of Cancer, and Tropic of Capricorn

What I need help understanding:

renewable and nonrenewable resources

Environmental processes: weathering, glaciation, vegetation

Vocabulary:

lithosphere

hydrosphere

atmosphere

biosphere

prime meridian

Tropic of Capricorn

Tropic of Cancer

culture

economy

vegetation

weathering

landforms

regions

natural resources

renewable resources

nonrenewable resources

Where can I practice talking about this?

When I ride in the car, I can talk about the natural resources I see.

My Guide can help me locate my community on a map and globe.

CONTINUED ->

1. In which region of the United States would you be most likely to find this scene?

○ the Southeast   ○ the Midwest

○ the Northeast   ○ the Southwest

2. Which of these would have been commonly found in early American cities, but **not** in modern cities?

○ horse-drawn carriages   ○ paved highways

○ large factories   ○ traffic lights

3. How did the steamboat change transportation?

○ River travel became slower than ever.   ○ Less cargo could be carried on the rivers.

○ People could travel both upstream and downstream.   ○ Land travel became easier and cheaper.

4. What term best describes this kind of community?

○ urban   ○ rural

○ suburban   ○ town

5. Which city can be located on the map using these coordinates?

Latitude: 40 degrees south, Longitude: 20 degrees east

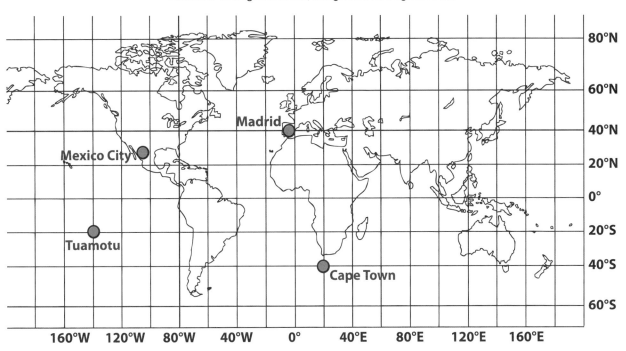

○ Tuamotu   ○ Cape Town

○ Madrid   ○ Mexico City

LESSON 23   IMPROVE YOUR NOTES

0:20

21-40

When you create study sheets, you are actually using your textbook and your notes from class and organizing them on one sheet. You will not use all the information from the textbook or your notes, just the important information you still need to understand or learn. Study sheets can be organized in many different ways, such as flash cards, vocabulary lists, and by study topics like the example in Lesson 22. Another strategy is to use an outline to help you organize information. Outlines are useful when you have a main idea and details. It allows you to focus on all the information that supports a main idea.

In Lesson 22, we represented the themes of geography using a study sheet. Look at the outline below. You and your Guide can decide which study sheet works best for your learning style. An outline study sheet takes a lot of time but allows you to organize the topic by all the major points you need to know. In this example, you will be able to study the spheres of the earth first, and then you can concentrate on the five themes of geography. As you organize your main idea, minor details, and subpoints, leave spaces just in case you want to add something later. You and your Guide can find the answers to the questions below in Section 2, page 248.

Outline

Topic: _Themes of Geography_   Subject: _Social Studies_   Text Pages: _XX – XX_

I.   (main idea) Earth: the third planet in our solar system
    A.   (minor detail) spheres: system of interdependent parts
        1.   (subpoint) lithosphere: earth's surface, rocks under the crust, and liquid core
        2.   (subpoint) hydrosphere: solid, liquid, and gaseous water
        3.   (subpoint) biosphere: all living organisms
        4.   (subpoint) atmosphere: all of the planet's air
II.   Geography: study of earth's surface
    A.   themes
        1.   location: poles, latitude, coordinates, equator, prime meridian, tropics, hemisphere
        2.   place: physical and human features, population, culture, economy, politics
        3.   human environment interaction: natural resources, capital resources, human settlement, weather, vegetation
        4.   movement: travel, industry, transportation, landforms
        5.   regions: five regions of the United States, states, capitals
            a.   Northeast
            b.   Midwest
            c.   Southeast
            d.   Southwest
            e.   West

---

1. The western part of the Northwest is along the _____.

   O   Pacific Ocean   O   Atlantic Ocean

   O   Rocky Mountains   O   Gulf of Mexico

2. The hilly areas between flat lands and mountains are called _____.

   O   plains   O   highlands

   O   coasts   O   plateaus

3. The northern and southern halves of Earth are called the _____.

   O   prime meridian   O   hemispheres

   O   fault   O   axis

4. A map that shows about how many people live in an area is a _____.

   O   climate map   O   weather map

   O   population map   O   physical map

5. Identify the two lines that divide Earth into hemispheres.

LESSON 24   WHAT'S IN A NAME?

0:20

21-40

At this point, you probably realize how important study sheets are to effectively manage your study time. You also need to know and use other strategies to help you remember information. One strategy you can use is mnemonics. **Mnemonics** is using words that you already know to remember information. You have already learned a mnemonic. The ACE strategy for answering extended response questions is a tool to help you remember to answer a question or solve a problem, cite evidence from the text or story, and explain your answer in your own words. If you write the word ACE next to each extended response question, you can easily remind yourself what you will need to answer a question properly. There are other types of mnemonic devices you can use. You probably already learned the rhyme "*i* before *e* except after *c* or when sounded like *a*, as in *neighbor* or *weigh*." You can remember how to spell difficult words using mnemonics. For example, for the word *rhythm* you could use: **r**hythm **h**elps **y**our **t**wo **h**ips **m**ove. Read the following mnemonic devices and see if you and your Guide can add two more to the list.

Mnemonic	Definition
Roy G Biv	Colors spectrum: red, orange, yellow, green, blue, indigo, violet
My Very Energetic Mother Just Served Us Nachos	The planets of the solar system: Mercury, Venus, Earth, Mars, Jupiter, Saturn, Uranus, Neptune (Pluto is no longer considered a planet.)
HOMES	Great lakes: Huron, Ontario, Michigan, Erie, Superior
30 days hath September, April, June, and November. All the rest have 31, except February, for it is great and has only 28, except when it steps out of line and brings to us 29.	Days in each month

LESSON 25

A DICTIONARY IS STILL YOUR FRIEND

Do you remember all the strategies that you use when you come to a word you don't know while reading? You can pause and try to sound it out, you can look for smaller words in the word, or you can try to see if you can figure it out using context clues. Words that you have difficulty with during class are the best vocabulary words to put on a study sheet and review during your weekly scheduled study time(s). When you are building your vocabulary list, a good strategy to use is to have a dictionary and an encyclopedia to reference.

A dictionary will help you learn new words. With a dictionary, you can check the meaning, check the parts of speech, and learn different meanings of a word. It will also show you how to pronounce a word. While reading, you may come across a new word that you don't understand. Usually that causes you to stop reading and try to use strategies to figure it out. Sometimes you may even skip over the word, which can lead you to not understand what the sentence or passage means. It is important to develop good comprehension skills while reading in order to learn important information. For example, you may read the following passage:

The world has many different political systems. Each is distinctive, but all greatly influenced the lives of their citizens and the society in which the political system was practiced.

The highlighted word may be new to you. At this point in your reading, you may pause and try to sound out the word. You can break it down into smaller pieces (dis-tinc-tive) to help sound it out. You may even try to understand the meaning using the sentences around the word. However, do you also know what that word means? If you look in the dictionary (http://dictionary.kids.net.au/word/distinctive) you would find the following definition:

> **dis·tinc·tive** (dĭ-stĭngk-tĭv) *adjective*
> 1. of a feature that helps to distinguish a person or thing; "Jerusalem has a distinctive Middle East flavor"- Curtis Wilkie; "that is typical of you!" 2. serving to distinguish or identify a species or group; "the distinguishing mark of the species is its plumage"; "distinctive tribal tattoos"; "we were asked to describe any identifying marks or distinguishing features" 3. possible to classify

This may be an important fact for the second theme of geography: places that you would need to know. In your study notes, you may want to put that sentence in your own words. Don't forget to set up your weekly schedule and study time(s). You can try out all the strategies you learned so far.

Discuss with your Guide how you could rewrite the sentence in your own words now that you know the definition of the word *distinctive*.

_____

_____

LESSON 26   NOTE TAKING FOR SUCCESS

0:20

21-40

Rachel Carson

Many know Rachel Carson as the mother of the environmental movement. She was born in rural Pennsylvania in 1907. There she showed an early interest in nature. As a girl, Carson collected fossils. She went bird watching. She also loved to write stories about woodland animals.

Carson's family was very poor, but she earned a scholarship for college. She studied English at first, but after one year, Carson changed her focus to science. She wished to become a scientist. She did very well, but there was trouble back at home. Over the years, Carson's family farmland had been ruined by factories. Carson's family moved in with her. Soon, she had to drop out of school to care for them. Distressed, she began to write for comfort. Magazines paid for her stories and articles. In this way, Carson supported her family.

Her articles became popular, so Carson began to write books. Her third book, *Silent Spring*, is her most famous. It warned about the effects of pollution on wildlife. She had seen these effects at her ruined family farm. The book was a worldwide hit. It inspired millions to care for the environment. Sadly, soon after the book was published, Rachel Carson died at age 56. After her passing, she was honored with the Presidential Medal of Freedom.

You will learn many new note taking strategies to use in language arts. Taking notes will help you no matter what class you are studying. Taking notes will help you remember the main idea and details from the text.

When you create your study notes, you do not need to write down or copy down every word. You are writing down the main ideas and the most important details from the material you are reading or studying. The main ideas are the focus of your study notes. You can keep your study notes either in a notebook or on a running word document on your computer.

Let's look at a passage that you have studied before:

Many know Rachel Carson as the mother of the environmental movement. She was born in rural Pennsylvania in 1907. There she showed an early interest in nature. As a girl, Carson collected fossils. She went bird watching. She also loved to write stories about woodland animals.

While you are reading a passage, you want to focus on and write down the main ideas. Look at the passage line by line.

Many know Rachel Carson as the mother of the environmental movement.

With this sentence, you would focus on the "who," *Rachel Carson*, and the "what," *mother of environmental movement*.

She was born in rural Pennsylvania in 1907.

With this sentence, you would focus on the "where" and the "when" she was born: *Pennsylvania in 1907*.

There she showed an early interest in nature.

With this sentence you can create a section of Rachel Carson's interests. You may write in your notes: *interest in nature*.

As a girl, Carson collected fossils.

With this sentence, you are adding to your new interests section that she collected fossils.

> She went bird watching.

With this sentence, you can also add that she did bird watching.

> She also loved to write stories about woodland animals.

The final sentence would complete your section on Rachel Carson's interests. Your notes might say that she wrote stories about woodland animals.

Here is an example:

(Main Idea) Rachel Carson (Detail) She was the mother of the environmental movement. Born: 1907 in Pennsylvania Interests: nature, collecting fossils, bird watching, writing stories about woodland animals

This paragraph is solely focusing on Rachel Carson. It is up to you to determine the key elements and main points that you need to take away and retain while reading this passage.

Complete the study notes for the passage with your Guide. You will need to reference this passage in later lessons. You and your Guide can find the answers in Section 2, page 250. Good luck!

_____

_____

_____

_____

_____

LESSON 27   WHAT'S THE POINT?

0:20

Let's continue looking at ways to be an effective note taker. You read information in each of your classes and are asked to understand and remember it. Summarizing is one way to support your study notes. Summarizing means that you are able to read a passage or selection and then restate or recall the important events in the story in the order they happened.

Summarizing is an action that occurs on a daily basis. A friend might ask what happened during the school day, and you proceed to provide the details of the day. That is summarizing. You might have the chance to go see a play, a movie, a musical, or a competition and upon returning from it, you might be asked to recall the action that happened. Your response would be an example of summarizing.

Let's continue to look at a familiar passage and practice summarizing:

Many know Rachel Carson as the mother of the environmental movement. She was born in rural Pennsylvania in 1907. There she showed an early interest in nature. As a girl, Carson collected fossils. She went bird watching. She also loved to write stories about woodland animals.

Carson's family was very poor, but she earned a scholarship for college. She studied English at first, but after one year, Carson changed her focus to science. She wished to become a scientist. She did very well, but there was trouble back at home. Over the years, Carson's family farmland had been ruined by factories. Carson's family moved in with her. Soon, she had to drop out of school to care for them. Distressed, she began to write for comfort. Magazines paid for her stories and articles. In this way, Carson supported her family.

Her articles became popular, so Carson began to write books. Her third book, *Silent Spring*, is her most famous. It warned about the effects of pollution on wildlife. She had seen these effects at her ruined family farm. The book was a worldwide hit. It inspired millions to care for the environment. Sadly, soon after the book was published, Rachel Carson died at age 56. After her passing, she was honored with the Presidential Medal of Freedom.

After reading the first paragraph of the passage, what if your teacher asked you to summarize and recall? What would you say or what details would you provide?

Here is an example of the summary.

Rachel Carson is known as the mother of the environmental movement. Being born in the rural part of Pennsylvania in 1907, she took an early interest in nature. Three nature interests she did included collecting fossils, watching birds, and writing stories about woodland animals.

Remember that when you are summarizing, you are recalling the main ideas or main events that happen as they occur in the story or passage. You and your Guide can find the answers to these questions in Section 2, page 251.

1. When Rachel was a child, what were her interests in nature?

   ○ factories

   ○ reading magazines

   ○ writing about woodland animals

   ○ science experiments

2. Why did Rachel drop out of college?

   ○ Rachel did not have good grades.

   ○ Rachel needed to care for her parents.

   ○ Rachel no longer wanted to become a scientist.

   ○ Rachel's parents' farm burned down.

3. Why was Rachel Carson's third book, *Silent Spring*, so famous?

   ○ Rachel died and it then became a bestseller.

   ○ Rachel wrote about the effects of pollution.

   ○ Rachel talked about the effects of her family farm.

   ○ Rachel was awarded the Presidential Medal of Freedom.

4. What does the term *scientist* mean?

   ○ person that takes care of wild animals

   ○ person that warns against environmental dangers

   ○ person having expert knowledge of natural science

   ○ all of the above

LESSON 28 PREPARE TO WRITE

0:20

21:40

As the school year passes, you will continue to work on being an effective note taker. One way to help support your study notes is to prepare an outline from your reading. This outline will help you focus on the main ideas and details. You will see a lot of different types of outlines; it is important to understand that each layout serves a different purpose. Outlining helps you understand the bigger picture and narrow down the finer details. Outlining also prepares you for the writing stage.

One strategy you can use is to identify the main idea and supporting details from every paragraph of a story or passage. This type of outline will focus on the theme of the main topic for each paragraph and provide the supporting details that summarize the topic sentence. Let's continue to review the passage about Rachel Carson and use an outline to support your ability to construct study notes.

Many know Rachel Carson as the mother of the environmental movement. She was born in rural Pennsylvania in 1907. There she showed an early interest in nature. As a girl, Carson collected fossils. She went bird watching. She also loved to write stories about woodland animals.

Main Idea	Detail
Rachel Carson was the mother of the environmental movement.	She loved to write stories about woodland animals.

Carson's family was very poor, but she earned a scholarship for college. She studied English at first, but after one year, Carson changed her focus to science. She wished to become a scientist. She did very well, but there was trouble back at home. Over the years, Carson's family farmland had been ruined by factories. Carson's family moved in with her. Soon, she had to drop out of school to care for them. Distressed, she began to write for comfort. Magazines paid for her stories and articles. In this way, Carson supported her family.

Main Idea	Detail
Carson's family struggled financially.	Carson began to write for comfort and this is how she supported her family. Magazines paid for her stories and articles.

Her articles became popular, so Carson began to write books. Her third book, *Silent Spring*, is her most famous. It warned about the effects of pollution on wildlife. She had seen these effects at her ruined family farm. The book was a worldwide hit. It inspired millions to care for the environment. Sadly, soon after the book was published, Rachel Carson died at age 56. After her passing, she was honored with the Presidential Medal of Freedom.

Main Idea	Detail
Carson began to write books.	Her articles became popular. *Silent Spring* is her most famous book and is known worldwide.

When you summarize each paragraph, you can almost use the main idea and details to write a summary of what you have read:

Rachel Carson, mother of environmental movement. She loved to write stories about woodland animals. Carson's family struggled financially. Carson began to write for comfort and this is how she supported her family. Magazines paid for her stories and articles. Carson began to write books. Her articles became popular. *Silent Spring* is her most famous book and known worldwide.

Discuss with your Guide: Would you have made any changes to a main idea or supporting detail?

_____

_____

LESSON 29 HOW MANY Ws?

0:20

21-40

Along with taking notes, you can use the reading strategy that is called 5W-How Strategy. This strategy enables you to focus on those main ideas and most important details you need to grasp from the passage.

This strategy focuses on five keywords that start with the letter *W* (*who*, *what*, *where*, *when*, and *why*) and the word *how*.

Who are the main characters?

What has happened so far, and what might happen next?

Where are the events taking place?

When are the events taking place?

Why are the events happening?

How do the characters resolve the conflict?

You will continue to review the passage about Rachel Carson and use the 5W-How Strategy to accompany your note taking. While reading, jot down the answers to the above questions.

Rachel Carson

Many know Rachel Carson as the mother of the environmental movement. She was born in rural Pennsylvania in 1907. There she showed an early interest in nature. As a girl, Carson collected fossils. She went bird watching. She also loved to write stories about woodland animals.

Carson's family was very poor, but she earned a scholarship for college. She studied English at first, but after one year, Carson changed her focus to science. She wished to become a scientist. She did very well, but there was trouble back at home. Over the years, Carson's family farmland had been ruined by factories. Carson's family moved in with her. Soon, she had to drop out of school to care for them. Distressed, she began to write for comfort. Magazines paid for her stories and articles. In this way, Carson supported her family.

Her articles became popular, so Carson began to write books. Her third book, *Silent Spring*, is her most famous. It warned about the effects of pollution on wildlife. She had seen these effects at her ruined family farm. The book was a worldwide hit. It inspired millions to care for the environment. Sadly, soon after the book was published, Rachel Carson died at age 56. After her passing, she was honored with the Presidential Medal of Freedom.

Check your answers to compare if they are similar to the ones below.

Who are the main characters?
Rachel Carson and her family

What has happened so far, and what might happen next?
Carson is interested in nature from an early age and is known as the mother of the environmental movement.

Where are the events taking place?
Events are taking place in rural Pennsylvania.

When are the events taking place?
Events are taking place while her parents are financially struggling throughout Rachel's life.

Why are the events happening?
Carson's family farmland is ruined by factories.

How do the characters resolve the conflict?
Carson begins writing articles and magazines. She receives pay for her articles. Her articles became popular, so she started writing books. Her writing supported her family financially. In her book, Silent Spring, *she was able to talk about the effects of pollution on wildlife and inspired people to start caring for the environment.*

You will continue to see and utilize this strategy throughout your schooling. It helps to narrow the focus on five keywords that start with the letter *W* (*who*, *what*, *where*, *when*, and *why*) and the word *how*. By focusing on these keywords, you will be able to focus your note taking on the important and main events from the passage.

You and your Guide can practice this strategy using stories that you have already read. What is the name of the last book you read for pleasure?

_____

_____

21-40

LESSON 30   GRAPHIC ORGANIZER

0:20

21-40

You can utilize a visual aid, or what is commonly known as a graphic organizer, to help your note taking skills. The graphic organizer in this lesson enables you to take notes using a visual aid to pinpoint specific details found in the passage.

You place the topic in the middle circle. You add details that further support the main idea in the surrounding smaller circles. You can add circles when needed. This strategy also prepares you for the writing process and for timed tests.

Let's read this passage about Rachel Carson. Create the graphic organizer in your notebook or create it on your computer. To create it in a Word document on your computer, open the Word document, click Insert, click Shapes, and then click on the circle. Place the circle on the page.

Rachel Carson

Many know Rachel Carson as the mother of the environmental movement. She was born in rural Pennsylvania in 1907. There she showed an early interest in nature. As a girl, Carson collected fossils. She went bird watching. She also loved to write stories about woodland animals.

Carson's family was very poor, but she earned a scholarship for college. She studied English at first, but after one year, Carson changed her focus to science. She wished to become a scientist. She did very well, but there was trouble back at home. Over the years, Carson's family farmland had been ruined by factories. Carson's family moved in with her. Soon, she had to drop out of school to care for them. Distressed, she began to write for comfort. Magazines paid for her stories and articles. In this way, Carson supported her family.

Her articles became popular, so Carson began to write books. Her third book, *Silent Spring*, is her most famous. It warned about the effects of pollution on wildlife. She had seen these effects at her ruined family farm. The book was a worldwide hit. It inspired millions to care for the environment. Sadly, soon after the book was published, Rachel Carson died at age 56. After her passing, she was honored with the Presidential Medal of Freedom.

Rachel Carson is found in the middle circle since the passage is about her. The circles surrounding the main topic include the various supporting details about Carson and her life.

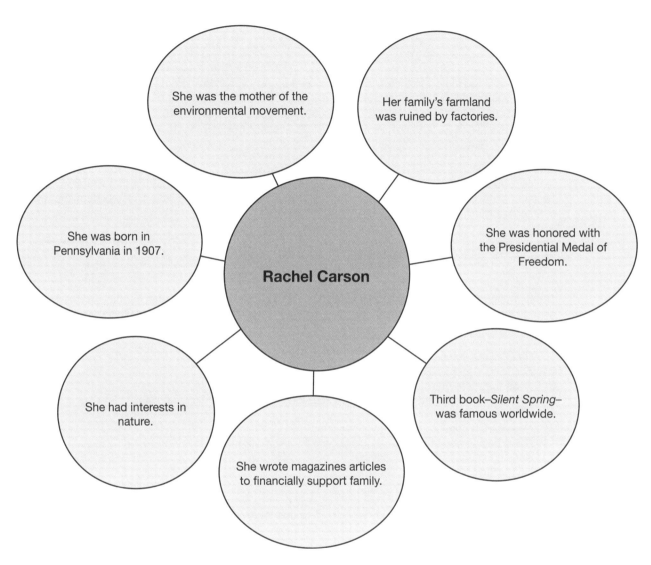

Don't forget to plan out your weekly and monthly schedule for study time, clubs and sports, and for test days. It is important to develop these habits without being reminded.

What other graphic organizer might help you create a story map?

_____

_____

LESSON 31   PREPARATION IS KEY!

0:20

21-40

We have reviewed many strategies for developing strong study habits and note taking skills. These strategies will help you prepare for quizzes, tests, and exams. It is important to develop strong study habits and learn how to be an effective test taker. We will review test taking strategies that will help you develop skills for tackling every test with a positive attitude. By developing proper study habits, you are already better prepared for taking tests.

Your Guide uses the results of a test to figure out what you know and don't know. Your Guide will use the results to make a plan for what needs to be concentrated on. It is very important that you always do your best and show your work. Don't be afraid to ask questions; questions help your Guide understand what you are having difficulty with.

You will spend time reviewing your study notes and eliminating topics that you feel you know well. It is important to study what you don't know and have confidence in what you do know, so you can focus your study time.

The first test taking strategy is to ask questions until you are comfortable that you have learned what you need to know. This should happen every day during the time you spend with your Guide. We will review the following strategies:

1. Read all the directions on a test.
2. Focus on one question at a time.
3. Read the entire question and all answer choices.
4. Eliminate answers and focus on the choices left in a multiple choice question.
5. Check your work.
6. Use scratch paper to plan out your answer.
7. Learn how to create or answer questions with graphic organizers.
8. Keep short answer questions short.
9. Understand rubrics.
10. Complete the ACE strategy.

If you follow all these strategies, you will soon find that fourth grade will be a great year for you.

Discuss with your Guide: Name one thing that you are concerned about before you take a test.

_____

_____

LESSON 32

0:20

DID YOU READ THE DIRECTIONS?

Following directions is a skill that you will use throughout your life. Directions can be as simple as your Guide telling you to open an activity book to a certain page, or they can be complicated, such as written directions used to build a piece of furniture. It is very important to master the art of following directions. State standardized assessments are filled with directions, but they have important information to help you be successful on the test.

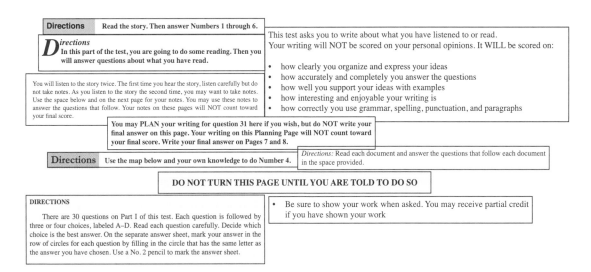

| Directions | Read the story. Then answer Numbers 1 through 6. |

Directions
In this part of the test, you are going to do some reading. Then you will answer questions about what you have read.

You will listen to the story twice. The first time you hear the story, listen carefully but do not take notes. As you listen to the story the second time, you may want to take notes. Use the space below and on the next page for your notes. You may use these notes to answer the questions that follow. Your notes on these pages will NOT count toward your final score.

This test asks you to write about what you have listened to or read. Your writing will NOT be scored on your personal opinions. It WILL be scored on:

- how clearly you organize and express your ideas
- how accurately and completely you answer the questions
- how well you support your ideas with examples
- how interesting and enjoyable your writing is
- how correctly you use grammar, spelling, punctuation, and paragraphs

You may PLAN your writing for question 31 here if you wish, but do NOT write your final answer on this page. Your writing on this Planning Page will NOT count toward your final score. Write your final answer on Pages 7 and 8.

| Directions | Use the map below and your own knowledge to do Number 4. |

Directions: Read each document and answer the questions that follow each document in the space provided.

DO NOT TURN THIS PAGE UNTIL YOU ARE TOLD TO DO SO

DIRECTIONS

There are 30 questions on Part I of this test. Each question is followed by three or four choices, labeled A–D. Read each question carefully. Decide which choice is the best answer. On the separate answer sheet, mark your answer in the row of circles for each question by filling in the circle that has the same letter as the answer you have chosen. Use a No. 2 pencil to mark the answer sheet.

- Be sure to show your work when asked. You may receive partial credit if you have shown your work

Before you begin any exam, you should follow all directions from your Guide. Directions such as putting your name and date on the top of the page, clearing off your work space, and taking out materials you will need are important to make sure you are prepared to take a test and that you get credit for your work. If you didn't put your name on the test, how would your teacher know who gets credit for the great work?

Make sure you have read or listened to all the directions before you begin any work. Sometimes you will see directions that appear to be the same directions you have read before; however, it may have a different word or an extra direction at the end. If you don't read the directions entirely, you could miss important information. Today, you will read a set of directions. Once you have completed the directions, hand your paper to your Guide. Your Guide will check your answers in Section 2, page 253 of this book. Good luck!

Directions:

1. Read all the directions. There are 10 steps; be sure to read all of the steps first. Don't do any work on your paper until you have read each direction.

2. Take a piece of paper out of your supply box or notebook. Place it on your work space in front of your Guide.

3. Take a No. 2 pencil and a red crayon out of your supplies and place them on your desk. Tell your Guide to initial the right corner of your paper once you have all your writing tools.

4. Count the number of doorways in your room. Write the number here in pencil. _____

CONTINUED ->

5. Complete the following math problem on your paper. Show all your work:

$$456 - 279 =$$

6. Draw an outline of your hand in red crayon in the center of your paper.

7. Write your Guide's name in pencil at the bottom of your paper.

8. Turn the paper over on your workspace. You will now let your Guide check your work.

9. Leave your work area and give your Guide five minutes to check your work in Section 2, page 253 of this book.

10. Instructions: Do not do any of the work in directions 1 – 9. All you need to do is write your name and date and hand your paper to your Guide.

Were the directions easy to follow?

_____

Did you read all the directions before you started working?

_____

Now that you have completed this activity, do you have a better understanding of the importance of following directions?

_____

What did you learn?

_____

LESSON 33 A FEW MORE TIPS

0:20

21-40

Imagine it is the day of your state standardized test. Are you prepared? You've gotten a good night's sleep. You ate a great breakfast. You arrived at school on time. You have studied all your notes. Now what? A little anxiety is normal because test taking can be overwhelming. You will have to trust that you have prepared yourself to be successful. You will learn to rely on the test taking strategies you are learning in this book. State standardized tests usually have four question types: multiple choice, show your work, short answer, and extended response. Knowing how to tackle each of these question types will help you feel confident. Don't forget to read all directions before beginning any section. Most state standardized tests begin with multiple choice questions. There are strategies for answering multiple choice questions. You will begin to learn them today.

Most multiple choice questions you have seen have **one best answer**. Your job is to find that answer. If you are ever unsure of your answer, put a little question mark next to the number on the test. Leaving a question unanswered is not a good strategy. When you have completed the test, you can go back to the questions with question marks and check your work.

It is a good strategy to use a piece of blank scratch paper to cover up answer choices and other questions so that you can focus on the question you are working on, as shown below.

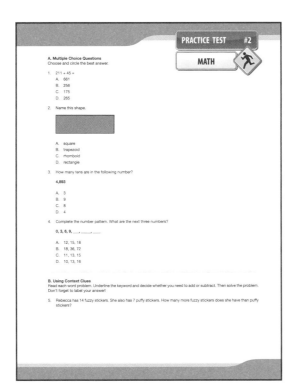

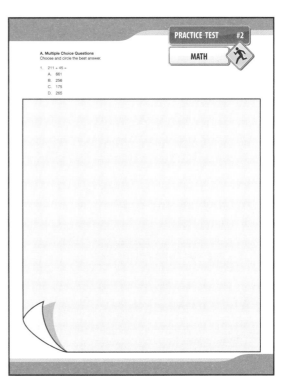

Give it a try! Use the sample questions on the next page. Use a blank piece of paper to cover up the other questions.

CONTINUED ->

Practice Test

You will complete five practice questions. Each question has four answer choices. Read each question carefully. Decide which answer choice is the best. Use a single line to cross out the other three answer choices. You can review your answers in Section 2, page 254 of this book.

1. Terry went outside at 9:00 a.m. on a sunny morning and looked at his shadow. He went back out at 10:00 a.m., 11:00 a.m., and noon. Which answer **best describes** the length of Terry's shadow?

    ○ His shadow did not change.

    ○ It was shorter each time Terry looked.

    ○ It was longer each time Terry looked.

    ○ It was shorter at 9:00 a.m. than it was at 11:00 a.m.

2. The primary energy source in all living communities is _____.

    ○ the sun

    ○ the animals

    ○ the plants

    ○ the soil

3. When light hits a dark object, most of the light is _____.

    ○ absorbed

    ○ reflected

    ○ diffused

    ○ refracted

4. Which statement **best** describes the relationship between a lion and a gazelle?

    ○ The lion is the consumer, and the gazelle is the producer.

    ○ The lion is the predator, and the gazelle is the decomposer.

    ○ The lion is the prey, and the gazelle is the consumer.

    ○ The lion is the predator, and the gazelle is the prey.

5. A ball is thrown up into the air. Which force causes the ball to fall to the ground?

    ○ friction

    ○ gravity

    ○ magnetism

    ○ electricity

LESSON 34

MULTIPLE CHOICE QUESTIONS

0:20

21-40

When you answer multiple choice questions, try to locate the keyword. Below, you will find examples of keywords in multiple choice questions and a sample of how the word might appear in a question. When you can locate the keyword and understand what you are supposed to answer, then you will be able to focus on selecting the correct answer choice. You practice reading comprehension skills all the time, especially in language arts. Whenever you read, your Guide may ask questions to determine if you understand the text. Knowing what is expected of you when answering multiple choice questions is important, but it is more important that you read for pleasure every day. This allows you to practice reading comprehension skills all the time.

Word or Phrase	How to Answer	Example
which	Select one answer choice that best answers the question.	• Which animal could be added to this web? • Which holiday honors all the men and women who fought to defend the United States? • Which two magnets are attracting each other? • Which expression can be used to find the total number of toy cars Joe has?
what	Think about what you read, see in a diagram, or evaluate in a process.	• What did Johnny's teacher write at the top of the page? • What was the approximate population of New York in 1900? • What simple machine is the person using to help roll the barrel? • What is the name of the shape?
why	Determine the best reason that explains a passage or process.	• Why does the author **most likely** include the information about Boston? • Why would this bulb be lit?
how	Understand an event, a fact, or a process that occurs.	• How would Marcy **most likely** describe evaporation? • How are these seeds **most likely** dispersed? • Using the graph below, how many students take the bus to school on Friday?
based on (the passage, the information, the diagram, the chart)	Make sure you reread passages, diagrams, or charts to get your answer.	• In the passage, the most important lesson Ally learns is_____. • Base your answers to questions 1 and 2 on the map below. • Based on the food web, frogs prey on _____. • Base your answer to question 3 on the illustration below.

CONTINUED ->

best, most, mostly, most likely	Use the process of elimination to find the best answer. These types of questions are commonly missed.	• Which of these details is **most** important to what happens in the passage? • What is the **best** title for this graphic organizer? • Which physical change would **most likely** help an animal survive during winter? • Based on the pictograph, how many people will **most likely** visit the museum in July?
least to greatest, smallest to largest, next, first, right after, last, which step	Determine the order or the sequence of numbers, objects, or events of a story.	• Based on what you read in the passage, Delores **first** tries the experiment on her _____. • Which number has the **greatest** value in the thousands place? • Which sequence shows the lifecycle of some insects? • What is the **next** step for a bill to become law?
true, except, NOT	These are the most commonly missed questions because they ask you to select an answer choice that does not answer a question.	• According to the article, which statement about the rainforest is **true**? • Which natural resource grows in all states in the Southeast **except** Florida? • Which of the following is **NOT** an adaptation of a desert fox?

LESSON 35

PROCESS OF ELIMINATION

0:20

21·40

When you take a state standardized exam, the first questions you will answer are multiple choice questions with four answer choices. Your task is to choose the answer that best or completely answers the question. Read the question carefully so you understand what the question is asking. A multiple choice question can be a phrase or a stem. A stem is a question that asks you to complete the sentence. An example of a stem is: *In the passage, the most important lesson Ally learns is _____.* This is a stem because the sentence needs to be completed using one of the answer choices.

It is important that you approach all multiple choice questions using the strategies outlined below—even if you think you are sure of your answer. Try to develop the habit of approaching all multiple choice questions the same way because shortcuts don't help. Shortcuts include only reading half the question, picking the answer you may think is correct without checking all answer choices, and not taking the time to make sure you understand the question. These examples are not good strategies to develop. It may seem that the strategies below will take a lot of time to complete; however, once you practice and develop these habits, you will soon find it doesn't take any more than thirty seconds of your time.

Below are strategies that will help you be a successful test taker.

Step 1: Cover the answer choices with a piece of scratch paper before you read the question. Read the question or stem and try to answer the question on your own. This will give you time to make sure you understand the question.

Step 2: Read the question or stem statement with each answer choice. You can read each answer choice aloud in your head to see what the best answer choice is. Ask yourself if the answer makes the stem true or completely answers the question.

Step 3: Eliminate answer choices that you know are absolutely **not** correct. If you are stuck on a question, the process of elimination allows you to **go back to Step 2** and review only answers that you know could possibly make the question or stem correct.

Let's review an example. Here is the question with the answer choices removed, so you can see how each step would look during a test.

Question:

Which colony was **most** influenced by Quaker settlements in the 1600s?

Step 1: Discuss with your Guide. Can you tell your Guide anything you know about early settlers to the United States? Do you know who the Quakers were? Do you know where in the Northeast the Quakers settled?

Step 2: Read the question with each answer choice.

Which colony was **most** influenced by Quaker settlements in the 1600s?

    O Georgia

Which colony was **most** influenced by Quaker settlements in the 1600s?

    O Pennsylvania

Which colony was **most** influenced by Quaker settlements in the 1600s?

    O Delaware

CONTINUED ->

Which colony was **most** influenced by Quaker settlements in the 1600s?

○ Maryland

When you do this step, you have had time to think about each answer and if it correctly answered the question. You may have even had a discussion in your head to try to figure out if the answer could make the question true. Your brain doesn't need a lot of time to do this because it is looking for the clues in your memory.

Step 3: This is the most important part to this process. The question above is a difficult question because there are no context clues to help you figure out the answer. This is basic knowledge that you must learn in fourth grade.

Which colony was **most** influenced by Quaker settlements in the 1600s?

○ ~~Georgia~~ (eliminated because it was formed in the 1700s)

○ Pennsylvania

○ ~~Delaware~~ (eliminated because it was formed in the 1700s)

○ Maryland

Were you able to eliminate any choices? You may have known that the Quakers were people that left England in the 1600s because they wanted religious freedom. The Quakers were being put in jail back in England because of their views on worship. William Penn was a famous Quaker. He led a group of Quakers out of England. Have you figured it out yet? The state of Pennsylvania is named after William Penn. He was given the state to pay off a debt to his father. He and other Quakers from the Society of Friends settled in Pennsylvania to live with the freedom to practice their religion.

Follow these steps each time you answer a multiple choice question. You will get faster at it as you develop good habits.

LESSON 36

PRACTICE MULTIPLE CHOICE STRATEGIES

0:20

21:40

In this sample test, you will answer multiple choice questions. Use a blank sheet of scratch paper to cover the answer choices as you read each question carefully. Each question will be followed by four answer choices. Use the multiple choice strategies you learned to help you with this practice test: cover answer choices, read each question carefully and look for keywords, read each question with the answer choices, and eliminate any answers that don't answer the question completely. Choose the answer choice that best answers the question. Fill in the bubble next to your choice completely. You and your Guide can review the answers in Section 2, page 256 of this book. Good luck!

Practice Test

1. Choose the sentence that uses **to**, **too**, or **two** correctly.

   ○ Amanda likes to dance and she likes to read, **two**.

   ○ If Jim had **to** make a choice, he would rather play the drums than the clarinet.

   ○ Todd always wanted **too** be a doctor.

   ○ Lydia hopes **too** help animals when she finishes veterinary school.

2. Choose the sentence that uses **there**, **they're**, or **their** correctly.

   ○ The baseball team was well prepared for **they're** game.

   ○ Can you hand me that book over **their** on the floor?

   ○ **Their** boots are by the front door.

   ○ **There** studying science.

3. Choose the sentence that is written **correctly**.

   ○ Yes you may open your test booklet.

   ○ The temperature outside, I think, is perfect.

   ○ Timothy, on the other hand likes baseball.

   ○ He believes, that going to school is important.

4. Which of these is an example of alliteration?

   ○ wonderful pancakes

   ○ huge feet

   ○ marvelous milkshakes

   ○ glass houses

CONTINUED ->

5. Which of these is an example of an idiom?

○ The moon is like a light of fire in the sky.

○ The bees buzzed, the horses neighed, and the dog woofed when the farmer went into the barn.

○ The lizard laughed at the silly snake.

○ He thought the test was a piece of cake.

21-40

LESSON 37

NEGATIVES, ABSOLUTES, AND OTHER TRICKY WORDING

Imagine that you are sitting in front of a state standardized test. You are confident because you have practiced good test taking strategies all year. You are reading all the directions, you are rereading the questions and adding each answer choice to see if it fits, you are using the process of elimination, you are checking your work, and you are using the ACE strategy to answer extended response questions. Then you come across the following three questions or statements:

1. All of the following words are spelled correctly **except**:
2. Which of the following statements about the passage is **not** true?
3. Which of the following plans would Daniel **least likely** choose?

These types of questions or statements are not meant to be a trick to confuse you, but are meant to be tricky. You are being tested on your reading comprehension skills. The best strategy is to be alert for words like *not*, *except*, or *least*. You must select the answer that is most wrong.

Beware of words like *not*, *but*, *except*, *always*, *never*, and *only*. You will need to rephrase the questions or statements into a positive question or statement. The strategy is to know what you are looking for instead of what you are not looking for. When you see the words *always*, *never*, and *only* in an answer choice, eliminate those answers because they are almost never correct. This is because they mean *all of the time*, not just *some of the time*.

In the first example, the stem states:

All of the following words are spelled correctly **except**:

What the stem is really asking is:

Which of the following words is spelled incorrectly?

This makes the question a positive statement and provides a clear idea of what the question is asking you to do.

In the second example, the question states:

Which of the following statements about the passage is **not** true?

The question is really asking:

Which of the following statements about the passage is false?

The final question states:

Which of the following plans would Daniel **least likely** choose?

The question is really asking:

Which of the following plans would Daniel not choose?

CONTINUED ->

Once you understand the question, you can use all of the multiple choice strategies you learned to answer it. This is why you were taught to cover up the answer choices; you need time to figure out what the question is asking.

Change the following questions or statements to positive questions or statements. You and your Guide can review your answers in Section 2, page 258 of this book.

1. All of the following are supporting details for the story **except**:

   _____

2. According to the passage, which statement about Athena's dog is **not** false?

   _____

3. Mimi is planning a vegetable garden. Mimi is **least likely** to grow:

   _____

LESSON 38

`0:20`

PRACTICE POSITIVE STATEMENTS

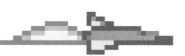

In this sample test, you will read a passage and answer multiple choice questions. Use a blank sheet of scratch paper to cover the answer choices as you read the questions carefully. Each question will be followed by four answer choices. Use the multiple choice strategies you learned to help you with this practice test: cover answer choices, read each question carefully and write a positive statement above the printed question, read each question with the answer choices, and eliminate any answers that don't answer the question completely. Choose the answer choice that best answers the question. Fill in the bubble next to your choice completely. You and your Guide can review the answers in Section 2, page 259 of this book. Good luck!

A Visit to Beaker's Lab
by Michael Scotto

Elsa and her friend Kai strolled together down a dirt road. She was telling Kai about her weekend as they walked.

Elsa was just getting toward the end of her story. Her voice lowered to a whisper. "I dropped the baking soda into the vinegar, and then…."

She trailed off and walked in silence.

After a few seconds, Kai finally looked over. "Then what?" he whispered back.

Elsa raised her eyebrows. "POW! FIZZ!" she shouted, making Kai jump. "Foam started shooting everywhere! I tried catching the foam in my hands, but I couldn't keep up. It spilled all over the kitchen floor."

"Wow," Kai replied.

"Gadzooks, it was fast!" said Elsa. "And then my mom told me, 'That is why we shouldn't live next door to a volcano.'"

Kai laughed. He loved to hear about Elsa's science adventures. Elsa's mother was a scientist. She did fun experiments with Elsa on the weekends.

"I still think living near a volcano could be neat," said Elsa. "You could toast marshmallows whenever you wanted!"

"It sounds kind of dangerous to me," Kai stated.

"That's why I want to ask Beaker about it," said Elsa. "I want to know what she thinks."

"She's not far away," Kai said. He pushed his blond hair out of his eyes and looked down the road. In the distance, he spotted the roof of the University of Midlandia Science Lab peeking over a hilltop.

"I can't wait to see her," said Elsa.

Elsa liked everyone who lived in Midlandia, but Beaker was her favorite. Beaker was a scientist, just like Elsa's mom. Whenever Elsa made a trip to Midlandia, she always tried to visit Beaker first.

When Elsa and Kai opened the doors to the lab, they found that Beaker was not alone. She and her friend Brick were each searching through a different area of the lab.

"Brick?" said Elsa. "What are you doing here?"

Both Midlandians turned. "Elsa and Kai!" Beaker cried. Her boot heels clicked as she trotted over to greet the kids. "Perfect timing!"

"What do you mean?" asked Kai.

"We have a bit of a mystery on our hands," answered Beaker. "You two might be just the pair to help us."

CONTINUED ->

1. All of the following statements can be used to describe Elsa **except**:

   ○ Elsa was surprised by the reaction of the baking soda and the vinegar.

   ○ Elsa does not live next door to a volcano.

   ○ The only friend that Elsa has in Midlandia is Kai.

   ○ Elsa enjoys conducting science experiments with her mother.

2. All of the following are examples of onomatopoeia **except**:

   ○ woof, meow

   ○ tick, tock

   ○ bang, clink

   ○ massive mountains

3. The author uses many examples of onomatopoeia in this passage. All of the following are **not** examples of onomatopoeia **except**:

   ○ Her boot heels clicked as she trotted over to greet the kids.

   ○ "You could toast marshmallows whenever you wanted!"

   ○ "Foam started shooting everywhere!"

   ○ Beaker was a scientist, much like Elsa's mom.

LESSON 39

HIGHLIGHT ONLY THE MAIN IDEA

`0:20`

21-40

You have read about the importance of reading comprehension skills. Part of developing strong reading comprehension skills is to be able to identify the main idea and supporting details in text. When you take a state standardized assessment, you will read passages, excerpts, or articles. These can be pieces of a larger story. If you recognize the passage from a story, make sure you only focus on what you are reading and do not include details from the rest of the story in your answers. It is important to only use the text given in the test to answer the questions.

The best strategy to use when you are reading a passage is to highlight only the main idea of the story. Highlighting allows your eyes to focus on an area of a passage. If you highlight too much of the text, then you will not be able to locate the paragraph or section that could help you answer a question correctly. State standardized tests assess whether you are able to find the main idea and supporting details of a passage. In previous lessons, you learned how to create study notes for language arts to use when summarizing a story or studying main ideas. During a state standardized test, you will not have time to be as detail oriented when answering multiple choice questions that follow a passage. The multiple choice section of a state standardized test is often limited in time; therefore, highlighting the main idea is a great strategy.

Read the following informative text; it will be the basis of the next three lessons. Read the entire text once all the way through. The second time you read the passage, use a highlighter to identify only the main idea in each paragraph. The main idea is the sentence or phrase that best explains the entire paragraph. The sentences around the main idea will provide the supporting details. You will use this passage to compare your work in Section 2, page 261 of this book.

The Importance of Protecting Endangered Species
by Nicole Costlow

The word *extinction* is a scary term. It means that a species of plant or animal has been eliminated from existence on the earth forever. Extinction is a very real threat to thousands of plants and animal species. Sadly, many species face extinction because of human actions. It is important not only to understand how our actions affect wildlife, but also to understand why humans should protect endangered species.

Awareness of endangered species began to grow in 1973 when government leaders passed the Endangered Species Act. This act is enforced by the US Fish and Wildlife Service. This act protects species that fall into two main categories: endangered and threatened. A species becomes *endangered* when it is very close to extinction. A *threatened* species is one that is not yet endangered, but is likely to become so soon. As of 2011, there were 1,383 endangered or threatened species of plants and animals in the United States alone.

Many animals are placed on the endangered or threatened list because humans are destroying their habitats, or where they live. In states like California and Utah, the habitat of the desert tortoise is shrinking due to the construction of new homes. Not only are desert tortoises losing their habitat, but many are killed by the heavy machinery used to build the new homes. Scientists estimate that only about one hundred thousand desert tortoises remain in the wild.

Another species that has suffered due to human interaction and development is the brown bear, commonly known as the grizzly bear. As the bears' natural, wooded habitat changes and disappears, they are forced into areas where humans live in order to find new food sources. When this happens, grizzlies are often shot and killed to keep humans safe. Also, during hunting season, hunters often mistake brown bears for black bears and kill them for sport. Today, brown bears are listed as a threatened species.

CONTINUED ->

Global warming, or climate change, is another serious threat to endangered species. Scientists have found that our planet's temperature is rising. Most believe that this is due to gases released from the fuels many humans use in their daily lives. These gases get trapped in the earth's atmosphere and cause the planet's temperature to become warmer over time. The rising temperatures cause ice to melt in places like the Arctic. This process has caused creatures such as polar bears to be considered threatened animals under the Endangered Species Act.

Polar bears depend on the natural sea ice in the Arctic for their habitat and for hunting. Without it, they will have fewer places to find food and will have to swim father distances to find a resting place. Scientists estimate that there are only about twenty-five thousand polar bears left in the wild. Two-thirds of that population may vanish within the next fifty years if Arctic temperatures continue to rise. That equals more than sixteen thousand polar bears that may be lost due to global warming.

The world's tiger population has suffered some of the greatest loss at the hands of humans. At one time, there were nine different types of tigers in the world. Over the past seventy years, three of those species have become extinct. Today, only a little more than three thousand tigers remain in the wild. The tiger population is shrinking for several reasons. Many were hunted for their fur; others lost their habitat as the human population expanded in countries such as India and China. Luckily for the tiger, organizations such as the World Wildlife Fund have begun efforts to save the species. Their goal is to double the world population of tigers by the year 2022.

There are many reasons why it is important for humans to help save endangered species from extinction. Our own survival may depend on it. Our planet is made up of many different ecosystems. Ecosystems are specific areas of living organisms that all depend on each other for survival. If one species in a particular ecosystem becomes extinct, all of the other living things in that ecosystem will be affected by the loss.

To understand how the extinction of a species can impact humans, it is important to think small. For example, in a forest ecosystem, a certain type of moss growing on a tree could provide shelter for hundreds of insects. Those insects leave their home in the moss to eat certain types of plants in the same forest. While feeding on those plants, the insects pollinate other plants in the forest that feed deer in the area. Humans who live near the forest use the deer as a food source. If the species of moss becomes extinct, the insects have no shelter and eventually die off. This harms the plants, which are no longer being pollinated and cannot grow. Without a plant supply, the deer are forced to move away to find another food source. Once the deer are gone, the humans in the area must find another source of meat for their meals. With the loss of just one species in an environment—even something as small as moss—the entire ecosystem could change forever.

In addition to saving endangered animal species, science has also proven that endangered plants could be extremely valuable to humans. Many medicines commonly used today contain substances from plants, including antibiotics and pain medications. In addition, medicines used to treat serious diseases, such as cancer, have come from plants. Today, there are 794 species of plants listed as endangered or threatened under the Endangered Species Act. Even if only a few of these species become extinct, scientists will lose the chance to study them. They could miss out on finding cures and treatments for diseases that affect people all over the world.

It is very important to understand how our actions on the planet affect the natural world around us. Once extinct, a species, whether beautiful or valuable, is gone forever. When we allow a plant or animal to become extinct, we are not just hurting nature; we could be hurting ourselves.

LESSON 40 — HIGHLIGHT ONLY THE MAIN IDEA

`0:20`

When you highlight just the main idea in a passage, you will be able to locate any supporting details that might help you answer a multiple choice question correctly. That is because the passages on state standardized tests are often long and span across two pages. You may find that flipping back and forth between pages can be overwhelming and may even result in you forgetting what the question is asking. The first thing to remember is to stay calm and do not give up. This is the reason you should always practice good highlighting skills. In the passage from the last lesson, you identified ten sentences or phrases that describe the main ideas. Reading ten sentences is a lot more effective then reading ten paragraphs over and over. When you come to a multiple choice question that asks you to use the text to help with the answer, you will be able to pinpoint the exact location you need.

In the passage "The Importance of Protecting Endangered Species," you should have highlighted ten sentences. Your sentences may not match the ones highlighted in Section 2, page 261 of this book. In this lesson, you will use these highlighted sentences to think about details.

The main idea of paragraph 1 is:

Extinction is a very real threat to thousands of plants and animal species.

This sentence identifies that the passage will be about animals and plants around the world that are facing extinction. In this paragraph, the supporting details provide you with a definition for extinction and a reason that animals and plants are in danger. If you had a multiple choice question that asks you to define extinction, you would use the context clues in this paragraph to help you.

The main idea of paragraph 2 is:

This act protects species that fall into two main characters: endangered and threatened.

Imagine that you are reading a question about the Endangered Species Act; you may be asked what year it was enacted, what the act provided, who passed the act, or how many species are endangered and threatened. All of these supporting details are in paragraph 2. By highlighting just the main idea sentence, you can locate that information quickly.

The main idea of paragraph 3 is:

In states like California and Utah, the habitat of the desert tortoise is shrinking due to the construction of new homes.

By now, you should see a pattern developing for how main idea sentences can help you quickly identify details of a passage. This skill takes a lot of practice. Earlier in this book, you read that reading comprehension skills are learned through practice and reading for pleasure. In this paragraph, you could answer questions about desert tortoises: where they live, how many are affected, and what is causing their extinction.

The main idea for paragraph 4 is:

Another species that has suffered due to human interaction and development is the brown bear, commonly known as the grizzly bear.

You may have noticed that this is the first time that the first sentence was used as the main idea. It is important to know that the main idea is not always the first sentence in a paragraph. It is the sentence that

CONTINUED ->

helps you to identify supporting details in a passage. It is important to limit the number of sentences that you need to read so that you can quickly locate information that will help you.

Now it's your turn to try. In Paragraph 5, the following sentence can be used as the main idea:

Scientists have found that our planet's temperature is rising.

From reading this paragraph, what questions may you be able to answer because of the supporting details? You and your Guide can check your answer in Section 2, page 263 of this book.

_____

_____

_____

LESSON 41

HIGHLIGHTING CHARTS AND DIAGRAMS

0:20

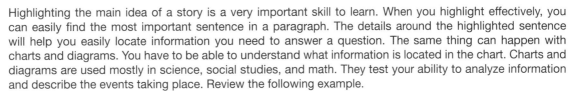

Highlighting the main idea of a story is a very important skill to learn. When you highlight effectively, you can easily find the most important sentence in a paragraph. The details around the highlighted sentence will help you easily locate information you need to answer a question. The same thing can happen with charts and diagrams. You have to be able to understand what information is located in the chart. Charts and diagrams are used mostly in science, social studies, and math. They test your ability to analyze information and describe the events taking place. Review the following example.

Base your answers to the questions on the diagram below and your knowledge of science.

A group of students in science class were completing an experiment about objects that would float or sink. They had four objects to test. The students dropped a steel nail and a steel spoon into a bucket of water and watched them sink to the bottom of the bucket. They had two experiments left.

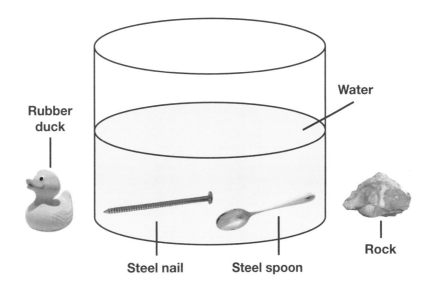

Without reading the questions, you have to be able to interpret the information in this diagram. The first thing you will want to do is read through the explanation and highlight the main idea.

This diagram is a picture of an experiment on objects that would sink or float in water. Then you should think about an experiment that you conducted for science class that may be similar. You will need to use your knowledge of science to help you decide which objects would sink and which objects would float. Next, you should write notes on the graph to help you focus on the important information.

In lesson 42, you will answer questions on this diagram. Today, however, all you need to do is interpret the diagram. When you take time to read all the directions and look at the graph with your knowledge of a subject, it helps you focus your attention on the important information. By the time you get to the questions, you will have an idea in your mind about the types of questions that can be asked. Answer the questions below to help you think about the diagram.

Discuss and complete with your Guide, then check your answers in Section 2, page 264.

1. Use a pencil to write above the rubber duck whether you think it will sink or float.
2. Use a pencil to write above the rock whether you think it will sink or float.
3. Use your knowledge of science to write a sentence explaining why objects sink or float.

STEP 2: READ THE QUESTIONS

`0:20`

In lesson 41, you were given only the diagram portion of this assessment. The assessment questions are now ready for you to answer. You can focus on the strategies you learned about answering multiple choice questions: cover up the answers and read the question only, read the question with each answer choice, and eliminate incorrect answers. It is important that you develop the strategies that you learn in this book. You want to take your time and practice these during every exam you take in fourth grade. More importantly, by learning these strategies now, you will be able to take these skills with you for the rest of your school years and into college. When you develop the habits that make these strategies part of your test taking routine, you can be confident that you have all the tools to be a great student.

Answer the questions that go with this diagram. You will check your answers in Section 2, page 265.

Base your answers to the questions on the diagram below and your knowledge of science.

A group of students in science class were completing an experiment about objects that would float or sink. They had four objects to test. The students dropped a steel nail and a steel spoon into a bucket of water and watched them sink to the bottom of the bucket. They had two experiments left.

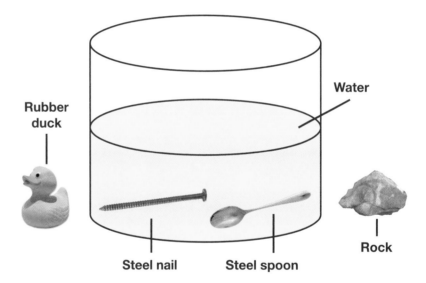

Practice Questions

The following questions only have three answer choices.

1. When the rock is placed in the bucket, the water level will _____.

   O decrease   O remain the same

   O increase

2. The group places the rock in the bucket. Which property can be used to best describe the reason the rock sinks?

   O texture   O color

   O density

3. The group places the rubber duck in the bucket. Which property can be used to best describe the reason the duck floats?

   O mass   O color

   O texture

41-60

LESSON 43   INFORMATION IN A TABLE

0:20

41-60

What types of diagrams or charts might you see on a state standardized assessment? That question is difficult to answer because the state creates the tests. The important point is not to worry; your classwork, homework, and exams will prepare you to answer any question. You have almost an entire school year to learn new information, practice good study skills, organize your time on a calendar, and practice the skills for effective test taking.

When you get to a social studies question on a map, a math question with a bar graph, or a science question with a food web, you will know great strategies to answer the question. If you take the time in your weekly schedule to practice all the skills you will learn, then it will not matter what type of question you see on a state standardized test.

In the previous lessons, you were given a science diagram to interpret. In this lesson, you will interpret information on a table. Today, you will be given only the information in the table. Take the time to organize your thoughts and write notes to help you interpret what you see. You can check your answers in Section 2, page 267.

Four friends have savings accounts. Each friend adds the same amount of dollars to his or her savings account each month. The table below shows the total amount of money each student has at the end of the month.

Savings Accounts

Month	Account Balance (in dollars)			
	Jason (+3)	Corey	Tyler	Brianne
January	$38.00	$34.00	$32.00	$35.00
February	$41.00	$38.00	$38.00	$40.00
March	$44.00	$42.00	$44.00	$45.00
	$47.00			
	$50.00			
	$53.00			

The table above shows a math question in a chart. The first step is to read the information above the chart and look for the main idea; the highlighted section in the question shows that you are being asked to figure out a number pattern. The question may ask you to extend each friend's number pattern or it may ask you to choose a number pattern that is similar to one of the friends. That gives you two choices to think about. Answer the questions below to help organize your thoughts.

1. Write the number pattern next to each friend's name that is added to that friend's savings account each month. The number for Jason has been provided for you.
2. Extend the chart for each friend three more months. Jason's has already been provided for you.
3. Circle the name of the friend who has the most money at the end of the sixth month and circle the amount.

LESSON 44 · INTERPRET AND ANSWER

0:20

Now that you understand what the chart is asking you to interpret, you can work on answering the questions. You will need to use your multiple choice strategies to help you get the correct answer. You should have all these skills memorized by now and they should be part of your regular strategy every time you answer a multiple choice question. List the three strategies to answering multiple choice questions. You can check your answers in Section 2, page 268.

1. Step 1: _____

2. Step 2: _____

3. Step 3: _____

Four friends have savings accounts. Each friend adds the same amount of dollars to his or her savings account each month. The table below shows the total amount of money each student has at the end of the month.

Savings Accounts

Month	Account Balance (in dollars)			
	Jason	**Corey**	**Tyler**	**Brianne**
January	$38.00	$34.00	$32.00	$35.00
February	$41.00	$38.00	$38.00	$40.00
March	$44.00	$42.00	$44.00	$45.00

Practice Questions

1. If each friend continues saving the same amount of dollars each month, who will have the **most** money at the end of the fifth month?

    O Corey   O Tyler

    O Brianne   O Jason

2. Which pattern is the same as Corey's?

    O 71, 77, 83, 89   O 10, 15, 20, 25

    O 33, 36, 39, 42   O 23, 27, 31, 35

41-60

LESSON 45 IT'S ON THE MAP

`0:20`

You may be required to complete a social studies state standardized test in fourth grade. You will also have many assessments over the school year in social studies; both will likely have a map or globe question. These questions are similar to the questions based on charts and diagrams because you have to interpret the information on the map in order to answer the questions. Take your time to understand what the map is showing you. Use your knowledge of maps to help organize your thoughts. Most importantly, remember the key elements that make up a map: the title, the key, the compass rose, and the map scale. The title tells you exactly what the map represents, the key will let you know what all the symbols on the map represent, the compass rose will give you the direction (north, south, east, and west), and the map scale will explain the distance between two points. You already have all the knowledge you need to interpret the map; you just need to take the time to do so before you attempt to answer any questions. You can check your answers in Section 2, page 269.

Base your answers to the questions on the map below.

Rivers and Lakes of Pennsylvania

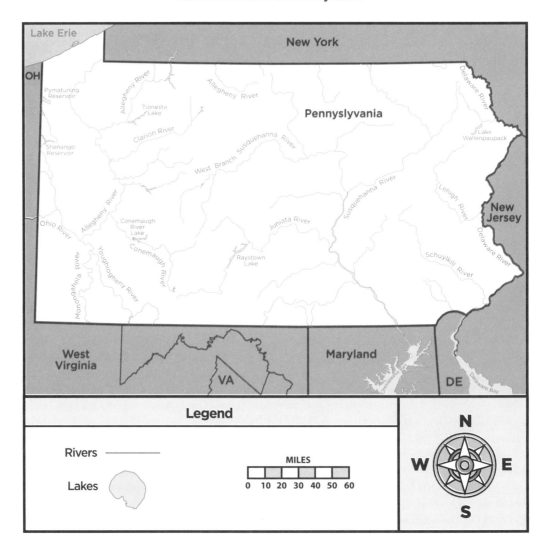

1. Which river forms a boundary between the states of Pennsylvania and New York?

   ○ Delaware River   ○ Monongahela River

   ○ Susquehanna River   ○ Ohio River

2. Which Pennsylvania river flows into the Chesapeake Bay in Maryland?

   ○ Delaware River   ○ Ohio River

   ○ Susquehanna River   ○ Allegheny River

41-60

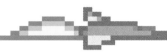

LESSON 46   WHAT'S A RUBRIC?

0:10

41-60

Earlier in this book, you learned about using the **A**nswer, **C**ite, **E**xplain strategy for extended response questions. These types of questions are also called open-ended questions, essay questions, or brief constructed response questions. Whatever they are called, these questions are very challenging. They test your ability to extend your thinking using your knowledge of a subject. When you answer closed-ended questions, like multiple choice or short answer, there is usually only one answer. They are called closed-ended questions because you only have to get to the one correct answer choice.

In open-ended questions, each student uses his own knowledge and writing style to help him "explain his brain." In this type of question, you are graded on a rubric. A rubric is a list of tasks that you will need to include in your writing. It tells you what you're expected to do when you answer an open-ended question. In fourth grade, your rubrics will be graded on a scale of 0 – 3; a zero is given when you do not attempt to provide any answers for the task or have little information related to the task. The key is to attempt every extended response question.

In state standardized assessments, rubrics do not get changed over to a letter grade like they do in your fourth grade formal assessments. State standardized tests are reported back to your state's Department of Education and tells them whether you are achieving at a high level as it relates to your grade. Each state decides what tasks you should be able to complete independently; this is called a standard of excellence. Every lesson you complete in fourth grade will have objectives that translate, in student vocabulary, what you should be able to complete after the lesson. Each of those objectives is used to write assessment questions in formal assessments and then in state standardized assessments.

Here is an example of what each task's "grade" means:

3 – Advanced: This means that you have demonstrated a high level of achievement, or at a level that exceeds fourth grade standards, on the task. You were easily able to demonstrate that you have knowledge of the subject matter, were able to apply your knowledge to the task at hand, and that you can extend the concept with your own thinking.

2 – Proficient: This means that you have clearly demonstrated that you have met the achievement standard. You demonstrated your knowledge of subject matter and were able to apply your knowledge with limited errors.

1 – Basic: This means that you are approaching meeting the achievement standard. You have demonstrated that you understand the subject matter but may be having difficulty applying your learning to a task.

0 – Below Basic: This means that you have not met the achievement standard. You will need further guidance and instruction to help you with the subject matter.

LESSON 47   HOW ARE RUBRICS USED?

You will complete many writing assignments in fourth grade; each will be accompanied by its own rubric. A rubric will list all the tasks that you need to include in your writing assignment, and it tells your teacher the key elements to grade. The purpose of a rubric is to share with you all the elements you have to include in your writing. This is done so that you can monitor your progress, check your work, and have an outline so you can produce a document that is complete. In other words, a rubric is like a checklist of writing elements to make sure you have done the best work in your written document. A great strategy to use when you are completing a writing assignment is to review the rubric completely, highlight any tasks that are required to demonstrate proficiency in, and then review the rubric with your rough draft and check off all the requirements that can be found in your writing. In the end, you should have a check next to each task.

The list below is **some** of the writing pieces that you will create:

- descriptive paragraph
- reading response journals
- opinion essay
- speech
- research paper
- persuasive essay
- poem
- personal narrative
- fictional story
- ***biographical writing***
- letter to an author
- informative essay
- compare and contrast writing

The rubric on the next page is an example of the one you may see in your biographical narrative writing. The left side of the rubric lists all the tasks that you will need to include in your writing. Those will be the elements that the teacher will grade you on. The top part of the rubric lists the scores that you can earn depending on how well you cover the tasks. As you can see when you move from 0 to 3 in the rubric, you are expected to show a higher level of achievement. Each of the tasks represents a performance standard you need to demonstrate achievement in for fourth grade. It is very important that you fully understand the rubric before you begin writing. Your Guide and you should review and discuss each of the elements that need to be included in the task to demonstrate proficiency.

CONTINUED ->

Biography Rubric				
Task	**0**	**1**	**2**	**3**
Used a Variety of Sources	I did not rely on any source.	I used only one source for my biography.	I used two sources for my biography.	I used at least three sources for my biography.
Opening Paragraph	I did not create a thesis for my biography's opening paragraph.	I did not include a strong opening paragraph in my biography.	I included an opening paragraph in my biography, but it does not grab the reader's attention.	I included an opening paragraph in my biography that grabs the reader's attention.
Early, Middle, and Late Life	I excluded references to early, middle, and late stages of my subject's life.	I did not include factual information about the early, middle, and late stages of my subject's life.	I included factual information from most, but not all, of the stages of my subject's life.	I included factual information from each stage of my subject's life, including the early, middle, and late stages.
Transition Words	I used fragmented sentence structure.	I did not use transition words in my biography.	I used some transition words in my biography.	I effectively used transition words in my biography to connect ideas.
Clear and Logical Order	My biography does not have a logical order or not one that could be determined.	My biography does not present information in a clear and logical order.	At times, my biography presents information in a clear and logical order.	My biography presents information in a clear and logical order.
Fair and Balanced View of Subject	I presented a one-sided view of my subject.	I did not present a fair and balanced view of my subject.	At times, I presented a fair and balanced view of my subject, but at other times there is a bias present.	I presented a fair and balanced view of my subject without bias.
Concluding Paragraph	My biography does not have a concluding paragraph.	My biography has a concluding paragraph, but it doesn't address the thesis statement.	My biography has a concluding paragraph, but it does not summarize the important parts and bring it to a close.	My biography has a concluding paragraph that summarizes the important parts and brings it to a close.

Discuss with your Guide: A student earns the following score on his biography rubric.

Used a Variety of Sources: 3
Opening Paragraph: 3
Early, Middle, and Late Life: 3
Transition Words: 3
Clear and Logical Order: 0
Fair and Balanced View of Subject: 3
Concluding Paragraph: 3

List one reason that can explain why the student earned a *0* on the task *Clear and Logical Order*.

_____

_____

LESSON 48

HOW DO YOU READ A RUBRIC?

0:20

You may be wondering why your written work is graded with a rubric and not with a letter grade or a percentage. Even though you have been working with rubrics for a while now, you may be wondering, "How do I read a rubric to help me with my writing?" You know that a rubric is a scoring tool that lists all the tasks that you need to complete in your writing and how those tasks are graded by your teacher. A rubric is simply "the stuff that counts" when you write. The second benefit of a rubric is that it lets you know what achievement level you need to attain in your writing to be considered advanced, proficient, or basic. Reading the criteria for excellence next to each task will let you clearly know what will be considered quality work. Also, rubrics allow you to measure your own work before you submit it to your teacher. It is a tool that you can use to develop an outline and notes for you written work, guide your writing and thinking, and create a checklist of tasks to include in your writing to reference when you finish your final draft. A final benefit to a rubric that is important to mention is that it helps teachers, too. When your teacher grades your work, he knows exactly what you are supposed to include in your writing and can provide you with great feedback on how well you did within a task.

It is important that you learn how to read a rubric so that you can outline the expectations of your writing piece and understand what skills you need to demonstrate in order to prove you are achieving at the highest level of success. Below, you will see a rubric for a compare-contrast essay. This rubric has been highlighted and written on by a student before he began his work on his essay. He also wrote an outline on his first rough draft to remind him of his tasks. It is important to always choose the highest level of achievement in the rubric to highlight because it contains all the key information to achieve at an advanced level.

Review the rubric with your Guide and discuss strategies that can help you work with a rubric. Rubrics are a tool for skill building, just like a hammer is a tool for building houses. You should learn how to make them an important part of your writing.

41-60

Notes

Purpose and Supporting Detail	Topic Sentence and Concluding Sentence	Comparison Paragraph: Organization and Structure	Contrasting Paragraph: Organization and Structure
title introduction	every paragraph	specific examples similarities point by point organized logical	specific examples differences point by point organized logical

CONTINUED ->

Compare – Contrast Essay Rubric				
Task	**0**	**1**	**2**	**3**
Introductory and Concluding Paragraphs	My essay does not include an introductory paragraph and/or a concluding paragraph.	My essay includes an introductory paragraph that provides minimal background of the two topics. My essay includes a concluding paragraph, but does not include new information.	My essay includes an introductory paragraph that provides background of the two topics. My essay includes a concluding paragraph with new information about the two topics.	My essay includes a detailed introductory paragraph that clearly provides background of the two topics. My concluding paragraph provides informative and relevant new information about the two topics.
Purpose and Supporting Details	My essay does not include a title and my introductory paragraph does not use compare and contrast words to inform the reader of the two topics.	My essay includes a title and an introductory paragraph, but does not clearly use compare and contrast words to inform the reader of the two topics.	My essay has a title and an introduction that clearly uses compare and contrast words to inform the reader of the two topics.	My essay has a title and an introduction that clearly informs the reader of the point-by-point comparison with compare and contrast words.
Topic Sentence and Concluding Sentence	My paragraph construction does not begin with a topic sentence and end with a concluding sentence.	Some of my paragraphs contain a topic sentence and a concluding sentence.	My paragraphs all have topic sentences and concluding sentences, but the transition of ideas is unclear.	Every paragraph in my essay has a topic sentence and a concluding sentence that clearly transition the reader through a topic.
Comparison Paragraph: Organization and Structure	I did not include any details to compare the two topics and my writing is not logically organized for a comparison.	I included some evidence to show the similarities between the two topics, but did not follow a consistent order when discussing the comparison.	I included a paragraph that shows clear evidence of similarities in a point-by-point structure between the two topics, but I did not include specific examples and/or a logical structure.	I included a paragraph using specific examples that clearly show evidence of a point-by-point structure of similarities between the two topics and I presented the information in an organized, logical, and expected order.
Contrasting Paragraph: Organization and Structure	I did not include any details to explain the difference between the two topics and my writing is not logically organized to demonstrate a clear contrast.	I included some evidence to show the differences between the two topics, but did not follow a consistent order when discussing the contrasts.	I included a paragraph that shows clear evidence of the differences in a point-by-point structure between the two topics, but I did not include specific examples and/or a logical structure.	I included a paragraph using specific examples that clearly show evidence of a point-by-point structure of differences between the two topics and I presented the information in an organized, logical, and expected order.

41-60

LESSON 49 — YOU BE THE JUDGE

0:20

Over the last two lessons, you have been doing a lot of reading about rubrics; it is time to use a rubric. Below is a rubric for a friendly letter. This letter contains several errors so you will need to read it carefully. You will review the rubric with your Guide and highlight all the elements that students will need to score a 3. Then you will read the letter and assign a score for each task based on the rubric. Finally, you will compare your answers to a teacher's grade in Section 2, page 271.

Friendly Letter Rubric				
Task	**0**	**1**	**2**	**3**
Salutation and Closing	I did not include a salutation and/or a closing.	I have a salutation and a closing but both have errors in placement, punctuation, and/or capitalization.	I have a salutation and a closing but one has an error in placement, punctuation, and/or capitalization.	I have a salutation and a closing and they have no errors in placement, punctuation, and capitalization.
Body of Letter	My sentences are mostly fragment sentences and I have no evidence of paragraphing.	My sentences and paragraphs are mostly complete and well written but my paragraphs are unorganized.	My sentences and paragraphs are complete and well written with no sentence fragments or run-ons.	My sentences and paragraphs are complete, are well written, and have varied transition words, sentence structure, and vocabulary.
Conventions of Writing	I have many errors in the body of my letter that make the letter illegible.	I have errors in capitalization, grammar, and/or punctuation that interfere in understanding the meaning of my writing.	I have some errors in capitalization, grammar, or punctuation that do not interfere with meaning.	I have no errors in grammar or spelling in the body of my letter.

41-60

CONTINUED ->

506 Memory Lane
Pittsburgh, PA 15232
August 10, 2010

Dear Amanda,

It feels like forever since school ended and we were able to see each other. I can't beleve I only saw you a few weeks ago because it feels like forever. My summer vacation has been amazing until this week; boredom has finally set in.

I went to visit my grandmother for a couple of weeks then we went on a family vacation to the beach. At my grandmother's, we went to an amusement park and the zoo. Most days we swam in her pool all day. I was very proud of myself because I learned to dive off a diving board. At the beach I played in the sand went boogie boarding and read lots of books. My tan looks great!

This is my first week back at home and there is nothing exciting going on. My mom is starting to buy me school clothes, a new book bag, and school supplies. Most days I just go out and ride my bike. That is definitely not as exciting as the first part of my summer.

I hope the summer time has been good for you too. I can't wait to here about your summer vacation.

Your friend,

Elise

Grade:

Salutation and Closing: _____

Body of Letter: _____

Conventions of Writing: _____

41-60

LESSON 50   YOU GRADE THIS ONE!

You will look at one more rubric and a sample of a fourth grade student's opinion essay. Take your time and review the rubric. Make sure you review the required tasks and the criteria included for achieving those tasks. You and your Guide should discuss whether the student has achieved at the highest level of performance and then work backward through the levels until you both agree on a score. You can check your answers in Section 2, page 272.

Opinion Essay Rubric				
Task	**0**	**1**	**2**	**3**
Opening Paragraph	My opening paragraph does not contain an opinion statement.	My opening paragraph contains an opinion statement that does not make much sense and might be confusing for the reader.	My opening paragraph contains an opinion statement that clearly states my opinion and is easy to understand.	My opening paragraph contains a strong opinion statement that grabs the reader's attention and clearly states my opinion.
Reason Paragraphs	I did not include any reason why I have the opinion I do about the topic.	I included 1 reason why I have the opinion I do about the topic but it is not clear and might be confusing for the reader.	I included 1 – 2 reasons why I have the opinion I do about the topic and clearly outline them in only one paragraph with a clear opening statement and concluding sentence.	I included 2 – 3 clear, exact reasons why I have the opinion I do about the topic. Each of my reasons has its own paragraph with an opening statement and concluding sentence.
Examples	I did not include any examples of my reasons for my opinion about the topic.	I included examples for some of my reasons I feel the way I do about the topic but they did not help the reader form a clear picture in his mind.	I have included examples for every reason I feel the way I do about the topic but all of them do not help the reader form an opinion in his mind.	I have included an example for every reason I feel the way I do about the topic. My examples help the reader clearly form a picture in his mind and his own opinion about the topic.

41-60

CONTINUED ->

Closing Paragraph	My essay has no closing paragraph.	My essay has a closing paragraph but doesn't restate my original opinion.	My essay has a closing paragraph with an opening statement and concluding sentence that clearly restates my opinion.	My essay has a closing paragraph with an opening statement and concluding sentence that clearly summarizes my reasons and restates my opinion.
Conventions of Writing	My essay was not written in my "voice" and has consistent mistakes in grammar, spelling, and punctuation.	My essay sounds like my "voice" but has some errors in grammar, spelling, and punctuation that make it difficult to follow.	My essay sounds like I wrote it because I used my "voice," expressions, and sayings. I have minimal errors in grammar, spelling, and punctuation.	My essay sounds exactly like my "voice." I used my slang, expressions, phrases, and sayings in my writing. Also, I have no punctuation, grammar, or spelling errors.

School Uniforms Should Not Be Required

Some teachers say that uniforms are a great way for schoolwork to be a priority. I don't think that is true because kids are going to learn whatever they want. After thinking about the way I feel there is no way uniforms should be required in school.

My parents don't think that I what I wear is important or gets in the way of my schoolwork. However teachers feel that letting kids where the latest fashions causes many fights in school that interferes with class. I think my parents are right and your only going to get a grade that is for how smart you are and not for what clothes you wear. It must be the kid's that can't dress as nice as I do that are jealous. These are all the reasons that some teachers insist that school uniforms should be worn.

For all of these reasons and a ton more, no one should require schools to make students wear school uniforms.

Score:

Opening Paragraph: _____

Reasons Paragraph: _____

Examples: _____

Closing Paragraph: _____

Conventions of Writing: _____

LESSON 51

USING A RUBRIC IN A WRITING ASSIGNMENT

`0:20`

Over the next few lessons, you will create a fictional story from planning through grading. You will add personal elements to the story, such as you as the main character. Review the rubric below to help guide your writing. In the previous lesson, you were given a strategy of looking at the tasks under the *3* in order to see exactly what your story needs to include. This will help you create a checklist for your work. As you plan your writing, decide whether you have met the criteria in the rubric, then decide how well you covered each task. The key is that you are planning your own grade. An important point to remember is to ask the most questions before you start writing. If there is something in the rubric that you are unclear about, take the time to ask your Guide for help. It is easier to ask questions in the planning stage of writing then in the final draft stage.

You have learned to write out a checklist for the tasks that you are expected to complete. For today, you will not plan out any of your writing; you will focus on writing out your checklist with your Guide. A checklist for the *Setting* section has been provided for you. You should also take the time to ask any questions about the rubric, specifically any task or criteria that you are having difficulty understanding.

In the following lessons, you will plan out your story using a graphic organizer, you will create a rough draft of your writing, you will give it an action and descriptive words review, you will write your final draft, and then you will grade your own work.

41-60

Rubric Checklists

Organization and Creativity	Character(s)	Setting	Problem and Solution of the Story	Conventions of Writing
		where story takes place describe the setting descriptive verbs		

CONTINUED ->

Fictional Story Rubric

Task	0	1	2	3
Organization and Creativity	My story lacks imagination, and the ideas are random and unclear.	My story has some elements of imagination but the transitions make it difficult for the reader to follow.	My story contains creative details that distract from the story and some parts of the story do not have a clear transition.	My imaginative story contains many creative and descriptive details. The structure of my story easily transitions the reader through the story.
Character(s)	I did not define the main character(s) of the story.	I defined the main character(s) of the story but did not provide a description to the reader. The reader does not really get to know the character.	I provided the reader with a brief description of the main character(s). The reader will be able to get to know the character's appearance.	I provided the reader with a well-developed character. I clearly described the character's appearance, actions, thoughts, and speech.
Setting	My story does not inform the reader when and where the story takes place.	My story informs the reader where and when the story takes place but doesn't give any details of the setting.	My story informs the reader where and when the story takes place and uses descriptive words in the details of the setting.	My story uses many vivid and descriptive details to inform the reader where and when the story takes place. The reader can visualize the setting in his head.
Problem and Solution of the Story	My story does not describe the main character's problem and offers no solution.	My story describes the main character's problem but it is unclear. The solution does not develop from events in the story.	My story easily describes the main character's problem then develops the solution towards a logical conclusion.	My story creates a problem for the main character that leaves the reader wondering about a solution. The story guides the reader towards a solution that provides the right closure for the tone of the story.
Conventions of Writing	My story contains numerous errors in spelling, capitalization, punctuation, and grammar that make reading difficult.	My story contains frequent errors in common words. There are distracting errors in capitalization, grammar, and punctuation that interfere with the story's message.	My story contains a few errors in difficult to spell words. Capitalization, grammar, and punctuation usage provides the reader with a pleasant tone throughout the story.	My story has no spelling, capitalization, punctuation, or grammar errors.

41·60

LESSON 52

PREWRITING A FICTIONAL STORY

0:20

In Lesson 51, we reviewed the steps you will use to plan out your fictional story. You will be given the idea for the story and then you will add some information of your own. In today's lesson, you will only work on your graphic organizer. In later lessons, you will create a rough draft, then you will complete an action and descriptive words review. Finally, you will write your final draft and grade your work. Are you ready? …3…2…1…let's write an awesome fictional story!

Story Plan

Title

(insert your name) "_____ the Phenomenal" Saves the Day

Character:	**Setting:**
You are a superhero that has to save the day.	You are a regular fourth grade student. Every day you ride home from school through a park.
1. Hair color: _____	
2. Special costume: _____	6. What are the features of your park?
	_____
3. Transportation: A bike with a _____ _____	_____
	7. What street do you live on?
4. Name one other main character: _____	_____
5. Decide that character's role: **Friend Foe** (circle one)	

Problem:	**Solution:**
A group of fifth graders is not using the playground equipment at the park properly. One of them is bound to get hurt.	8. Your superhero springs into action by _____
	9. How do you save the day? _____

41-60

LESSON 53

YOUR FICTIONAL STORY ROUGH DRAFT IS A WORKING COPY

`0:20`

You will begin the rough draft of your story. It is important to know one thing about creating a fictional story before we begin a rough draft; in a state standardized assessment or on a formal assessment, you will write your rough draft on scratch paper and your final draft in the test booklet. It is important to write a rough draft before you write your story in the test booklet. You are given plenty of time to work on the writing part of your state standardized assessment. There are no extra points for being done quickly, so use all of the strategies you are learning in this book to plan and write on your fourth grade standardized test.

The first thing to do before you begin writing is to quickly review the rubric and your task checklist. You completed a rubric checklist in Lesson 51. This strategy will allow you to focus your attention on the criteria you need to demonstrate in your writing. The following draft below contains suggestions for paragraph openings and closings. You can add your own story ideas in the lines provided or you can rewrite the entire paragraph to your liking on a separate piece of scratch paper. Remember, this is only a rough draft and not the final submission; therefore, you can experiment with the story and make changes later.

"_____ the Phenomenal" Saves the Day

It was a typical Monday morning; I was in the bathroom looking in the mirror brushing my hair. I was thinking this would be the week that would pass without incident. I finished up and started down

_____

_____

_____

You may not know me. I go by _____ most days, of course, because that is my name. However, I'm on my way home from school and this is usually when the trouble begins.

_____

_____

I jumped on my bike with the expectation of getting home quickly so I could complete my schoolwork.

_____

_____

_____

As I rode into the park, I spotted _____ (insert second character). (She or He) was just ahead

_____

_____

_____

41-60

It was time for me to spring into action and quickly! I shouted, "_____

_____

_____

_____

As always, another disaster thwarted by "_____ the Phenomenal!" I smiled to myself and grabbed my bike

_____

_____

_____

41-60

IF YOU GET
STUCK MAKE
SURE YOU LOOK
BACK AT THE
RUBRIC FOR ALL
THE WRITING
REQUIREMENTS.

LESSON 54

FICTIONAL STORY RUBRIC CHECK

0:20

41-60

During the rough draft stage of your writing, you should be referencing your rubric to make sure you are meeting the criteria set forth for each task. As a writer, you need to decide if you want to do a quick check at the end of your rough draft or as you go along in your writing. The rubric will guide you to your final draft. In this lesson, you and your Guide will use your rubrics checklist if you have included important elements. You and your Guide can review the guide questions in this rubric checklist, then read your rough draft out loud to your Guide. As you complete each paragraph:

- Pause and think about the tasks in the rubric that apply to that paragraph.
- Discuss your ideas with your Guide.
- Make any changes you feel are appropriate.

Rubric Checklist

Task	Checklist	Guide Questions
Organization and Creativity	creative details descriptive details transitions take reader through story	Does each paragraph have an opening sentence and closing sentence? Does the story have a proper sequence? Does each paragraph include the next logical step to the story? Does my story have creative elements?
Character(s)	well-developed appearance actions thoughts speech	Did I describe one characteristic of my main character(s) appearance? Did my main character(s) speak or think in my story?
Setting	where story takes place describe the setting descriptive verbs	Did I briefly describe at least one characteristic of all places included in my story?
Problem and Solution of the Story	leaves reader wondering about solution guides the reader to the solution right closure for tone of story	Is my problem clear? Did I create suspense in my story? Is the solution the right choice for the story?
Conventions of Writing	spelling grammar punctuation capitalization	Did I read my final draft out loud?

LESSON 55

ADDING ACTION AND DESCRIPTIVE WORDS

0:20

41-60

You are almost to the final draft of your fictional story. If you look at your story right now, you probably have a whole bunch of corrections, crossed out words, and added or deleted sentences. That is why your scratch paper is called a rough draft. A smart strategy to use at this point is to add some descriptive vocabulary. This is where your knowledge of adverbs and adjectives comes into your writing because they are both modifying words.

For example, you can write:

It was a typical Monday morning; I was in the bathroom looking in the mirror brushing my hair. I was thinking this would be the week that would pass without incident.

You can add some descriptive modifying words to change the sentence to:

It was a typical Monday morning; I was in the **upstairs** bathroom looking in the **small** mirror brushing my **blonde** hair. I was thinking this would be the week that would pass without **another crazy** incident.

When you add descriptive words to your writing, you create a better picture in the reader's mind. In the first example, the reader is given a clear idea of what is happening in your story; however, in the second example, by adding describing words you help the reader picture what is occurring. The second example enables you to earn a score of 3 in the *Organization and Creativity* task because you are including "many creative and descriptive details" in your story. Another difference in the two paragraphs is the last sentence where the narrator wishes that the week would pass without incident. In the first paragraph, the narrator is thinking that he wants the week to pass without a problem. However, the reader is left to wonder why the narrator would want that to happen. In the second paragraph, the use of *another crazy incident* tells the reader that the narrator has had something occur every week in his life.

In this example, that may be placed in your story, the main character rides into the park:

I rode through the entrance of the park. There were many people enjoying the day. As I approached the playground, I noticed a group of fifth graders I recognized from school.

Here is an example of how you can use descriptive words to describe nouns and actions:

I **slowly** rode through the **tree-lined** entrance of the park. *I passed people biking, having picnics, and throwing baseballs on the grassy knolls*. ~~There were many people enjoying the day~~. As I approached the **big** playground, I noticed a group of **trouble making** fifth graders I recognized from **my elementary** school.

As you read through your rough draft with your Guide, use the caret (^) symbol to add descriptive words to your text. This allows you to add elements to your story without erasing any of your original text. Your rough draft will begin to look like this:

CONTINUED ->>

> **my best friend**   **We've known each other**   **leisurely**
> As I rode into the park, I spotted ∧ Nathan. ~~Nathan and I have been best friends~~ since kindergarten. He was ∧ walking
>
>   **easily**   **trusted**
> just ahead of me and I knew I would ∧ catch up to him. Nathan is not only my best friend, he is my ∧ sidekick.

It is now your turn to work on your rough draft with your Guide. It is important to remember that you are adding descriptive and action words that will improve the reader's experience. You want to make sure that the reader is visualizing the places and actions taking place. When you tell the reader that a bike is being ridden slowly or quickly, he can create a mental image in his head. When you give descriptions of the color and size of an object, the reader can create mental images. Have you ever read about a main character in a book and made a mental image of what the character may look like? You might have even made the character look like a famous person. When you add describing and action words to your fictional story, you are giving the reader the best experience possible.

LESSON 56

FICTIONAL STORY: FINAL DRAFT

`0:20`

In the previous five lessons, you completed a fictional story from the prewriting stage through the rough draft review. Today, you will write your final draft. Your final draft will include all the revisions you made when you completed the descriptive and action word review. This is a very important step on a state standardized test because whatever you write will be used to generate your score. This is why rubrics are important, because you have to judge your own work. You get to earn your score because you were given the exact tool that the teacher will use to assign a grade. Rubrics are great because a teacher knows how to judge your work and you know exactly what you need to demonstrate to get the best score possible.

The best strategy to use for writing final drafts on a state standardized test is to write each sentence and then reread the sentence out loud to your Guide. Rereading the sentence will help you make sure the sentence makes sense, has proper punctuation, and has proper grammar. While rereading the sentence, check for capitalization of the first word and proper nouns. Remember rules such as days and months are capitalized, but not seasons.

Once you have written your final draft, you will have completed the writing assignment on a state standardized test. This portion of the test is usually given to you separate from the multiple choice and the reading comprehension parts. Sometimes you are even given a day between those two parts and the writing test. Take your time writing your final draft. Good luck!

41-60

Title

_____

_____

_____

_____

_____

_____

_____

_____

_____

_____

_____

_____

CONTINUED ->

41-60

LESSON 57 — FICTIONAL STORY GRADE

0:20

41-60

Today, you and your Guide will grade your fictional story. You have been working on this fictional story over quite a few lessons. It is important to remember that you will not have this amount of time to complete your writing assignment on the state standardized test. You will have about two to three hours depending on the number of writing samples you are required to complete. Normally, your writing test is one writing sample, but it can also be two. The entire process you completed will need to be done in a short amount of time. It is important that you practice these strategies with all of your fourth grade writing assignments; reading this book alone will not help you be a better test taker. You need to practice the strategies you learned.

Review the rubric and give yourself a score for each task in the column marked *Scores*, in the *Your Score* box. Then give your fictional story to your Guide. Have your Guide review the tasks and criteria and then read your fictional story. Your Guide will then grade your fictional story. You should review your scores together and discuss ways to improve your fictional story.

Fictional Story Rubric					
Task	**0**	**1**	**2**	**3**	**Scores**
Organization and Creativity	My story lacks imagination, and the ideas are random and unclear.	My story has some elements of imagination but the transitions make it difficult for the reader to follow.	My story contains creative details that distract from the story and some parts of the story do not have a clear transition.	My imaginative story contains many creative and descriptive details. The structure of my story easily transitions the reader through the story.	Guide Score Your Score
Character(s)	I did not define the main character(s) of the story.	I defined the main character(s) of the story but did not provide a description to the reader. The reader does not really get to know the character.	I provided the reader with a brief description of the main character(s). The reader will be able to get to know the character's appearance.	I provided the reader with a well-developed character. I clearly described the character's appearance, actions, thoughts, and speech.	Guide Score Your Score

Setting	My story does not inform the reader when and where the story takes place.	My story informs the reader where and when the story takes place but doesn't give any details of the setting.	My story informs the reader where and when the story takes place and uses descriptive words in the details of the setting.	My story uses many vivid and descriptive details to inform the reader where and when the story takes place. The reader can visualize the setting in his head.	Guide Score
					Your Score
Problem and Solution of the Story	My story does not describe the main character's problem and offers no solution.	My story describes the main character's problem but it is unclear. The solution does not develop from events in the story.	My story easily describes the main character's problem then develops the solution towards a logical conclusion.	My story creates a problem for the main character that leaves the reader wondering about a solution. The story guides the reader towards a solution that provides the right closure for the tone of the story.	Guide Score
					Your Score
Conventions of Writing	My story contains numerous errors in spelling, capitalization, punctuation, and grammar that make reading difficult.	My story contains frequent errors in common words. There are distracting errors in capitalization, grammar, and punctuation that interfere with the story's message.	My story contains a few errors in difficult to spell words. Capitalization, grammar, and punctuation usage provides the reader with a pleasant tone throughout the story.	My story has no spelling, capitalization, punctuation, or grammar errors.	Guide Score
					Your Score

41·60

LESSON 58 — YOU GRADE 1

0:20

All of the scoring rubrics provided in this book have been adapted from their original teacher form. Rubrics were originally intended as a teacher's tool. Now they are also used as a tool for you to grade your own learning. You will spend the next several lessons grading original student work.

You and your Guide will read the fictional story together. Then you will use the listed criteria to grade the story on your own in the *Scores* section, in the *Your Score* row. Your Guide will then grade the student's work. You will then have a brief discussion to share reasons you chose the scores. Finally, you and your Guide will review your answers and the teacher explanation provided in Section 2, page 274.

Scores					
Task	Organization and Creativity	Character(s)	Setting	Problem and Solution of the Story	Conventions of Writing
Guide Score					
Your Score					

Fictional Story Rubric				
Task	**0**	**1**	**2**	**3**
Organization and Creativity	My story lacks imagination, and the ideas are random and unclear.	My story has some elements of imagination but the transitions make it difficult for the reader to follow.	My story contains creative details that distract from the story and some parts of the story do not have a clear transition.	My imaginative story contains many creative and descriptive details. The structure of my story easily transitions the reader through the story.
Character(s)	I did not define the main character(s) of the story.	I defined the main character(s) of the story but did not provide a description to the reader. The reader does not really get to know the character.	I provided the reader with a brief description of the main character(s). The reader will be able to get to know the character's appearance.	I provided the reader with a well-developed main character. I clearly described the main character's appearance, actions, thoughts, and speech.
Setting	My story does not inform the reader when and where the story takes place.	My story informs the reader where and when the story takes place but doesn't give any details of the setting.	My story informs the reader where and when the story takes place and uses descriptive words in the details of the setting.	My story uses many vivid and descriptive details to inform the reader where and when the story takes place. The reader can visualize the setting in his head.

41-60

Problem and Solution of the Story	My story does not describe the main character's problem and offers no solution.	My story describes the main character's problem but it is unclear. The solution does not develop from events in the story.	My story easily describes the main character's problem then develops the solution towards a logical conclusion.	My story creates a problem for the main character that leaves the reader wondering about a solution. The story guides the reader towards a solution that provides the right closure for the tone of the story.
Conventions of Writing	My story contains numerous errors in spelling, capitalization, punctuation, and grammar that make reading difficult.	My story contains frequent errors in common words. There are distracting errors in capitalization, grammar, and punctuation that interfere with the story's message.	My story contains a few errors in difficult to spell words. Capitalization, grammar, and punctuation usage provides the reader with a pleasant tone throughout the story.	My story has no spelling, capitalization, punctuation, or grammar errors.

41-60

Circle, Circle, Dot, Dot
by Brianne Kovacs

I saw her lying there on her belly in the grass field during our recess. She was sitting there under the sun, picking petals off of a flower. "He loves me, he loves me not," she said so quietly, almost in a whisper. This poor golden-haired girl! Has anyone ever told her that boys have cooties? I know for a fact. I've seen it!

She picked her head up from the flower and drew her attention to the boys playing tag by the swings. I followed her eyes and realized who she was staring at, Todd. "Oh no, not Todd!" I thought to myself, "He's almost as awful as Gregg!" Last week at lunch, Gregg stuck gum in my hair and Todd fell out of his seat laughing at me. I was so humiliated that I had to go home. At this moment, I knew she needed a best friend to educate her, and that best friend would be me!

I took in a deep breath and marched in her direction. As my shadow drove the sunshine out from her face, she peaked at me with a curious look. I let out my breath and plopped myself down beside her, "Hi, I'm Maggie."

She lowered her eyes back to the ground and almost in a whisper she said her name, "I'm Gertrude."

I watched her freckled face as she continued to pick at the puffy, yellow flowers. Without thinking, I grabbed her arm, pulled it onto my lap, and drew on it with my finger, "Circle, circle, dot, dot, now you've got your cootie shot!" As she looked up at me confused, I reassured her, "You should be good now." Without missing a beat I announced, "Let's go do something fun!" Getting up I dashed towards the swings. Gertrude followed behind me spinning on her toes the whole way.

We swung back and forth on the swings for quite some time without saying anything to each other. I pumped my legs hard, swinging higher and higher, as Gertrude stayed low to the ground at a gentle pulse. I looked at the sky preparing to ask her a question and just as I went to take a breath, THUMP! My foot had kicked Gregg right in the head! He fumbled backwards and fell to ground. Holding his hand to his head he started crying and Todd tried to help him up. My mouth dropped open as I watched Gregg struggle to his feet and run screaming to the teacher. Then I noticed it, I turned my head and saw Gertrude laughing so hard at Gregg, she almost fell off the swing. At that moment, I was optimistic she would be just fine!

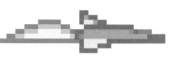

LESSON 59   YOU GRADE 2

0:20

You and your Guide will read the fictional story together. Then you will use the listed criteria to grade the story on your own in the *Scores* section, in the *Your Score* row. Your Guide will then grade the student's work. You will then have a brief discussion to share reasons you chose the scores. Finally, you and your Guide will review your answers and the teacher explanation provided in Section 2, page 275.

	Scores				
Task	Organization and Creativity	Character(s)	Setting	Problem and Solution of the Story	Conventions of Writing
Guide Score					
Your Score					

Fictional Story Rubric				
Task	**0**	**1**	**2**	**3**
Organization and Creativity	My story lacks imagination, and the ideas are random and unclear.	My story has some elements of imagination but the transitions make it difficult for the reader to follow.	My story contains creative details that distract from the story and some parts of the story do not have a clear transition.	My imaginative story contains many creative and descriptive details. The structure of my story easily transitions the reader through the story.
Character(s)	I did not define the main character(s) of the story.	I defined the main character(s) of the story but did not provide a description to the reader. The reader does not really get to know the character.	I provided the reader with a brief description of the main character(s). The reader will be able to get to know the character's appearance.	I provided the reader with a well-developed character. I clearly described the character's appearance, actions, thoughts, and speech.
Setting	My story does not inform the reader when and where the story takes place.	My story informs the reader where and when the story takes place but doesn't give any details of the setting.	My story informs the reader where and when the story takes place and uses descriptive words in the details of the setting.	My story uses many vivid and descriptive details to inform the reader where and when the story takes place. The reader can visualize the setting in his head.

41·60

Problem and Solution of the Story	My story does not describe the main character's problem and offers no solution.	My story describes the main character's problem but it is unclear. The solution does not develop from events in the story.	My story easily describes the main character's problem then develops the solution towards a logical conclusion.	My story creates a problem for the main character that leaves the reader wondering about a solution. The story guides the reader towards a solution that provides the right closure for the tone of the story.
Conventions of Writing	My story contains numerous errors in spelling, capitalization, punctuation, and grammar that make reading difficult.	My story contains frequent errors in common words. There are distracting errors in capitalization, grammar, and punctuation that interfere with the story's message.	My story contains a few errors in difficult to spell words. Capitalization, grammar, and punctuation usage provides the reader with a pleasant tone throughout the story.	My story has no spelling, capitalization, punctuation, or grammar errors.

I Made It out Alive, Barely

I woke up and it was a day just like any other. I rolled out of bed to peek out of the frosty window, making sure no more snow had fallen. In maine it is always best to check for a snow day before getting ready. Seeing that I would have school today I turned my back to the window and with a ready, set, go, I ran and dove onto my bed, bouncing off and landing with a crash on the other side. My clock read 6:45 a.m., I'm late! Why didn't my mom wake me up? I rushed around the room getting dressed, bouncing on one foot to get my last sock on and I dashed out my door and down the stares.

She was standing there in her pajamas and robe. She hadn't brush her hair yet. She slid the pancakes from the skillet onto my plate. Seeing that I was confused because she was not ready to drive me to school yet. She smiled and pointed to the calendar "You have a doctor appointment today, Ill drive you to school afterward." My heart dropped into my stomach as I took a huge gulp. I hated going to the doctor. I knew I was getting a shot. I sat nervously in my chair, barely able to eat as my mom went to get ready for the day.

We sat bundled up in the car driving down the snowy street heading into town. Before I knew it we had arrived at the office. I walked as slowly as I could toward the door, watching my breath turn into clouds that swept pass my head. We walked in the door and I headed for the chairs as my mom went to check in at the counter. It's not fair, making me sit and wait. I could feel my nerves building up and my hands starting to shake. Shortly after my mom sat down a nurse came out, "Bobby, you ready?" Here we go.

I sat on the cold table looking around at all the cartoon characters that were plastered on the walls. Thats it , I couldn't take it anymore. I hopped of the table and hid underneath it. Raising my head up to my mom I whispered "They can't find me under here!" With a giggle she told me to get back on the table and I reluctantly did. There was a knock on the door and the doctor came in and did the exam with ice cold hands. He finished and said the nurse would be in to give me my shot.

She came in carrying her tray with the needle and bandage on it. I looked at her panicked and she said with a smile, "Don't worry it'll be over before you know it." I closed my eyes and started crying, I know it is going to hurt! She might as well just chop off my arm! Oh how awful it will feel, I won't be able to move my arms for days. "Okay, you're done," she said, "I told you it wouldn't be bad!" I looked down at the bandage on my arm wondering if I actually got a shot.

LESSON 60   YOU GRADE 3

You and your Guide will read the fictional story together. Then you will use the listed criteria to grade the story on your own in the *Scores* section, in the *Your Score* row. Your Guide will then grade the student's work. You will then have a brief discussion to share reasons you chose the scores. Finally, you and your Guide will review your answers and the teacher explanation provided in Section 2, page 277.

0:20

Scores					
Task	**Organization and Creativity**	**Character(s)**	**Setting**	**Problem and Solution of the Story**	**Conventions of Writing**
Guide Score					
Your Score					

Fictional Story Rubric				
Task	**0**	**1**	**2**	**3**
Organization and Creativity	My story lacks imagination, and the ideas are random and unclear.	My story has some elements of imagination but the transitions make it difficult for the reader to follow.	My story contains creative details that distract from the story and some parts of the story do not have a clear transition.	My imaginative story contains many creative and descriptive details. The structure of my story easily transitions the reader through the story.
Character(s)	I did not define the main character(s) of the story.	I defined the main character(s) of the story but did not provide a description to the reader. The reader does not really get to know the character.	I provided the reader with a brief description of the main character(s). The reader will be able to get to know the character's appearance.	I provided the reader with a well-developed character. I clearly described the character's appearance, actions, thoughts, and speech.
Setting	My story does not inform the reader when and where the story takes place.	My story informs the reader where and when the story takes place but doesn't give any details of the setting.	My story informs the reader where and when the story takes place and uses descriptive words in the details of the setting.	My story uses many vivid and descriptive details to inform the reader where and when the story takes place. The reader can visualize the setting in his head.

Problem and Solution of the Story	My story does not describe the main character's problem and offers no solution.	My story describes the main character's problem but it is unclear. The solution does not develop from events in the story.	My story easily describes the main character's problem then develops the solution towards a logical conclusion.	My story creates a problem for the main character that leaves the reader wondering about a solution. The story guides the reader towards a solution that provides the right closure for the tone of the story.
Conventions of Writing	My story contains numerous errors in spelling, capitalization, punctuation, and grammar that make reading difficult.	My story contains frequent errors in common words. There are distracting errors in capitalization, grammar, and punctuation that interfere with the story's message.	My story contains a few errors in difficult to spell words. Capitalization, grammar, and punctuation usage provides the reader with a pleasant tone throughout the story.	My story has no spelling, capitalization, punctuation, or grammar errors.

41·60

stuff my grandma talks about

My grandma likes to take me out to lunch when she comes to visit. I do not like it very much because she likes to tell the same story and its like boring. She is coming over today to take me to lunch to some lame diner. When she picked me up she was wearing this ugly purple and red hat. Gross, she taking me to lunch with her Red Hat club. Doesnt she understand that I would rather go play soccer on this nice day then sit around listening to loud women talk about purses and necklaces? I think she wishes I was a girly girl but I think my dad calls me joey for a reason. Oh well. Here we go. I will climb into her car that is blasting doo wop music from her generation and spit out the feathers from that like feathery, scarfy thing she wears for these meetings. So we drive to this place and get out of the car to meet up with the women my grandma is friends with. Great. Here comes the pinching my cheeks. There so weird, haven't the heard of personal space? We went inside and sat down and I could tell our waiter was annoyed because he was going to deal with these loud overly happy old women talking about girly things that no one else really cares about. I looked around for a tv, or anything related to sports. Nothing, just an old jukebox playing music that made my ears sad. I mean like really. Couldn't my grams send me to a game with pap instead or does she enjoy torturing me. At least I can order as many milkshakes as I want and draw on the paper on the table. I got a burger and fries. I guess it didnt taste to bad, its nothing like an arena hotdog? Maybe I will day dream about becoming a professional soccer player. I'm on the field of the biggest soccer field in the world and almost everyone in the stand has my jersey on. I have the ball and I head to towards the goal and then my dream is interrupted by my grandma's squeal. Joey would look so cute in these holding earrings up to ears. I just like wrolled my like eyes. I just want to go home.

LESSON 61

OPEN-ENDED SCORING RUBRICS: LANGUAGE ARTS

`0:10`

Now that you have reviewed rubrics for the writing portion of a state standardized test, you should have a clear understanding of how to use rubrics in your writing. Rubrics allow you to be the judge of your own work. The rubric for the writing test provides you with all the tasks and criteria on which your teacher will grade your work. A rubric gives you a checklist to help you visualize what should be included in your writing. As a student, you should take responsibility for your writing by using a rubric as a tool instead of a grading instrument.

Over the next several lessons, we will review a new type of rubric. These rubrics are used on state standardized assessments for open-ended response questions. Open-ended response questions require you to answer a question and then explain how you got your answer. Earlier in this book, you learned about the ACE (**A**nswer, **C**ite, **E**xplain) strategy to use when you answer these extended response questions. Before we begin reviewing the ACE strategy, look at the scoring rubric below. These rubrics are similar to the ones you will see on your reading, math, and science state standardized tests. If you are in a state that has a social studies assessment, you will also have one that is written for that subject.

The rubric below is an example of the criteria that you need to demonstrate when you answer open-ended questions on a language arts state standardized assessment. This is the rubric that is used by the state to determine if you were able to answer an open-ended question. This rubric is identical to the ACE strategy that you will use, except it is written for a teacher.

By understanding how to use these rubrics, you will begin to focus your attention on the type of open-ended questions that are on the state standardized test. In language arts, you will usually see open-ended questions in the reading comprehension section of your test. Review the following rubric with your Guide, and then see if you can pick out criteria that are similar to Answer, Cite, Explain.

61-80

YOU AND YOUR GUIDE SHOULD READ THROUGH THE NEXT SEVERAL LESSONS CAREFULLY. YOUR GUIDE CAN HELP ANSWER ANY QUESTIONS.

Language Arts Rubric	
0	• Response is absent • Does not address task
1	• Demonstrates minimal understanding of the task • Provides an ambiguous reference or makes no use of the text • References to the text may be inaccurate resulting in an incomplete interpretation that is relevant to task • Response may be insufficient to demonstrate that criteria are met
2	• Demonstrates a partial understanding of the task but may still complete all requirements of the task • Demonstrates a limited understanding of the text by using information from the text incorrectly, resulting in an inconsistent or weak explanation • Makes basic interpretations of the text without using significant ideas or making relevant reference to other situations or personal perspectives
3	• Demonstrates an understanding of the task • Provides some explanation using ideas from the text as support • Uses information from the text to interpret main ideas • Uses connections to other situations or personal perspectives logically through analysis, evaluation, or by comparison and contrast • Uses relevant but general references from the text that may not be fully supported • Provides a partially unsupported interpretation of the text
4	• Clearly demonstrates understanding of the task • Demonstrates an accurate understanding of important information in the text by focusing on the main ideas factually presented or implied by meaning • Uses information from the text to logically interpret important concepts or make connections to other situations or personal perspectives through analysis, evaluation, inference, or by comparison and contrast • Uses relevant, specific, and accurate references from the text • Integrates a balanced interpretation of the text with text-based support

LESSON 62

OPEN-ENDED SCORING RUBRICS: MATH

Last year, you completed your first state standardized assessment in language arts and math. On your math assessment, you were presented with a chart, graph, or mathematical problem that you had to answer and then explain the process you used. In other words, you had to use math vocabulary to "explain your brain." Fourth graders consistently make mistakes on the open-ended questions in the state standardized math tests because it is difficult to use words to explain how you selected a math algorithm. An algorithm is a set of steps for solving math problems. For example, if you were given the following word problem, you would need to explain the steps you took to solve the math problem.

Lilly and Mark are playing a word game. Lilly made the word MATH.

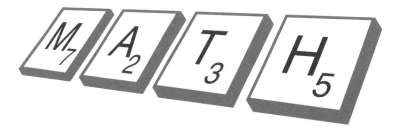

Add the points on each letter to find Lilly's score.

The step-by-step solution would be to add the scores from the first two tiles, then add the score of the third tile to the total, and finally add the score of the fourth tile to the sum of the first three numbers. The sum of all the numbers is Lilly's score.

That is the description that needs to be part of your answer on an extended response question. You can see that this explanation uses math terms such as *sum*, *total*, and *add*. You will have to solve the problem in order to demonstrate and explain the solution and score a 4 (Advanced) on the state standardized test.

The following rubric is an example of a rubric given to teachers that score the math state standardized test. When you completely review the ACE strategy, you will see how any open-ended response question can be answered to achieve all the criteria and tasks of these teacher rubrics. Please review the rubric with your Guide.

	Math Rubric
0	• No answer attempted • Did not explain strategies used or provide a written explanation of the solution
1	• Demonstrates limited understanding of the problem's mathematical concept and principles • Shows limited to no understanding of the algorithm to employ, which results in an incorrect answer • Fails to use mathematical terminology • Attempts to identify some of the important elements of the question with limited success • Demonstrates an inappropriate strategy to solve the problem correctly • Explanation for the solution does not match the computation used • If applicable, solutions to a chart or diagram are unclear and lack explanations of elements
2	• Demonstrates limited understanding of the problem's mathematical concept and principles • Shows limited understanding of the algorithm to employ, which results in major computational errors • Uses some appropriate mathematical terminology • Identifies some of the important elements of the question but demonstrates a limited understanding of the relationship between elements • Demonstrates some strategies to solve the problem correctly • Explanation for the solution does not completely match the computation used • If applicable, includes a solution to a chart or diagram with unclear explanations of elements
3	• Demonstrates a partial understanding of the problem's mathematical concept and principles • Demonstrates understanding of the appropriate algorithm to employ but computation contains minor errors • Uses mostly appropriate mathematical terminology • Identifies most of the important elements of the question and demonstrates a general understanding of the relationship between elements • Demonstrates an incomplete strategy to solve the problem correctly • Clearly explains the "what was done" but can't explain the "why it was done" of the solution • If applicable, includes a solution to a chart or diagram with some explanations of elements
4	• Clearly demonstrates an understanding of the problem's mathematical concept and principles • Demonstrates understanding of the appropriate algorithm to employ and performs all computations completely and correctly • Uses appropriate mathematical terminology • Identifies all important elements of the question and explains complete understanding of the relationship between elements • Demonstrates an appropriate strategy to solve the problem correctly • Clearly explains the "what was done" and "why it was done" of the solution • If applicable, includes a solution to a chart or diagram with explanations of all elements

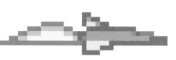

LESSON 63

OPEN-ENDED SCORING RUBRICS: SCIENCE

In science class, you learn about the process and theories used to investigate the world around you. You practice science every time you ask questions: *Why does the moon have phases? How does a fly buzz? What happens to the salt if all the water evaporates? When will we be able to reach the planet Mars?* All of these questions begin the process of the scientific method. The scientific method process allows us to answer the questions that we want to investigate by giving clear steps to use.

Understanding and using the scientific method is a large part of what you will be tested on when you complete a science state standardized assessment. All your investigations, facts you learned about the world, theories, and skills will be tested. Part of what you learn in science is also how to observe the world around you. You will need to know how life cycles, food webs, water cycles, simple machines, and many other cycles and processes work and react with the world.

Open-ended questions on the state standardized science test require you to provide thorough explanations of the solutions presented in diagrams, graphs, images, and general questions. The most important thing to remember in an extended response question for science is to provide a written explanation for your complete answer, especially if it contains a graph, chart, or diagram. The following is an example of a teacher rubric used on a state standardized test. You and your Guide should review the rubric so you can build an understanding of what skills you will have to demonstrate. Later in this book, we will review how to use the ACE strategy to meet the requirements on an open-ended science question.

	Science Rubric
0	• No answer attempted • Did not explain strategies used or provide a written explanation of the solution
1	• Provides insufficient evidence to demonstrate a grade level understanding of the scientific content, concepts, and procedures as required by the task(s) • Does not demonstrate grade level scientific skills related to a main idea or learning standards within the task(s) • May show only information copied or rephrased from the question
2	• Demonstrates minimal understanding of the scientific content, concepts, and procedures required by the task(s) • Response is somewhat correct with an emerging grade level understanding of the required scientific content, concepts, and procedures demonstrated and/or explained The response contains some work that is incomplete or unclear • Demonstrates emerging grade level science skills related to the main idea being assessed by the task(s) • Demonstrates emerging understanding of the grade level science concepts The procedure or concepts selected are inconsistent with the task(s)
3	• Provides a clear and correct understanding of grade level science content as required by the task(s) • Demonstrates a thorough understanding of grade level scientific content, concepts, and procedures required by the task(s) The response may contain minor errors or omissions in the response that does not detract from demonstrating a thorough understanding • Demonstrates grade level science skills related to the main idea and standard being assessed by the task(s) • Demonstrates understanding of the grade level science concepts required to complete the task(s) with minimal errors
4	• Provides a clear, complete, and correct understanding of grade level science content required by the task(s) • Demonstrates superior understanding of grade level scientific content, concepts, and procedures required by the task(s) • Demonstrates superior grade level science skills related to the main idea and standard being assessed by the task(s) • Demonstrates superior understanding of the grade level science concepts required to thoroughly complete the task

08-19

LESSON 64

OPEN-ENDED SCORING
RUBRICS: SOCIAL STUDIES

0:10

In social studies, you study the past, present, and future of politics, civics, economics, cultures, and societies. Studying social studies gives you a viewpoint and understanding of the past so you can determine the effects the past has on the present and the future. You also study social studies so you can understand your role and responsibilities to society. Finally, by studying social studies, you are taught problem-solving and decision-making skills so you can become a responsible citizen in your community and the world. Some states do not have a social studies state standardized assessment for fourth graders, though all fourth graders study social studies. Even if you will not complete a state standardized assessment in social studies, you will take plenty of formal assessments this year where you will need to demonstrate the skills identified in this rubric.

When you answer an open-ended question on a social studies test, it will be a geography question, a government or civics question, or an economics question. The goal is to see if you can demonstrate decision-making skills and understand the cause and effects of your decisions using a social studies concept. This teacher rubric is used to grade how well you answered an open-ended response question. When you use the ACE strategy to answer questions, you will learn the best strategies to earn a 4 on each question. You and your Guide will review this rubric together and discuss key ideas of the types of topics you should study during your weekly study times. Don't forget to fill out your weekly and monthly calendar, too.

	Social Studies Rubric
0	• No answer attempted • Did not explain strategies used or provide a written explanation of the solution
1	• Demonstrates some knowledge but not consistent to the material presented • Is unable to show grade level proficiency in understanding the content and concepts of main historical events in the study of social studies • Does not apply the social studies content, concepts, and skills required to the material presented • Does not expand upon the topics with relevant information that supports material presented • Does not describe material presented with historical understanding (if applicable) • Cannot locate relevant regions or geographical features to the material presented (if applicable) • Does not demonstrate an understanding of the role government and civics has to the material presented • Does not demonstrate an understanding of basic economic concepts and how they relate to historical events
2	• Demonstrates some knowledge of material presented • Shows only minimal knowledge and understanding of the content and concepts of main historical events in the study of social studies • Shows minimal knowledge and understanding to apply the social studies content, concepts, and skills required to the material presented • Expands upon the topics with additional information that may not support the information presented • Describes material with little historical understanding but cannot expand upon the information using a cause and effect explanation (if applicable) • Locates some regions or geographical features of historical significance but cannot relate information presented to relevant historical information (if applicable) • Demonstrates some knowledge of the role government and civics has to the material presented (if applicable) • Demonstrates some knowledge of basic economic concepts but cannot relate them to historical events presented in the material

61-80

3	• Demonstrates an accurate knowledge of material presented • Shows knowledge and understanding of the content and concepts of main historical events in the study of social studies • Shows evidence of the ability to apply the social studies content, concepts, and skills required to the material presented • Expands upon the topics studied with additional information presented from the text • Describes material presented with historical understanding and can somewhat expand upon the information using cause and effect explanations (if applicable) • Locate by regions or other geographical features of historical significance but has difficulty associating relevant information to location and historical information to expand upon the material presented (if applicable) • Demonstrates an accurate knowledge of the role government and civics has to the material presented (if applicable) • Demonstrates an accurate knowledge of basic economic concepts and how they relate to historical events in the materials presented (if applicable)
4	• Demonstrates an exceptional and consistent knowledge of material presented • Shows evidence of superior understanding of the content and concepts of main historical events in the study of social studies • Shows evidence of superior ability to apply the social studies content, concepts, and skills required to the material presented • Expands upon the topics studied with additional relevant information consistent with the material presented or by inference from the text, time period, or relevant facts • Describes material presented with relevant historical understanding and can expand upon the information using cause and effect explanations (if applicable) • Locates by regions or other geographical features of historical significance and associates relevant information to location and historical information to expand upon the material presented (if applicable) • Demonstrates an exceptional and consistent knowledge of the role government and civics has to the material presented (if applicable) • Demonstrates an exceptional and consistent knowledge of basic economic concepts and how they relate to historical events in the materials presented (if applicable)

LESSON 65   PUTTING IT ALL
TOGETHER

`0:10`

You are about to begin the process of learning how to effectively use the ACE strategy to answer extended response questions for all subjects. Over the next few weeks, you will learn about the ACE strategy, and then you will practice grading actual student work using your student ACE rubric. The teacher rubrics were shared with you so that you have a good understanding of what you are expected to learn in fourth grade. Those rubrics help teachers design their lessons and tell them what subjects, ideas, and tasks on which you need to be tested. You and your Guide can use those rubrics to help identify what to include in your study time. You will not need those rubrics to grade work.

Before you begin, it is important to share some important information with you about state standardized extended response questions. Please take the time to review the section below with your Guide.

1. Extended response questions are not a writing test. When you answer open-ended extended response questions, you are being tested on your comprehension and/or decision-making skills. That is the purpose of using evidence from the text in your answer. You are interpreting what the information in the text is saying and explaining that information in your answer. You will not be tested on your creativity or organization of your answer. The key is to provide a complete answer and explain your thinking.

2. Extended response questions should never include a summary of the passage or text—you are using evidence from the text only to support your answer. The key is to paraphrase or reference a sentence or paragraph in a passage. Simply quoting a passage doesn't let the reader know why that particular sentence or paragraph helped you get your answer.

3. Extended response questions are not graded on writing conventions because they are not a writing test. You are being graded on your ability to effectively and completely answer, cite, and explain a task. Your sentence phrasing and spelling has to be accurate enough to determine the meaning of your answer but no points will be deducted for misspelled words. The key is for you to concentrate on a great answer.

The information above does not translate to the requirements you have on fourth grade formal assessments in school. When you complete formal assessments, you will be required to demonstrate superior conventions of writing skills. Punctuation, spelling, and grammar are extremely important to learn and demonstrate in all of your school work. However, state standardized tests are used to show how well you learned all the fourth grade material and how well you apply your knowledge. Therefore, whenever you take a formal assessment in school, make sure you use good spelling, punctuation, and grammar.

61-80

LESSON 66

YOUR OPEN-ENDED RESPONSE RUBRIC

0:10

It is time to learn how to effectively use the ACE strategy to answer extended response questions for all subjects. You have been given teacher rubrics for all subjects in order to help you understand what you have to know before taking your state standardized test. The rubrics are written by teachers for teachers. You and your Guide can use these rubrics to make sure your study sheets target the skills you will need. You will need to know all the content you will study this year. This book will not help you know social studies, science, math, or language arts content. The questions you see may come from the content you are learning, but the intention of this book is to teach you how to be an effective test taker by learning strategies that every student should know.

The rubric below is part of a strategy for answering open-ended questions on formal assessments and state standardized tests. The rubric's goal is to make you think about the strategies you need to answer the questions effectively. Starting today, we will review each step in the ACE process so that you can build a full understanding of how to use it. The strategies you are about to learn will only work if you take the time to learn the content. Using a calendar, creating study sheets, and developing good study habits are the important parts of this book; this will allow you to use the strategies you learned in this book to succeed.

Rubric

0	The answer was left blank.
1a	Answer the question: • Restate the question/create a topic sentence using the question, problem, or statement. • Have you answered all questions? • Does your answer make sense?
2c	Cite evidence from the text, passage, or problem: • All requirements are met in the *Answer* section. • Use information from the story, passage, text, graphs, or diagrams. • Cite specific examples from the text in your own words. • The evidence demonstrates understanding of the reading. • Is there more than one example in the text? Pick which one is best or use both.
3e	"Explain your brain." • All requirements are met in the *Answer* and *Cite* sections. • Examine your answer. • Extend your thinking; use your own words. • Explain why your evidence/supporting details make your answer correct. • Explain why you chose that answer.

61-80

LESSON 67 — **RESTATE THE QUESTION**

0:20

In the last lesson, you learned that ACE is not really a grading rubric; it is a strategy to help you answer extended response questions on formal assessments or state standardized tests. Answering questions is a part of reading comprehension skills that you have learned about since kindergarten. When you follow the ACE strategy and use your knowledge of the content you studied, then you should be able to score a 4 (Advanced) or 3 (Proficient) on open-ended questions.

In this lesson, you will review the *A* of the ACE strategy. The **A**nswer to any question is always the most important part for students to master. Whether you are answering an oral question, a multiple choice question, or an essay question, you must make sure that your response provides a full answer to the question. Below is a review of the answer strategy.

Answer the question:
- Restate the question/create a topic sentence using the question, problem, or statement.
- Have you answered all questions?
- Does your answer make sense?

Restating a question is the easiest step in this process, but it is also a very important habit to develop for real life. When you answer a teacher's question out loud, restating the question gives you time to think of the exact answer you want to give and lets the teacher know you listened to the question. Your brain doesn't need a lot of time to think, so giving yourself a few more seconds is a great strategy. When you are answering open-ended questions, restating gives you a chance to get your answer on the right track because the right answer is the logical next step in your writing.

Read the following question and the student answer below.

1. If a mouse dies and is not eaten by an owl, how do the nutrients from the mouse go back into the food chain?

Monique's Answer:

It lies on the ground and decomposes and that provides nutrients to the grass, plants, and trees.

Monique did not restate the question. When you read this answer, it is difficult to determine who *it* is referring to when she starts her answer. *It lies on the ground* can be the mouse or the owl. The answer is unclear. When you get to the second part of the answer, it is difficult to determine what provides nutrients to the grass, plants, and trees. The use of the word *that* in *that provides nutrients to the grass, plants, and trees* doesn't clearly identify what is providing the nutrients. Is it the ground or is it the decomposing that provides the nutrients? Or is it that the mouse died and didn't get eaten?

You see, even though the answer is correct, it is unclear to the reader. That is why restating the question is so important.

How would you and your Guide restate the question? Provide your answer on the lines below. Use your knowledge of decomposers in your answer. You can check your answer in Section 2, page 278.

_____

_____

_____

LESSON 68 **RESTATE PRACTICE**

`0:20`

One of the common mistakes that fourth graders make on open-ended response questions is that they do not restate the question, so their answers demonstrate a failure to comprehend what was read. If your answer is confusing to the reader grading your work, then it will be difficult to score. When you don't restate your question, you are beginning your answer in the middle of nowhere. Today, you and your Guide will practice restating questions to begin answers. In the answer key provided in Section 2, page 279, you will compare your beginning statement with the restatements to the open-ended questions asked below. Good luck!

What did you do last night before you went to bed?

_____

_____

_____

Why is it important to begin each lesson day by making sure you have all the materials you need for a lesson?

_____

_____

_____

What would you do to save money for a new bike?

_____

_____

_____

If you did not know a friend's email address, how might you find it?

_____

_____

_____

61-80

LESSON 69 — OPEN RESTATEMENTS AND CLOSED RESTATEMENTS

0:20

Each time you restate a question, you must decide if you want to use an open restatement or a closed restatement. When you are taking a formal assessment or a state standardized assessment, you can choose either strategy. You do not get extra points or a better score for beginning your extended response questions with a certain type of restatement.

In the last lesson, you were asked to answer four questions. The answer key provided the following choices to the questions:

1. Last night before I went to bed, **I**…

2. It is important to have all of my materials before I begin a lesson, **because**…

3. I can save money for a new bike **by**…

4. If I needed to find a friend's email address, **I**…

Each one of these answers begins with an open restatement; they end in a transition word. Transition words like *because*, *I*, *to*, and *by* require you to finish the answer with an extended statement. The restatement is open for a wide variety of possible answers. Each student will be able to give his personal response by using an open restatement with a transition word after it. Open restatements are always good to use when you know there are multiple answers to the question.

Closed restatements are answers that have a complete sentence in the answer. Closed restatements end with a period. You will not be able to extend your answer or provide different answers. That is because you have answered the question in a complete sentence that ends with a period. Using the questions from the last lesson, you and your Guide will review the closed restatement responses below.

1. What did you do last night before you went to bed?

    Answer: Last night, I brushed my teeth before I went to bed.

2. Why is it important to begin each lesson day by making sure you have all the materials you need for a lesson?

    Answer: In order to be prepared to learn, it is important to have all of my materials ready before I begin a lesson.

3. What would you do to save money for a new bike?

    Answer: I would save half of my allowance to save money for a new bike.

4. If you did not know a friend's email address, how might you find it?

    Answer: If I didn't know my friend's email address, I would call him on the telephone and ask for it.

You might be asking yourself, "When do I use a closed restatement or an open restatement?" That depends on the subject, question, and your response. If you were answering a math question or a history question, you may choose to use a closed restatement because those questions usually only have one possible answer. In language arts and science, you may be able to explain a passage or a process (food chain, water cycle, and so on) in several different ways, so an open restatement allows you to lead the reader to the correct response. There is no one correct way to begin your answer to an extended response question. You have to do what feels right for you.

61-80

LESSON 70

THINKING ABOUT YOUR ANSWER

0:20

Rubric

Answer the question:
• Restate the question/create a topic sentence using the question, problem, or statement.
• Have you answered all questions?
• Does your answer make sense?

Now that you have a better understanding of how to restate a question, you will complete the final activity. For each question, restate the question using either a closed restatement or an open restatement. You and your Guide can review samples of each in Section 2, page 280. Your answer does not have to match the answers provided. The important skill to practice in this lesson is using both types of restatements in your answers.

1. What two commands would you train your puppy to perform if you want it to be well behaved?

_____

_____

_____

2. What advice would you give a new pet owner who is having difficulty training his puppy?

_____

_____

_____

3. How can seeds from plants and trees be dispersed?

_____

_____

_____

4. What is one responsibility of the judicial branch of the United States government?

_____

_____

_____

61-80

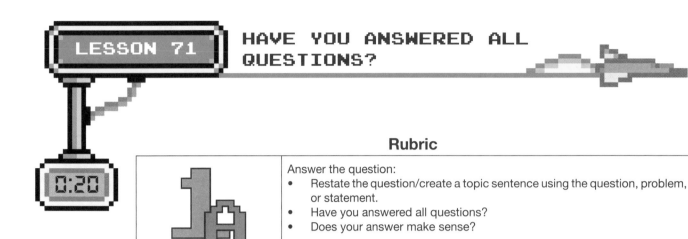

LESSON 71

HAVE YOU ANSWERED ALL QUESTIONS?

0:20

Rubric

Answer the question:
- Restate the question/create a topic sentence using the question, problem, or statement.
- Have you answered all questions?
- Does your answer make sense?

By this time, you should have a good understanding of how a restatement works in the ACE strategy. If you do nothing but answer the question, then you will score a 1. If you did this for all of the questions, you would pass the state standardized test with a score of *Basic*. Basic means that you have general knowledge of fourth grade content but can't apply your knowledge to extend your answer. Later on in this book, you will review the scoring summary of a state standardized test, how to read your results, and what the scoring criteria mean for you.

There will be times when an extended response question has more than one task that you have to complete. Earlier in this book, you learned about highlighting tasks and action verbs in a question.

Below, you will find an extended response question.

Mrs. Patel was testing for physical and chemical changes. First, she put an ice cube in an empty drinking glass. Next, she combined baking soda with vinegar and immediately observed bubbles forming. Identify each change as physical or chemical, and give an explanation for each change.

The question has two tasks. In the first, you must identify each change as either physical or chemical. In the second task, you must give a clear reason (performance verb: *explain*) for your choice. The best strategy to use is to create two or more restatement sentences to answer this question. Using this strategy will allow you to make sure you have covered all requirements in the *A* part of the ACE strategy.

For this example, your restatements might look like this:

Putting an ice cube in an empty drinking glass is an example of a physical change, and combining baking soda and vinegar is an example of a chemical change. A chemical change occurs when you combine substances to make new matter. A physical change occurs when you combine substances but the matter stays the same.

When you answer a question, whether it has one or more tasks, you should use the restatement strategy to your advantage. By using two restatements, you are able to make sure that each of the questions is answered completely. You will also not forget to answer any part of the question because the restatements keep you on track. The trick is to answer the question first. We will get to the explanation part of a good extended response question in a few lessons.

LESSON 72   TWO TASK RESTATEMENTS

0:20

Rubric

1a	Answer the question: • Restate the question/create a topic sentence using the question, problem, or statement. • Have you answered all questions? • Does your answer make sense?

Today, you will practice writing two restatements for extended response questions. You have probably noticed that multiple terms are being used to describe these questions. Earlier in this book, you learned that open-ended questions are also called extended response questions, brief constructed response questions, or constructed response questions. It is important to know all of the terms because each state uses one of these names on its test. No matter what it is called, an open-ended question requires you to complete a task and provide enough of an explanation so that the scorer can understand how you got your solution.

An open-ended question has no question marks. You have to use critical thinking to identify the tasks, conjunctions, and performance verbs. You should use highlighting strategies to help highlight, circle, or underline. Conjunctions like *and*, *or*, *but*, *then*, and *after* are important parts of a question because they give you important information to completely answer a question and they provide a clue to questions with two tasks. Conjunctions are connecting words that can join two tasks together and require you to provide answers for both tasks.

Today you will need three colored pencils or (a conjunction) crayons to complete your task. In the open-ended questions below, you will:
• highlight one of the tasks in the question in one color.
• highlight the second task in the question in another color.
• highlight the conjunction in the question that connects the two tasks in a third color.

You will then provide a restatement for each open-ended question. You and your Guide will review the answers in Section 2, page 281.

1. Latasha goes through a traumatic event but learns a very valuable lesson in *Latasha and the Little Red Tornado*. Use information from the passage and your own ideas or conclusions to describe the tragedy and the lesson learned.

    _____

    _____

    _____

2. Explain why Latasha chose to go on a walk with Ella alone instead of having Ricky accompany them and identify the consequences of her choice. Use information from the story and your own ideas to support your answer.

    _____

    _____

    _____

61-80

LESSON 73 — ANSWER THE QUESTION FIRST

0:20

You probably thought the ACE strategy was going to be quick to learn; but here we are almost five lessons later and all you have been working on is the *Answer* in ACE. However, the answer is the most important part of this strategy. The answer to an open-ended response question allows you to start off on the right foot. The answer naturally leads to the *Cite* and *Explain* parts of ACE. It is important for you to communicate with the reader who scores your test so that he understands the response you gave. When you write a clear, legible answer, the reader doesn't have to guess what you are trying to say. That is why a restatement is important; it allows you to have a good foundation for your answer and it lets the reader clearly see what your answer is to each task. When you don't write a restatement, you almost start the answer in the middle of a sentence.

For example, let's look at a conversation between two friends.

Sam: "What would you like to do this weekend, Nick?"

Nick: "to the movies."

Sam: "What about Saturday for the movies?"

Nick: "busy but Sunday, maybe."

In this example, Sam has to guess a little to help him understand Nick's answer. As a reader, you will also have to guess what this dialogue is about. Maybe Nick is saying that he will go to the movies this weekend with someone else but can go with Sam on Sunday, or maybe Nick is saying that a movie sounds good but his schedule is busy until Sunday.

Now let's look at the same discussion with restatements.

Sam: "What would you like to do this weekend, Nick?"

Nick: "I would love to go to the movies."

Sam: "What about Saturday for the movies?"

Nick: "Saturday I'm busy, but Sunday, maybe."

The conversation has now become clear for Sam. The reader also knows that the two friends chose to go to the movies together on Sunday. That's the key to a good answer; you need to explain your thinking to the reader. Starting an answer without a restatement could confuse the reader and cause him to view your answer as incorrect. It doesn't take long to write out a restatement and it will help you formulate a correct answer; that is what makes restatements a great strategy.

LESSON 74   AFTER THE ANSWER

It is important to remember that the ACE strategy is a strategy and not a rubric. In earlier lessons, you were given the teacher rubrics for grading open-ended response questions. Those rubrics identify the ACE strategy for each subject but are written in teacher language. By knowing the ACE strategy, you will be able to meet all the criteria for answering questions using your knowledge and understanding of the content of a subject. That means that you have to spend plenty of time studying your notes every day. You need to know everything you learned in fourth grade and how to apply that knowledge before each formal assessment and state standardized test. That is why this strategy works; you don't have to worry about what the teacher rubric says about content.

You and your Guide will read the following passage and answer the question below. Write a good restatement sentence with an answer on the lines. This question will be used in the next several lessons but an example is provided in Section 2, page 282.

Read the following passage with your Guide.

David and the Gull
by Debbie Parrish

Eight-year-old David strolled down the beach with his hands shoved in his pockets. He was thinking and letting the sand drift through his toes as he went. David had just moved to the coast of North Carolina. His dad had gotten a new job in that community. While he was going to miss his friends, David had to admit that living near the Atlantic Ocean was going to be fun. As he walked, he kicked around a bent up can that was lying on the beach. When he got near the pier, David grew a bit tired. He sat down on a thick piece of driftwood that had washed up on the shore under the pier. David sat quietly, tossing the can he had been kicking from one hand to the other.

You will read many longer passages on your state standardized test. Don't forget to use the strategies you learned about highlighting main ideas and details of a story or passage. The following is an example of an open-ended response question.

1. Identify how David feels about his move to North Carolina. Use evidence from the text to support your answer.

_____

_____

_____

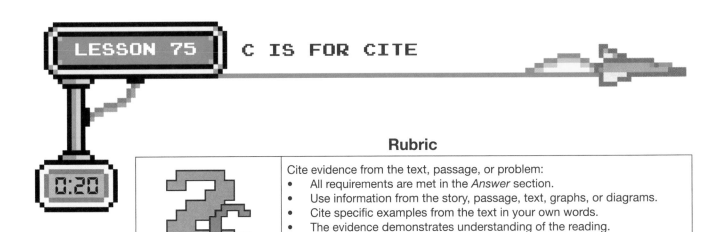

LESSON 75   C IS FOR CITE

Rubric

Cite evidence from the text, passage, or problem:
- All requirements are met in the *Answer* section.
- Use information from the story, passage, text, graphs, or diagrams.
- Cite specific examples from the text in your own words.
- The evidence demonstrates understanding of the reading.
- Is there more than one example in the text? Pick which one is best or use both.

Today, you will begin learning about using evidence from texts, charts, graphs, or passages to support your answer. That is what the word *cite* means; you use evidence from a passage to support your answer. Before we begin any lessons, you should have a deeper understanding of what it means to cite. In Lesson 74, you provided the answer to the open-ended assessment question below. You will now begin learning how to cite evidence from the text to support your answer.

David and the Gull
by Debbie Parrish

Eight-year-old David strolled down the beach with his hands shoved in his pockets. He was thinking and letting the sand drift through his toes as he went. David had just moved to the coast of North Carolina. His dad had gotten a new job in that community. While he was going to miss his friends, David had to admit that living near the Atlantic Ocean was going to be fun. As he walked, he kicked around a bent up can that was lying on the beach. When he got near the pier, David grew a bit tired. He sat down on a thick piece of driftwood that had washed up on the shore under the pier. David sat quietly, tossing the can he had been kicking from one hand to the other.

You will read many longer passages on your state standardized test. Don't forget to use the strategies you learned about highlighting main ideas and details of a story or passage.

The following is an example of an open-ended response question.

1. Identify how David feels about his move to North Carolina. Use evidence from the text to support your answer.

From reading this passage, you would be able to say that David is both sad and excited about his move to North Carolina. That is the answer to the question.

Using the ACE strategy, you would have the following answer.

Answer:

David is both sad and excited about his move to North Carolina. (closed restatement)

Now you have to tell the scorer for this question how you knew David was both sad and excited. That is why most questions on a state standardized test state to use your own knowledge, evidence from the text, and your knowledge of the subject to support your answer.

Read the following student answers.

Student A:

> David is both sad and excited about his move to North Carolina. I know David is sad because I would be sad if I moved away from all my friends.

Student B:

> David is both sad and excited about his move to North Carolina. In the story, David says that he was going to miss his friends but living near the Atlantic Ocean was going to be fun.

Student A uses some evidence from the text and adds his own experiences to explain the reason he answered the question the way he did; however, he doesn't fully support the explanation for David also being excited about the move. It is important that you never use your own personal feelings or knowledge to support your answer. Just because you know something or feel something does not provide the scorer with enough information to determine if you comprehended what you read and were able to apply your knowledge to support your answer.

Student B clearly uses the text to support his answer about David's sadness and excitement about the move. He summarizes the passage and the exact sentence that clearly demonstrates to a reader that David is both sad and excited.

LESSON 76

CITE IS PART COMPREHENSION

`0:20`

Earlier in this book, we talked about the importance of reading comprehension, or understanding what you are reading and being able to process the information. This is a very important skill to practice all your life. Think about reading the funniest fourth grade book but not laughing because you don't understand what you read, or trying to build a model car from the directions and it comes out looking like a bicycle. When you are using the ACE strategy to respond to an open-ended question, you are being tested on your ability to comprehend the text. Therefore, you can also think of the *C* in ACE as *cite* and *comprehension*. You have to show that you got the information in your answer from the text.

Today, you and your Guide will use all the strategies you learned about highlighting the main ideas of a passage to practice the *A* and *C* sections of the ACE strategy. You learned about highlighting strategies to identify the main idea of a passage so you can quickly locate details. You also learned about summarizing and taking study notes about a passage. You can use all these strategies for this lesson.

Directions:
* Read a short passage with your Guide.
* Highlight the main idea in each paragraph.
* Read the questions provided at the end of the passage.
* Circle all the performance verbs.
* Do not answer the questions provided. You are preparing yourself to answer the questions.
* Check your work in Section 2, page 283.

Vacation to Disney World
by Brianne Kovacs

Every year families take vacations. Vacations are the best way to relax and create bonding experiences with the family. There are many destinations to choose from, but Disney World is the perfect option. Disney World offers attractions for all ages, affordable options, and endless family activities.

Disney World has all kinds of attractions and foods that we all can enjoy. They have thrilling roller coasters, slower rides, and water rides. Throughout the year, they have all kinds of parades, musical shows, and fireworks. Favorite Disney characters are available to have their picture taken with everyone. Along with all of this, Disney offers entertaining dining and shopping for its visitors.

Disney offers packages for a place to stay and tickets to their park. For adventurous families, they offer camps to stay at. Hotels are available to cater to families with lower incomes. For families that want nothing but the best or would like to experience luxury, they offer five-star hotel stays. Disney has family and group packages, too.

Disney is one of the best ways to ensure the family has fun while bonding. Thrilling rides can cause siblings to hug each other and admit they really do love one another, while long walks from ride to ride allow families time to talk and laugh together. Disney also offers individual activities for when members of the family need a short break from each other.

Disney is the best option for our family vacation. Disney provides fun and educational bonding experiences and affordable options for all types of families. Adults and children can appreciate the opportunities provided by a Disney vacation. At the end of the day, hearing, "You're the best, mom and dad," will make it all worth it.

1. Identify the purpose of this essay and interpret the author's opinion. Use evidence from the essay and your knowledge of persuasive essays to support your answer.

2. Conclude whether the author was able to persuade or dissuade your opinion. Use evidence from the persuasive essay to support your answer.

LESSON 77

DEMONSTRATE YOUR COMPREHENSION

`0:20`

For this lesson, you and your Guide will complete the *Answer* and the *Cite* sections of the ACE strategy for the questions below the persuasive essay. In your *Cite* response, focus on demonstrating to the reader that you understood what you read and are able to interpret your knowledge into your own words. Before you begin, you and your Guide should read the persuasive essay again. You are writing your answer for your Guide, so be sure that you work independently; this will allow your Guide to provide you with honest feedback.

The most important part of this exercise is the *Cite* section. Here are several important tips:

- If this question was on a formal assessment, spelling, grammar, and punctuation would count toward your grade; but on a state standardized test they don't count. Do your best to avoid errors in conventions of writing by rereading your answer out loud in your head.
- Give only the information from the text that is needed. Be specific; avoid useless details that do not support your answer.
- Summarize information from the text; avoid copying sentences directly from the passage, and use your own words to explain what you understood (comprehended) from the text.

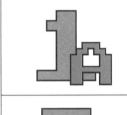	Answer the question: • Restate the question/create a topic sentence using the question, problem, or statement. • Have you answered all questions? • Does your answer make sense?
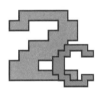	Cite evidence from the text, passage, or problem: • All requirements are met in the *Answer* section. • Use information from the story, passage, text, graphs, or diagrams. • Cite specific examples from the text in your own words. • The evidence demonstrates understanding of the reading. • Is there more than one example in the text? Pick which one is best or use both.

Vacation to Disney World
by Brianne Kovacs

Every year families take vacations. Vacations are the best way to relax and create bonding experiences with the family. There are many destinations to choose from, but Disney World is the perfect option. Disney World offers attractions for all ages, affordable options, and endless family activities.

Disney World has all kinds of attractions and foods that we all can enjoy. They have thrilling roller coasters, slower rides, and water rides. Throughout the year, they have all kinds of parades, musical shows, and fireworks. Favorite Disney characters are available to have their picture taken with everyone. Along with all of this, Disney offers entertaining dining and shopping for its visitors.

Disney offers packages for a place to stay and tickets to their park. For adventurous families, they offer camps to stay at. Hotels are available to cater to families with lower incomes. For families that want nothing but the best or would like to experience luxury they, offer five-star hotel stays. Disney has family and group packages, too.

CONTINUED ->

Disney is one of the best ways to ensure the family has fun while bonding. Thrilling rides can cause siblings to hug each other and admit they really do love one another, while long walks from ride to ride allow families time to talk and laugh together. Disney also offers individual activities for when members of the family need a short break from each other.

Disney is the best option for our family vacation. Disney provides fun and educational bonding experiences and affordable options for all types of families. Adults and children can appreciate the opportunities provided by a Disney vacation. At the end of the day, hearing, "You're the best, mom and dad," will make it all worth it.

Check your answers in Section 2, page 285.

1. Identify the purpose of this of this essay and interpret the author's opinion. Use evidence from the essay and your knowledge of persuasive essays to support your answer.

Answer:

Cite:

2. Conclude whether the author was able to persuade or dissuade your opinion. Use evidence from the persuasive essay to support your answer.

Answer:

Cite:

 **LESSON 78**

C IS FOR...
CITE CONCISELY!

How did your answers compare to the student examples? You and your Guide probably did a great job on your first attempt. Citing examples from the text doesn't have to be long and should never be copied directly from the passage. You have to be concise, which means short and to the point. When you cite from the text, you also have to summarize what you have read. That allows the reader to see that you understood the question, applied your knowledge, and supported your answer completely.

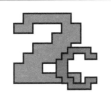	Cite evidence from the text, passage, or problem: • All requirements are met in the *Answer* section. • Use information from the story, passage, text, graphs, or diagrams. • Cite specific examples from the text in your own words. • The evidence demonstrates understanding of the reading. • Is there more than one example in the text? Pick which one is best or use both.

When you are working on an open-ended response question, you want to provide enough information so the person scoring the exam can quickly see that you comprehended what you have read. If you copy from the text or provide too much of an answer, it may seem to the scorer that you are unsure of how to answer and are just going to provide a lot of information and see if something is correct. That's like a batter asking for a pitcher to throw twenty baseballs so he can make sure that he hits at least one. That doesn't make sense, does it? That is why you want to be concise, so the reader scoring your exam knows that you got a hit on the first try. You and your Guide will have to practice this strategy each time you have an exam review or during your study time. You can do this!

1. Identify the purpose of this essay and interpret the author's opinion. Use evidence from the essay and your knowledge of persuasive essays to support your answer.

	Answer:
	The author's purpose is to persuade the reader that going to Disney World is the perfect option for a vacation.
	Cite:
	In the essay, the author states that Disney World is the perfect option because it has all kinds of attractions that everyone can enjoy.

2. Conclude whether the author was able to persuade or dissuade your opinion. Use evidence from the persuasive essay to support your answer.

	Answer:
	The author was able to convince me that Disney would be a great place to take a vacation.
	Cite:
	The author stated that Disney was a great place for families to have bonding time and that is a very important part to keep the love in a family.

61-80

LESSON 79 — PRACTICE A AND C; SAVE E FOR LATER

0:20

Directions:
- Read the following passage.
- Highlight the main ideas of each paragraph.
- Read each of the questions at the end of the passage.
- Circle the performance verbs.
- Respond to the *Answer* and *Cite* sections. Use the text to support your answer.

Circle, Circle, Dot, Dot
by Brianne Kovacs

I saw her lying there on her belly in the grass field during our recess. She was sitting there under the sun, picking petals off of a flower. "He loves me, he loves me not," she said so quietly, almost in a whisper. This poor golden-haired girl! Has anyone ever told her that boys have cooties? I know for a fact. I've seen it!

She picked her head up from the flower and drew her attention to the boys playing tag by the swings. I followed her eyes and realized who she was staring at, Todd. "Oh no, not Todd!" I thought to myself, "He's almost as awful as Gregg!" Last week at lunch Gregg stuck gum in my hair and Todd fell out of his seat laughing at me. I was so humiliated that I had to go home. At this moment I knew she needed a best friend to educate her, and that best friend would be me!

I took in a deep breath and marched in her direction. As my shadow drove the sunshine out from her face, she peaked at me with a curious look. I let out my breath and plopped myself down beside her, "Hi, I'm Maggie."

She lowered her eyes back to the ground and almost in a whisper she said her name, "I'm Gertrude."

I watched her freckled face as she continued to pick at the puffy, yellow flowers. Without thinking, I grabbed her arm, pulled it onto my lap, and drew on it with my finger, "Circle, circle, dot, dot, now you've got your cootie shot!" As she looked up at me confused, I reassured her, "You should be good now." Without missing a beat I announced, "Let's go do something fun!" Getting up I dashed towards the swings. Gertrude followed behind me spinning on her toes the whole way.

We swung back and forth on the swings for quite some time without saying anything to each other. I pumped my legs hard, swinging higher and higher, as Gertrude stayed low to the ground at a gentle pulse. I looked at the sky preparing to ask her a question and just as I went to take a breath, THUMP! My foot had kicked Gregg right in the head! He fumbled backwards and fell to ground. Holding his hand to his head he started crying and Todd tried to help him up. My mouth dropped open as I watched Gregg struggle to his feet and run screaming to the teacher. Then I noticed it, I turned my head and saw Gertrude laughing so hard at Gregg, she almost fell off the swing. At that moment, I was optimistic she would be just fine!

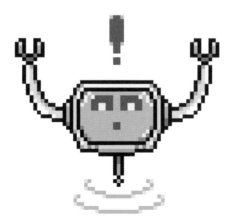

BEEP
DON'T FORGET TO
PRACTICE YOUR
HIGHLIGHTING
STRATEGIES.
BEEP

Check your answers in Section 2, page 286.

1. Maggie decides that Gertrude needs a best friend to help "educate" her. Identify one way in which Maggie educates Gertrude. Use evidence from the passage to support your answer.

1a	Answer:
2c	Cite:

2. In the story, Maggie injures Gregg while swinging on the swing set. Using evidence from the passage to support your answer, and your own personal knowledge, evaluate whether Maggie should have consequences for her actions.

1a	Answer:
2c	Cite:

08-19
61-80

LESSON 80 ONE MORE CITE PRACTICE

`0:20`

Directions:
• Read the following passage.
• Highlight the main ideas of the passage.
• Read each of the questions at the end of the passage.
• Circle the performance verbs.
• Respond to the *Answer* and *Cite* sections. Use the text to support your answer.

Amy's Pet
by Debbie Parrish

Five-year-old Amy came into the kitchen one morning. She had on a sad face.

"What's wrong, Amy?" asked her mom.

"I need a pet," was Amy's glum reply.

Mom smiled. "You need a pet, or you want a pet?"

Amy smiled back at her. "I guess I could live without one, but I really, really do want one!"

"If you could have a pet, what pet would you want?" her mom asked.

Amy thought for a minute. She said, "I would like a different, special kind of pet. I think, maybe, I would like a monkey. They are so cute!"

"Did you know that a monkey is a wild animal?" Mom asked.

"Yes, but I could tame it," insisted Amy.

"Even if you could tame it, would that be fair to the monkey?" asked her mom.

"What do you mean?" asked Amy.

"Monkeys have a different habitat than humans," answered Mom. "A habitat is where something or someone lives. Monkeys are used to living outside in a place with many trees. They love to climb and swing from tree to tree. They like to roam and be free to find the kinds of food they like."

Amy said, "Okay, then maybe I could have a seal. I saw a movie on television about a seal, and it was very sweet."

Mom shook her head and said, "A seal's habitat is different from ours, too. It needs a very cold place to live. They like to live where there is lots of water for swimming and hunting. Seals love to hunt for fish to eat. If we took a seal away from its habitat, it would not be happy and would not stay healthy."

"What about a raccoon?" asked Amy.

"Raccoons are wild animals, too," said her mom. "They are able to live in lots of different places, but they like to live near lakes and streams. They can find nuts, berries, and fish there. That's what raccoons like to eat."

Mom scratched her head and added, "Besides, raccoons mostly move around at night. They sleep during the day. That wouldn't be much fun since you sleep at night."

Mom continued by explaining, "Wild animals' needs are just very different from what we can give them in our homes."

Amy frowned. She still seemed very sad.

"I have an idea," said Mom. "Let's go for a ride."

Amy and her mom climbed into the car. "Where are we going, Mom?"

"We are going to a special place called an animal shelter," answered her mom.

"What is an animal shelter?" asked Amy.

"An animal shelter is a place where animals are taken when they have no home and no one to take care of them," Mom said. "I know the man who works at the shelter. His name is Mr. Rescue. He says they always have more animals than they can handle at the shelter."

When the car came to a stop, Amy hopped out and followed her mom into the front door. Mr. Rescue greeted them as they came in. He asked Amy's mom if she needed some help.

Mom told Mr. Rescue that they were there to look around a little bit. She told him that Amy had never been to an animal shelter.

Amy and her mom followed Mr. Rescue as he showed them around. They were about to turn and head back to the front of the building, but Amy suddenly heard a tiny cry. It was coming from over near a window. She looked behind the green plant in front of the window. There a tiny, yellow kitten lay crying. Amy bent down and said, "What's wrong, little fellow?"

Mr. Rescue told Amy that someone had left the little kitten on the steps of the shelter the day before.

"He is feeling pretty lonely right now," said Mr. Rescue. "I guess whoever he belonged to could not give him what he needed."

"What does he need?" Amy asked.

Mr. Rescue replied, "Well, kittens need food, water, shelter, playtime for exercise, and lots of love."

Amy looked at her mom and asked, "Can we take him home and let him be my pet?"

Her mom said, "But Amy, I thought you wanted a pet that was very different and special. Would this kitten be that kind of pet?"

"Oh, yes," smiled Amy. "He is different because he needs me, and he would be very special because he would be mine!"

Amy's mom laughed and said, "Well, I guess we had better get going. You need to show him all around his new home!"

With a huge smile on her face, Amy cuddled her new pet. On the ride home she would start thinking of a special name for her very special new pet.

61-80

CONTINUED ->

Check your answers in Section 2, page 287.

1. Amy's mother spends a lot of time explaining wild animals to her. Use evidence from the text to evaluate where Amy's mother was able to convince Amy that wild animals do not make good pets.

	Answer:
1A	
2C	Cite:

Read the following sentence from the passage:

"I need a pet," was Amy's glum reply.

2. Amy decides that she wants a pet but informs her mother that she "needs" a pet. Using evidence from the text and your knowledge of needs and wants, evaluate if Amy's statement is logical.

	Answer:
1A	
2C	Cite:

LESSON 81

E IS FOR "EXPLAIN YOUR BRAIN"

0:10

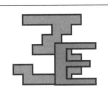

"Explain your brain."
- All requirements are met in the *Answer* and *Cite* sections.
- Examine your answer.
- Extend your thinking; use your own words.
- Explain why your evidence/supporting details make your answer correct.
- Explain why you chose that answer.

The last section of the ACE strategy is the *E*, which means to elaborate, expand, extend, or explain your answer. You have to make it clear that you know the answer by explaining the connection between the information you cited and the answer. Explaining your brain is letting your teacher, the reader, and/or the scorer know that the information in your *A* and *C* sections was an important and significant choice. You chose the specific text to support your answer because you can apply your own personal knowledge and experience to the topic.

The *Explain* section of the ACE strategy is the difference between scoring a 4 (Advanced) and a 3 (Proficient) on the state standardized test. This is your time to shine and dazzle the scorer with your brilliance. When you are able to score a 4 on an open-ended response question, you are demonstrating that you have knowledge of a subject matter, are able to apply your knowledge, and can demonstrate that you comprehend how to connect the information to reach a conclusion.

The *E* is the *how* of your answer. How did you know what process to use? How did you know that your summary of the passage provided an answer? How did you apply your knowledge of the subject matter? You have to let the scorer know, in detail, how you knew your response was appropriate. This is the section where you have to use your own personal experience and knowledge to support your response. Over the next lessons, you and your Guide will review good *E* responses, then you will begin to put all three sections of ACE together.

Discuss with your Guide:

Do you learn better by seeing, hearing, touching, or doing?

_____

_____

How can knowing how you learn help you in school?

_____

_____

81-100

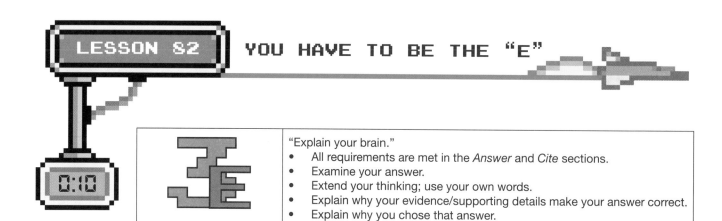

LESSON 82 — YOU HAVE TO BE THE "E"

"Explain your brain."
- All requirements are met in the *Answer* and *Cite* sections.
- Examine your answer.
- Extend your thinking; use your own words.
- Explain why your evidence/supporting details make your answer correct.
- Explain why you chose that answer.

You have read a lot about answering open-ended response questions on formal assessments and on state standardized tests over the course of this book. Today, you will begin to put all the pieces together. It is important that you always use this strategy, whether you are answering essay questions, open-ended response practice quizzes, or completing the state standardized assessment. This strategy will allow you to demonstrate your mastery of content and ability to apply strategies to solve problems. This is a very important skill to have for school and for life.

When you and your Guide first reviewed the *A* section of ACE, you learned that you need to demonstrate your reading comprehension. You learned to use a restatement sentence as a guide to your response. Later, you learned that the *C* section helps you demonstrate that you comprehended the chart, graph, or passage and were able to draw conclusions that helped support your answer. You may use sentences like "*According to the (text, graph, chart)...,*" "*The (author, narrator) states...,*" or "*The (chart, graph) information shows....*"

In the *E* section, you have to explain how you made connections from the text to yourself. You have to use your own experiences and knowledge to elaborate on the reason for your response. You can do this by writing down the steps that you took in your mind to reach the conclusion; in other words, explain how you came to the conclusion.

Read the following student explanations:

- I just know.
- It's easy because you just have to add five more to the first number.
- The graph has all the information you need to answer the question.
- We learned the food web in science so I knew that frogs ate crickets.

The answers above do not allow the reader to understand the student's knowledge of the content or concepts of the task. Explaining your brain means that you are making a connection to the text. Remember, there are three types of connections you make with text: text-to-text, text-to-self, and text-to-world.

When you begin your sentence for the *E* section of your response, it is a good strategy to begin your statement with one of the following sentence starters:

- The evidence of the text helped me...
- In the (map, chart, or graph), I was able to...
- I knew the math problem was addition because the question states...
- I had a similar experience one time (make a connection to self or world)...
- This story is similar to another text I read (make a connection to text)...

These sentence starters, like a restatement, will help you introduce the explanation to the answer and the citation. What other sentence starters can you and your Guide create to "explain your brain"?

LESSON 83   THE E IN A RUBRIC

0:20

"Explain your brain."
- All requirements are met in the *Answer* and *Cite* sections.
- Examine your answer.
- Extend your thinking; use your own words.
- Explain why your evidence/supporting details make your answer correct.
- Explain why you chose that answer.

When you extend, explain, or elaborate on your response to an open-ended response question, you increase your potential to score a 4 (Advanced) on the state standardized testing rubric. You and your Guide will review an actual open-ended scoring rubric from a state standardized test. When you read the criteria for each score, pay attention to the highlighted words that show evidence that you are expected to use the ACE strategy.

In the rubric, you can see that you will be expected to use an ACE strategy by making a connection to the text and your own personal knowledge to extend your thinking.

- Answer
- Cite
- Explain, Extend, Elaborate

Open-Ended Scoring Rubric State Standardized Assessment	
4 – Advanced	Demonstrates a clear and complete understanding of the task, completes all requirements, and provides an insightful explanation or connection to the text, or extends beyond the knowledge of the text.
3 – Proficient	Demonstrates an understanding of the task, completes all requirements, and provides some explanation using situations or ideas from the text as support.
2 – Basic	Attempts to address all of the requirements, but demonstrates only a partial understanding of the task and uses text incorrectly or with limited success resulting in an inconsistent or unsupported explanation.
1 – Below Basic	Demonstrates minimal understanding of the task that leads to partial completion of requirements for the task, and provides no reference or no use of the text.

Now that you have a complete understanding of the ACE strategy, it is time to put all three pieces together. In the next three lessons, you will complete the open-ended responses to the practice problems that only used the *A* and *C* strategies. Then you will practice open-ended response questions in math, science, social studies, and language arts. You and your Guide will also practice being the scorer. By the end of all the lessons, you will become an expert on open-ended response questions. Are you ready to begin?

81-100

LESSON 84   E IS FOR ELABORATE

0:20

In Lessons 76 and 77, you and your Guide read a persuasive essay about Disney World. You highlighted the main ideas of the essay and answered two questions. The example from the answer key in Section 2 is provided below. When you use the ACE strategy on a state standardized test, you may want to write a little *A*, *C*, and *E* on the right-hand corner of the space provided for writing. This will allow you to cross off the *A*, *C*, and *E* as you write. Today, you and your Guide will read the persuasive essay and review the entire ACE answer provided below each question.

In the *Explain* section of the answer, you will read a student's elaboration on his *Answer* and *Cite* sections. The student is trying to expand upon his answer and offer insight into his thinking. One of the connections that you can make when you elaborate on your answer is text-to-self; you can offer your own opinion or personal example. Read the answer choice with your Guide. Would you have elaborated the answer in a similar way? What may you have done differently?

Vacation to Disney World
by Brianne Kovacs

Every year families take vacations. Vacations are the best way to relax and create bonding experiences with the family. There are many destinations to choose from, but Disney World is the perfect option. Disney World offers attractions for all ages, affordable options, and endless family activities.

Disney World has all kinds of attractions and foods that we all can enjoy. They have thrilling roller coasters, slower rides, and water rides. Throughout the year, they have all kinds of parades, musical shows, and fireworks. Favorite Disney characters are available to have their picture taken with everyone. Along with all of this, Disney offers entertaining dining and shopping for its visitors.

Disney offers packages for a place to stay and tickets to their park. For adventurous families, they offer camps to stay at. Hotels are available to cater to families with lower incomes. For families that want nothing but the best or would like to experience luxury they, offer five-star hotel stays. Disney has family and group packages, too.

Disney is one of the best ways to ensure the family has fun while bonding. Thrilling rides can cause siblings to hug each other and admit they really do love one another, while long walks from ride to ride allow families time to talk and laugh together. Disney also offers individual activities for when members of the family need a short break from each other.

Disney is the best option for our family vacation. Disney provides fun and educational bonding experiences and affordable options for all types of families. Adults and children can appreciate the opportunities provided by a Disney vacation. At the end of the day, hearing, "You're the best, mom and dad," will make it all worth it.

1. Identify the purpose of this of this essay and interpret the author's opinion. Use evidence from the essay and your knowledge of persuasive essays to support your answer.

Answer Space	
	~~ACE~~
1a	The author's purpose is to persuade the reader that going to Disney World is the perfect option for a vacation.
2c	In the essay, the author states that Disney World is the perfect option because it has all kinds of attractions that everyone can enjoy.
3E	I have never been to Disney World but the author made it sound like a great place for me, my sister, and my parents. My parents would enjoy the slower rides, my sister likes water rides, and I could ride roller coasters all day.

The student sample shows a text-to-self connection using ideas from the passage to personally connect to the essay. In this example, he demonstrates that the author persuaded him about a Disney vacation because he could see himself enjoying the rides with his family. He also makes a connection to the *Cite* section by elaborating on the idea that there are attractions for everyone to enjoy.

2. Conclude whether the author was able to persuade or dissuade your opinion. Use evidence from the persuasive essay to support your answer.

Answer Space	
	~~ACE~~
1a	The author was able to convince me that Disney would be a great place to take a vacation.
2c	The author stated that Disney was a great place for families to have bonding time and that is a very important part of keeping the love in a family.
3E	The author provides me with a lot of useful information that I can use to convince my parents to choose Disney World for a vacation. I would be able to tell them they are the best parents in the world.

In this example, the student again elaborates his answer from the *Cite* section. His text-to-self connection expands his idea about love in a family. He uses the author's quote about a child telling his parents that they are the best to make a personal connection to the text. This is an excellent ACE answer and the elaboration allows the scorer to make a personal connection to the student's thinking. The scorer of this state standardized question could also see that the student was able to completely comprehend the text and make a connection to it.

81-100

LESSON 85

E IS FOR EXPLAIN A TEXT CONNECTION

0:20

In Lesson 79, you and your Guide read a fictional story about a growing friendship between two girls. Today, you and your Guide will read the story again and review the *Answer* and *Cite* section of each response to the questions below. In the *E* section of the answer, you will read a student's explanation for his *A* and *C* section based on a text-to-text connection. When you make text-to-text connections, it allows the scorer to know that you completely comprehend text and remember details that could be connected to another story. Making text-to-text connections is a great strategy to use in language arts. Read the answer choice with your Guide. Would you have used a different text to explain the answer in a similar way? Would you have made a text-to-self connection instead?

Circle, Circle, Dot, Dot
by Brianne Kovacs

I saw her lying there on her belly in the grass field during our recess. She was sitting there under the sun, picking petals off of a flower. "He loves me, he loves me not," she said so quietly, almost in a whisper. This poor golden-haired girl! Has anyone ever told her that boys have cooties? I know for a fact. I've seen it!

She picked her head up from the flower and drew her attention to the boys playing tag by the swings. I followed her eyes and realized who she was staring at, Todd. "Oh no, not Todd!" I thought to myself, "He's almost as awful as Gregg!" Last week at lunch Gregg stuck gum in my hair and Todd fell out of his seat laughing at me. I was so humiliated that I had to go home. At this moment I knew she needed a best friend to educate her, and that best friend would be me!

I took in a deep breath and marched in her direction. As my shadow drove the sunshine out from her face, she peaked at me with a curious look. I let out my breath and plopped myself down beside her, "Hi, I'm Maggie."

She lowered her eyes back to the ground and almost in a whisper she said her name, "I'm Gertrude."

I watched her freckled face as she continued to pick at the puffy, yellow flowers. Without thinking, I grabbed her arm, pulled it onto my lap, and drew on it with my finger, "Circle, circle, dot, dot, now you've got your cootie shot!" As she looked up at me confused, I reassured her, "You should be good now." Without missing a beat I announced, "Let's go do something fun!" Getting up I dashed towards the swings. Gertrude followed behind me spinning on her toes the whole way.

We swung back and forth on the swings for quite some time without saying anything to each other. I pumped my legs hard, swinging higher and higher, as Gertrude stayed low to the ground at a gentle pulse. I looked at the sky preparing to ask her a question and just as I went to take a breath, THUMP! My foot had kicked Gregg right in the head! He fumbled backwards and fell to ground. Holding his hand to his head he started crying and Todd tried to help him up. My mouth dropped open as I watched Gregg struggle to his feet and run screaming to the teacher. Then I noticed it, I turned my head and saw Gertrude laughing so hard at Gregg, she almost fell off the swing. At that moment, I was optimistic she would be just fine!

1. Maggie decides that Gertrude needs a best friend to help "educate" her. Identify one way in which Maggie educates Gertrude. Use evidence from the passage to support your answer.

Answer Space	
	ACE
1a	Maggie educates Gertrude by giving her a cootie shot.
2c	In the story, Gertrude is lying by herself in the grass pulling petals to see if Todd likes her but Maggie thinks boys have cooties and plans to save Gertrude.
3E	This reminds me of the story *Even Inks Need Friends.* Wilda, the zoo keeper, becomes friends with an Ink, who was banished from the Ink Cave for trying to educate the other Inks to do something nice for Midlandians. By the end of the story, Wilda and the Ink knew they would be friends.

Text-to-text connections are a great way to "explain your brain." The scorer on a state standardized assessment will see that you applied your reading comprehension skills to the passage. When you make a connection to another text, you are linking two story lines and telling the reader that the two stories made you understand the characters. This is an excellent application and extension of your knowledge.

2. In the story, Maggie injures Gregg while swinging on the swing set. Using evidence from the passage to support your answer, and your own personal knowledge, evaluate whether Maggie should have consequences for her actions.

Answer Space	
	ACE
1a	Maggie injures Gregg by accident when she wasn't paying attention so she should not have consequences for her action.
2c	Maggie was looking up at the sky when she was pumping her legs to swing higher and higher when she felt Gregg hit her legs and saw him go to the ground.
3E	This story reminds me of the time that Fixit and Brushy got into an argument in the story *Twin Trouble*. Chief was accidently hit in the head with a punch bowl. The Chief doesn't get too mad and he talks to Fixit and Brushy instead of giving them consequences.

In order to make good text-to-text connections, you have to read a lot of stories and books; however, you also have to take the time to apply reading comprehension skills, too. You and your Guide should not only read stories together, but also ask questions about the story. This is the only way that you will be able to make text-to-text connections that support your *Answer* and *Cite* sections of your open-ended response questions.

LESSON 86

E IS FOR EXTEND YOUR CONNECTION TO THE WORLD

0:20

The previous lessons demonstrated making a text-to-text connection and a text-to-self connection to support your *Answer* and *Cite* sections. The other strategy you can use to extend your answer is to make a text-to-world connection. When you use this strategy, you are explaining how your answer relates to what you have learned about the world around you. You can use your own personal experiences, opinions, or what you learned in a specific subject matter in fourth grade. As long as your extension for the *E* section supports your answer and citation from the text, then you can give the scorer/reader an opportunity to see how you came to your answer.

You and your Guide will read the following passage again and review the student response. When you have finished reviewing today's lesson, discuss the response with your Guide. Did the student "explain his brain?" Would you have given a different response? What personal experience can you use to change the text-to-world connection?

Amy's Pet
by Debbie Parrish

Five-year-old Amy came into the kitchen one morning. She had on a sad face.

"What's wrong, Amy?" asked her mom.

"I need a pet," was Amy's glum reply.

Mom smiled. "You need a pet, or you want a pet?"

Amy smiled back at her. "I guess I could live without one, but I really, really do want one!"

"If you could have a pet, what pet would you want?" her mom asked.

Amy thought for a minute. She said, "I would like a different, special kind of pet. I think, maybe, I would like a monkey. They are so cute!"

"Did you know that a monkey is a wild animal?" Mom asked.

"Yes, but I could tame it," insisted Amy.

"Even if you could tame it, would that be fair to the monkey?" asked her mom.

"What do you mean?" asked Amy.

"Monkeys have a different habitat than humans," answered Mom. "A habitat is where something or someone lives. Monkeys are used to living outside in a place with many trees. They love to climb and swing from tree to tree. They like to roam and be free to find the kinds of food they like."

Amy said, "Okay, then maybe I could have a seal. I saw a movie on television about a seal, and it was very sweet."

Mom shook her head and said, "A seal's habitat is different from ours, too. It needs a very cold place to live. They like to live where there is lots of water for swimming and hunting. Seals love to hunt for fish to eat. If we took a seal away from its habitat, it would not be happy and would not stay healthy."

"What about a raccoon?" asked Amy.

"Raccoons are wild animals, too," said her mom. "They are able to live in lots of different places, but they like to live near lakes and streams. They can find nuts, berries, and fish there. That's what raccoons like to eat."

Mom scratched her head and added, "Besides, raccoons mostly move around at night. They sleep during the day. That wouldn't be much fun since you sleep at night."

Mom continued by explaining, "Wild animals' needs are just very different from what we can give them in our homes."

Amy frowned. She still seemed very sad.

"I have an idea," said Mom. "Let's go for a ride."

Amy and her mom climbed into the car. "Where are we going, Mom?"

"We are going to a special place called an animal shelter," answered her mom.

"What is an animal shelter?" asked Amy.

"An animal shelter is a place where animals are taken when they have no home and no one to take care of them," Mom said. "I know the man who works at the shelter. His name is Mr. Rescue. He says they always have more animals than they can handle at the shelter."

When the car came to a stop, Amy hopped out and followed her mom into the front door. Mr. Rescue greeted them as they came in. He asked Amy's mom if she needed some help.

Mom told Mr. Rescue that they were there to look around a little bit. She told him that Amy had never been to an animal shelter.

Amy and her mom followed Mr. Rescue as he showed them around. They were about to turn and head back to the front of the building, but Amy suddenly heard a tiny cry. It was coming from over near a window. She looked behind the green plant in front of the window. There a tiny, yellow kitten lay crying. Amy bent down and said, "What's wrong, little fellow?"

Mr. Rescue told Amy that someone had left the little kitten on the steps of the shelter the day before.

"He is feeling pretty lonely right now," said Mr. Rescue. "I guess whoever he belonged to could not give him what he needed."

"What does he need?" Amy asked.

Mr. Rescue replied, "Well, kittens need food, water, shelter, playtime for exercise, and lots of love."

Amy looked at her mom and asked, "Can we take him home and let him be my pet?"

Her mom said, "But Amy, I thought you wanted a pet that was very different and special. Would this kitten be that kind of pet?"

"Oh, yes," smiled Amy. "He is different because he needs me, and he would be very special because he would be mine!"

Amy's mom laughed and said, "Well, I guess we had better get going. You need to show him all around his new home!"

With a huge smile on her face, Amy cuddled her new pet. On the ride home she would start thinking of a special name for her very special new pet.

81-100

CONTINUED ->

1. Amy's mother spends a lot of time explaining wild animals to her. Use evidence from the text to evaluate where Amy's mother was able to convince Amy that wild animals do not make good pets.

Answer Space	
	ACE
1A	Amy's mother was able to convince Amy that wild animals do not make good pets.
2C	Amy's mother explained how each animal has a habitat that is different than a human's habitat and it would be unfair for the wild animal.
3E	I agree with Amy's mother, wild animals belong in their own habitat so they can learn to survive in the wild. My house would not be a good place to raise animals because I wouldn't be able to provide them with the proper habitat or food chain.

In this example, the student is extending his thinking to what he learned in science and social studies about communities and food sources. This is a great answer because the student is applying his knowledge of other subjects to what he is reading. The scorer can see that the student understood the message Amy's mother was giving.

Read the following sentence from the passage:

"I need a pet," was Amy's glum reply.

2. Amy decides that she wants a pet but informs her mother that she "needs" a pet. Using evidence from the text and your knowledge of needs and wants, evaluate if Amy's statement is logical.

Answer Space	
	ACE
1A	Amy's statement that she needs a pet is not logical because a pet is not food, clothing, or shelter.
2C	In the text, Amy comes to the conclusion that she could live without a pet and really just wants one.
3E	Amy's statement was not logical because I learned that needs are food, clothing, and shelter. A pet is something I would want to have as part of my family for a long time.

In this answer, the student uses the explanation section to support the *Answer* and *Cite* sections. He clearly explains that he understands the difference between needs and wants. He also uses a nice concluding statement that again supports his opinion that Amy's statement was not logical.

LESSON 87 — THE C IN MATH IS FOR COMPUTE

In the next lessons, you and your Guide will begin scoring ACE answers for math. After that, you will practice the ACE strategy in each subject. In math state standardized assessments, the open-ended response questions will require a different strategy in the *C* section. You will be required to show your math work in detail. When you complete the *Cite* section, you are actually working out the math problem presented in the question. You have to *compute* your response; that means you have to show all your work in detail. Earlier in this book, you read about using good strategies for answering math questions and checking your work to make sure your answer is correct. The scorer of your state standardized assessment will look at your *Compute* section to determine if you used reading comprehension to understand the task required for a correct response.

The example below is an actual question from a state standardized test:

Directions for the Open-Ended Questions

The following questions are open-ended questions. Remember to:

- read each question carefully and think about the answer.
- answer all the parts of the questions.
- show your work or explain your answers.

You can answer the questions by using words, tables, diagrams, or pictures.

1. Nancy is making apple pies for a party. She bought 3 bags of apples. Each bag has 12 apples. She needs 8 apples to make each pie.

   - What is the greatest number of pies Nancy can make? Show all your work and explain your answer.
   - How many more bags of apples does Nancy need to buy in order to make a total of 6 pies? Show your work and explain your answer.

This open-ended question contains two tasks that each requires you to compute an answer and explain how you got your answer. Explaining math problems in words can be difficult because you have to explain four things: why you decided to use a certain computation (addition, subtraction, multiplication, division), what process you used to solve your problem, what each number was used for (addend, subtrahend, factor, divisor, dividend, and so on), and how you knew your answer was correct. Before you begin working on an open-ended response question for math, you and your Guide will review several student responses to get a clear understanding of how to cite and extend an open-ended math question.

LESSON 88

MATH: ANSWER, COMPUTE, EXPLAIN

0:20

Below is a student response to the question you read in Lesson 87. The response could score a 4 (Advanced) on a state standardized test. In the response, the student shows all his work, shows how he checked his work for accuracy, and uses math words to explain his thinking. The student clearly demonstrates his math knowledge and his comprehension of the task.

This example shows a great strategy to use for math extended response questions; the student explains his thinking as he works through the problem. When you complete math problems, you do not have to wait until the end to write one big paragraph with an ACE strategy. When you answer math extended response questions, the A is the answer you get at the end of your computations. The A and C rely on you using the correct math solution and computing it correctly. The E in the ACE strategy is then your description of the step-by-step process you took to reach a solution.

Almost all state standardized tests have multi-step, open-ended math questions. The best strategy is to "explain your brain" using math vocabulary through each step of the process. This doesn't make using ACE any less important from what you have seen in previous lessons; it just makes this ACE strategy slightly different.

You and your Guide will read the directions carefully and review the answer provided.

Discuss with your Guide: Would you have scored this answer the same way?

Directions for the Open-Ended Questions

The following questions are open-ended questions. Remember to:

- read each question carefully and think about the answer.
- answer all the parts of the questions.
- show your work or explain your answers.

You can answer the questions by using words, tables, diagrams, or pictures.

1. Nancy is making apple pies for a party. She bought 3 bags of apples. Each bag has 12 apples. She needs 8 apples to make each pie.

    - What is the greatest number of pies Nancy can make? Show all your work and explain your answer.
    - How many more bags of apples does Nancy need to buy in order to make a total of 6 pies? Show your work and explain your answer.

81-100

ACE

Student Work Area

```
    12
  x  3
    36
```

The first step was to figure out how many apples were in the 3 bags. In this problem, we had 3 groups with 12 apples each. When you have groups of something, you use multiplication to find out how many. That is why I used 12 groups of 3 as my factors to find the product of 36.

```
        4 r 4
  8 | 36
```

Next, I had to figure out how many pies Nancy could make with 36 apples. I had to break the 36 apples into groups of 8 to plan out each apple pie. When you make groups, you need to use division so I used 36 as the dividend and 8 as the divisor and found a quotient of 4 with 4 apples remaining. **Now I know that the greatest number of pies Nancy can make is 4.**

```
     2
  x  8
    16

  16 - 4 = 12
```

Nancy needs to make 2 more pies to have 6 pies. She needs 8 more apples for each pie which means that she will need 16 more apples. Nancy has 4 apples left over from the other pies. I can subtract 4 apples from the 16 new apples needed which means I only need 12 apples. I know there are 12 apples in 1 bag. **Nancy will need just 1 more bag of apples to make a total of 6 pies.**

81-100

This student used many outstanding strategies. First, he explained his thinking in logical steps. Then he used excellent math vocabulary to show that he can comprehend and apply his math knowledge; he used the proper terms for all numbers in his math problems. Last, he did not forget to use a restatement to answer the questions. It is important that you use words to give an answer. The C is the *computation* or the actual math work, but the answer is still in words.

LESSON 89 — YOU GRADE A MATH ACE

Today, you and your Guide will review and score a student's response to an open-ended response question. This open-ended response question is unique because the *Cite/Compute* section will be labeled on the diagram. You and your Guide will:

Underline the *Answer* to each task in RED.
Underline the *Explanation* in BLUE.

After you have marked the student's response, you and your Guide will score the student's work. You will decide if the student completely answered the question, was able to show evidence of his thinking as he computed his response using the graph, and whether he demonstrates that he applied his knowledge logically in his explanation. You and your Guide can review the scorer's response and score to the sample question in Section 2, page 288.

Directions for the Open-Ended Questions

The following questions are open-ended questions. Remember to:

- read each question carefully and think about the answer.
- answer all the parts of the questions.
- show your work or explain your answers.

You can answer the questions by using words, tables, diagrams, or pictures.

Look at the map below:

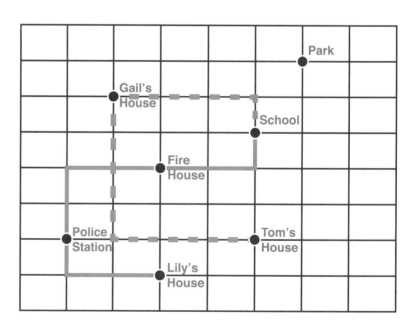

1. Lily left her house and followed this list of directions:

    1. Walk two blocks west.
    2. Walk three blocks north.
    3. Walk four blocks east.
    4. Walk one block north.

    Use the map to help you list all of the places Lily passed on her walk, including the place where she ended her walk.

2. After school, Gail is going to Tom's house to study for the big test. She wants to stop at home first to get her study notes.

    Make a list of directions that Gail can follow to walk from school to her house and then to Tom's house.

Student Work Area

1. Using the map, I determined that each square was one block that ended on the **+** between each block. I used a highlighter to trace the path Lily took using the compass rose to calculate my directions. When Lily leaves her house and follows the directions given to her, she passes the police station during the three blocks north and the fire house during her walk four blocks east. She ends her walk at the school after going one block north.

2. When I had to make directions for Gail to go home from school to grab her study notes and then to Tom's house, I had two choices. I could have sent Gail back to the school and then go south to Tom's house or I could have her walk south from her house. I chose to have Gail follow a new route. The list below is a set of directions that Gail needs to get to Tom's house.

    Leave school and walk one block north.

    Walk three blocks west; grab your study notes out of your house.

    Leave your house and walk four blocks south.

    Walk three blocks east; you are at Tom's house.

LESSON 90 — YOUR TURN TO RESPOND TO A MATH ACE

Today, you will try out your new skill! Use the ACE strategy to answer the following open-ended response question from a state standardized math assessment. You should work through this practice with your Guide. Discuss strategies for coming up with an answer. Demonstrate good computation strategies and extend your answer by giving a step-by-step description of how you applied your math knowledge. The purpose of this lesson is for you and your Guide to think about what you learned and apply it to an actual question. If it helps, you can use colored pencils each time you work on a different section of the ACE strategy. You won't be able to do that on an actual state standardized test, though, because you have to use a No. 2 pencil. In this extended response sample, the *C* section will definitely stand for *compute*. Check your math carefully. You and your Guide can review the scorer's response to the sample question in Section 2, page 290.

Directions for the Open-Ended Questions

The following questions are open-ended questions. Remember to:

- read each question carefully and think about the answer.
- answer all the parts of the questions.
- show your work or explain your answers.

You can answer the questions by using words, tables, diagrams, or pictures.

Pick a Plan

This month, Mr. Sadler's telephone bill included information about a new long distance plan being offered. The plans are listed below.

Current Plan	New Flat Rate Plan
Monthly service fee of $8.75	No monthly service fee
Plus $.09 for each call	$.30 for each call

Mr. Sadler generally makes fewer than 30 long distance calls each month. Which plan would you advise him to use to spend the least amount of money?

Show all your work. Explain in words how you found your answer. Tell why you took the steps you did to solve the problem.

Student Work Area

ACE

LESSON 91

PRACTICE YOUR MATH ACE SKILLS

0:20

Most open-ended response questions in math will have more than one task to complete. This is common on state standardized assessments because you will be required to demonstrate that you can apply your skills regardless of how the task is presented. In this example, you are asked to demonstrate your knowledge of patterns. In the directions, you will notice that you are allowed to use pictures to answer the question and cite from the text. Don't forget, though, to use math vocabulary words to describe the pattern; you can insert pictures for words where appropriate. You and your Guide can review the scorer's response and score to the sample question in Section 2, page 292.

Directions for the Open-Ended Questions

The following questions are open-ended questions. Remember to:

- read each question carefully and think about the answer.
- answer all the parts of the questions.
- show your work or explain your answers.

You can answer the questions by using words, tables, diagrams, or pictures.

1. Phyllis drew the following figures to make a pattern.

PART A

- Draw the next figure in the pattern. Use your knowledge of math patterns to describe the rule of the pattern in words.

PART B

Phyllis decided that she was going to try a new pattern using numbers to see if her classmate Aaron could find the missing numbers. Phyllis wrote the following pattern.

$$63, \_\_\_, 49, 42, 35, \_\_\_, \_\_\_, 14$$

Aaron wrote the following answer:

$$63, \underline{\mathbf{56}}, 49, 42, 35, \underline{\mathbf{28}}, \underline{\mathbf{22}}, 14$$

- Phyllis checks Aaron's work and finds an error. Evaluate Aaron's response and explain the error he made in the pattern. Demonstrate the correct number pattern, and describe the rule for the number pattern.

81–100

CONTINUED ->

ACE

Student Work Area

PRACTICE YOUR MATH ACE SKILLS

0:20

For the next two lessons, you and your Guide will evaluate a student's response to an extended response question taken from a state standardized assessment. In today's example, the student will compute an answer for the table and write the correct answer in the space provided. The student worked on his calculations on a piece of scratch paper. On state standardized tests, scratch paper is not given to the scorer for him to use in scoring open-ended response questions. That means that the answer to Part A will appear in the table, and the *Cite* and *Explain* sections will have to be in words. This is a common strategy used on most state standardized tests. In these types of questions, the scorer is evaluating whether the student could explain his process using math vocabulary.

As you and your Guide read the student's response, work through the process the student used on a piece of scratch paper. You can also use counters. If you can use the explanation to get the answer yourself, then the student used a successful ACE strategy and should be given a 4. As you review the response, you will follow the directions below:

- Highlight the answer in RED.
- Highlight the computation in GREEN.
- Highlight the explanation in BLUE.

You and your Guide will score the student response and check your answer in Section 2, page 294.

Directions for the Open-Ended Questions

The following questions are open-ended questions. Remember to:

- read each question carefully and think about the answer.
- answer all the parts of the questions.
- show your work or explain your answers.

You can answer the questions by using words, tables, diagrams, or pictures.

Corin, Darryl, and Leeann collected 14 leaves for science class. Darryl has 5 leaves. Corin has fewer leaves than Darryl. Leeann has twice as many leaves as Corin.

Part A

Use the scratch paper and the counters (   ) provided to complete Part A.

In the table below, write the number of leaves that Corin and Leeann have.

LEAVES COLLECTED

Name	Leaves
Corin	3
Darryl	5
Leeann	6
Total	14

CONTINUED ->

Part B

On the lines below, explain how you found your answer. Use words, symbols, or both in your explanation.

> ACE
>
> I started with 14 counters to represent the leaves and removed Darryl's 5 leaves. That was 14 – 5 = 9. I took the 9 counters and knew that Corin has fewer leaves than Darryl, which means that Corin has less than 5 leaves. So the answer is Leeann has to have 6 and Corin has to have 3.

Score:

Scorer Comments:

**PART 2:
HOW MANY LEAVES?**

In Lesson 92, you and your Guide evaluated a student's response to a math extended response question. The student correctly answered the question but did not apply good ACE strategies to help the scorer understand his process. When you answer questions, you have to provide enough detail to the scorer so that he can determine the process you used. In today's example, a student will compute and respond to the same question. As you and your Guide read the response provided by the student, work through the process the student used. You will need counters to work through the problem. If you can use the explanation to get the answer, then the student used a successful ACE strategy and should be given a 4. As you review the response, you will follow the directions below:

- Highlight the answer in RED.
- Highlight the computation in GREEN.
- Highlight the explanation in BLUE.

You and your Guide will score the student response and check your answer in Section 2, page 295.

Directions for the Open-Ended Questions

The following questions are open-ended questions. Remember to:

- read each question carefully and think about the answer.
- answer all the parts of the questions.
- show your work or explain your answers.

You can answer the questions by using words, tables, diagrams, or pictures.

Corin, Darryl, and Leeann collected 14 leaves for science class. Darryl has 5 leaves. Corin has fewer leaves than Darryl. Leeann has twice as many leaves as Corin.

Part A

Use the scratch paper and the counters (   ) provided to complete Part A.

In the table below, write the number of leaves that Corin and Leeann have.

LEAVES COLLECTED

Name	Leaves
Corin	3
Darryl	5
Leeann	6
Total	14

CONTINUED ->

Part B

On the lines below, explain how you found your answer. Use words, symbols, or both in your explanation.

ACE

I started with 9 counters because I had to remove Darryl's 5 leaves from the 14 total leaves collected. I checked my work using math, 14 − 5 = 9. I knew that Corin had to have fewer leaves than Darryl, so I started with 4, that split the counters to 5 leaves for Leeann and 4 for Corin. I checked my math, 9 − 5 = 4. In the problem, it says that Leeann has twice as many leaves as Corin but 5 is not twice as many as 4. I gave Corin 3 leaves and Leeann 6 leaves. Since 3 + 3 = 6, I knew that this was the correct answer. I checked my work, 3 + 5 + 6 = 14, and knew all the rules were followed.

Score:

Scorer Comments:

LESSON 94 — CAN YOU SCORE A 4?

⌧ 0:20

Today, you will practice your math ACE strategies with your Guide. In this assignment, you will be required to complete Part A in the space provided on the answer sheet. You will then use scratch paper to complete the computation of Part B but explain your answer using words. When you have completed the question, give your response and scratch paper to your Guide to score. You and your Guide will review the score together and use colored pencils or crayons to highlight the parts of the ACE strategy. Your Guide should also be able to compute the answer to Part B using only evidence from your response as a step-by-step process. Good luck!

You can check your work in Section 2, page 296. The answer key lists possible responses for each section of the ACE strategy.

Directions for the Open-Ended Questions

The following questions are open-ended questions. Remember to:

• read each question carefully and think about the answer.
• answer all the parts of the questions.
• show your work or explain your answers.

You can answer the questions by using words, tables, diagrams, or pictures.

Students in fourth grade track their homework assignments on a bulletin board in each class. When 1,000 homework assignments have been completed, they will earn an extra hour of recess. The chart below shows how many homework assignments have currently been completed by each class.

Homework Assignments Completed

Mrs. Simpson	Mr. Givens	Ms. Lewis
100 100 100 / 10 10 10 / 1 1 1	100 100 / 10 10 10 10 10 / 1 1 1 1	100 100 100 / 10 / 1 1 1 1 1 1 1

81-100

CONTINUED ->

Part A

Determine the number of homework assignments the three classes have currently completed.
Show all your work.

Part B

The students would like to know how many more homework assignments they need to complete to achieve their goal of 1,000. Using mental math, if you divided the remaining homework assignments among the three classes evenly, *about how many* would each class need to complete? Use words, symbols, and math to describe your answer.

_____

_____

_____

_____

_____

_____

_____

_____

_____

_____

_____

_____

_____

_____

LESSON 95 FINAL MATH ACE PRACTICE

0:20

Today you will complete the final practice activity for open-ended response questions in math. You should now have enough practice to begin developing this new skill. You can practice this new skill all school year on your formal assessments. When you practice ACE strategies, you will soon find that you think about all open-ended response questions differently. This means that you are developing critical thinking skills, or your ability to think about how a task is completed and break it down into meaningful steps. In math, thinking critically means that you can solve the same problem with multiple strategies but you use your experience and knowledge to choose the best one. If you spend time practicing your ACE strategies this year, you will soon find that you will not need to put an ACE on the side of extended response questions because your brain will naturally complete the process.

Complete the following example with your Guide. You can check your work in Section 2, page 298. The answer key lists possible responses for each section of the ACE strategy.

1. Edythe made a banner for her sister Emme. She taped the tall edges of 10 pieces of paper together as shown below.

Part A

Each piece of paper is 22 centimeters wide and 28 centimeters tall.

Solve for the perimeter of one piece of paper and show your work.

81-100

CONTINUED ->

Part B

Edythe and Emme's father would like to hang the banner on a wall in the entryway of the house. He measures the space on the wall at 250 centimeters wide by 300 centimeters tall. Analyze the measurements of the wall to the total width and height of the banner to determine if the banner can hang in the entryway wall space. Use words or symbols to explain your work.

LESSON 96 — SCIENCE OVERVIEW FOR ACE

You will begin practicing ACE strategies in science. When you study science this year, you should know, understand, and apply principles of natural sciences. You will work on combining processes and content to develop critical thinking skills about how the world around you works. Fourth grade science is about observations and measurements, classifying, experimenting, interpreting, communicating, and being inquisitive about the world.

You will study physical science, life science, space science, and earth science. Each of these content areas has a connection to each other that requires you to be observant and inquisitive, which means you have to know when to ask why. When you extend your open-ended response questions in science, you will want to focus on making text-to-world connections on the following items:

- energy, motion, light, and sound
- plants, animals, and other organisms
- our planet and the solar system

For science extended response questions, you will have charts and diagrams that you will be required to interpret. You will have to infer, conclude, and give an opinion about scientific methods, food webs, simple machines, and measurements using the metric system. As you create study notes this school year, you may want to focus on the following content areas:

- The metric system: grams, milligrams, meters, centimeters, millimeters, kilometers, time, degrees, liters, milliliters, and so on. You will also need to focus on the tools used in these measurements (metric rulers, graduated cylinders, thermometers).
- The scientific method: experiments, variables, independent variables, hypotheses, observations, and conclusions.
- Motion and electricity: push and pull, conductors, insulators, and open and closed circuits.
- Organisms: living and nonliving, environments, groups, and behaviors.
- Interpreting results: understanding information from tables, graphs, diagrams, and raw data.

When you know the content, using the ACE strategy to answer open-ended response questions will come naturally. This is because you will have all the tools you need to think critically about the task and how it relates to the real world. That is why you and your Guide should make every effort to continue setting up your weekly and monthly planning calendar and creating good study sheets to help you learn the content. When you develop the habits of a good learner, you also develop the habits of a good test taker. You can do it!

 **LESSON 97**

WHAT DOES THE C STAND FOR?

As in all subjects, the *C* in the ACE strategy stands for *cite*. When you cite, you use evidence from the question in your response to show that you interpreted what was being asked, applied knowledge, and comprehended what was required. In math, you learned that this is done through computing a response using the information from the question. You had to demonstrate that you understood what type of math problem (add, subtract, multiply, or divide) was being described and which numbers from the problem would help you solve it. In science, the *C* means you have to *cite* the *correct* information from the graphs, charts, diagrams, and/or texts. You will see many extended response questions with charts and graphs on your science state standardized test.

Today you and your Guide will review an open-ended response question from a state standardized test. The student response you will read scored a 4 (Advanced). The student's answer was correct, his citations from the text demonstrated understanding of the task, and his text-to-world insights were excellent examples of how well he can apply the concepts he learned in science.

Sample Question

1. A fourth grade class had a field trip to a local farm. During their trip, they visited the farm's pond. They observed a green frog, a brown beaver, and a smooth snake. Mrs. Friedman thought the frog was pretty. The students used nets to catch insects on the surface of the pond. The students looked at several insects. They counted six legs on each insect. Some students thought some of the insects looked scary.

Once the student's return from their field trip, they are given the following assignment:

*   Identify two observations that you made from the pond.

Using evidence from the text, identify two observations that the fourth grade students may choose for their response. There are several opinions stated in the paragraph, too. Explain the reason why an opinion can **NOT** be used as an observation.

ACE

Two observations that the fourth grade students made are that the frog was green, and they counted six legs on each insect. In the paragraph, Mrs. Friedman gave the opinion that she thought the frog was pretty. This can't be on the observation list because other students might not have thought the frog was pretty and you can't observe something pretty like you can observe something green. That is like saying that vegetables are good but not everyone thinks that, so it is an opinion.

LESSON 98 THINKING CRITICALLY

When you respond to an open-ended question in science, you must provide enough explanation so that the scorer can understand the solution. Diagrams, graphs, and charts can be used even when the question does not specifically request their use. It is important to remember that if you use diagrams or drawings in your response, then you must provide a written explanation. In science, the scorer is looking to determine if you can analyze and interpret information presented about the world around you, such as: *What would happen to food webs if an organism is removed? What type of simple machine can be used to get an object on a moving van? Is it better to measure liquid in liters or kilometers?* In these types of questions, you have to use scientific reasoning to explain your answer.

The following example has to do with the earth's environment and resources. As you and your Guide respond to this open-ended question, you will need to think about ways in which renewable and nonrenewable resources impact our environment (pollution) and living organisms. You and your Guide can check your answer in Section 2, page 300.

Sample Question

Material	Items Made with the Material
wood	paper, desks, birdhouses
metal	cans, chairs, paper clips
plastic	pens, bottles, bags

Part A

1. Identify and explain whether each material is a renewable or nonrenewable resource.

_____

_____

_____

_____

_____

Part B

2. Describe one way to conserve nonrenewable resources.

_____

_____

_____

_____

_____

81-100

LESSON 99

IS THERE A FULL ACE ANSWER? PART 1

0:20

An important skill you can develop is to recognize a good ACE answer when you read one; this allows you to review your work on a state standardized test's open-ended response questions. You need to be able to analyze your answer and determine where you used evidence from the text (cite) and where you show evidence of explaining your brain. You should be able to identify whether a text-to-text, text-to-self, or text-to-world connection is the best strategy to use. You should be aware that having an *Explanation* (*E*) section in your response doesn't automatically mean that you will be given credit by the scorer. Your explanation or expansion of your answer has to demonstrate comprehension of the text and content. You have to demonstrate that you can apply that knowledge to the world around you.

Today, you and your Guide will review the first of three responses you will see to an open-ended question. The student's answers are taken from a state standardized assessment in science. You and your Guide can review the scorer's comments and score in Section 2, page 301.

1. A group of fourth grade students in the Science Club constructed a weather station in the woods behind their school. They recorded the temperatures and amounts of precipitation during the days they were there.

Weather Observations

Day	High Temperature (°C)	Precipitation (centimeters per day)
Monday	26	1
Tuesday	20	3
Wednesday	22	0
Thursday	27	0
Friday	21	6
Saturday	28	2

- Explain how the Science Club collected data for the temperature.
- Explain how the Science Club collected data for precipitation.
- Identify another condition that the Science Club might include in describing the weather, and explain how information about this condition could be gathered.

81-100

ACE

The Science Club collected the temperatures using Celsius instead of Fahrenheit all week. The Science Club then collected data for precipitation by collecting precipitation and measuring it in centimeters each day of the week. The Science Club could have also included the number of cloudy and sunny days as another condition and not included the partly sunny or cloudy days so it doesn't get confusing.

Score:

Scorer Comments:

LESSON 100

IS THERE A FULL ACE ANSWER? PART 2

0:20

In the previous lesson's response, the student clearly attempted to respond to the open-ended question. Unfortunately, his answer made little sense and didn't provide an appropriate response to the task. The student didn't comprehend the task he was required to complete. Even though he wrote a lengthy response, he cannot be given any score because he didn't complete any of the ACE strategy.

When you respond to any open-ended response question, you must make sure that you understand the task. Although you can't ask a teacher questions during a state standardized test, you can reread directions, text, passages, and questions as many times as you need in order to understand. Most state standardized tests are not timed.

Today, you and your Guide will review the second of three responses to an open-ended question. The student's answers are taken from a state standardized assessment in science. You and your Guide can review the scorer's comments and score in Section 2, page 302.

1. A group of fourth grade students in the Science Club constructed a weather station in the woods behind their school. They recorded the temperatures and amounts of precipitation during the days they were there.

Weather Observations

Day	High Temperature (°C)	Precipitation (centimeters per day)
Monday	26	1
Tuesday	20	3
Wednesday	22	0
Thursday	27	0
Friday	21	6
Saturday	28	2

- Explain how the Science Club collected data for the temperature.
- Explain how the Science Club collected data for precipitation.
- Identify another condition that the Science Club might include in describing the weather, and explain how information about this condition could be gathered.

ACE

The Science Club collected data for the temperature by using a thermometer with Celsius degrees on it. The Science Club collected precipitation using a tool that had centimeters as a measurement. Another condition that the Science Club might include in describing the weather is the windy, cold, or raining conditions outside using words. They can gather this information by looking outside to see what the weather is like.

Score:

Scorer Comments:

81-100

IS THERE A FULL ACE ANSWER? PART 3

This is a tip you can use on state standardized assessments:

At one point, the C in ACE was described as *Concise*. When you give a concise response, it means that you don't add a lot of unnecessary information in your response but still give all the correct information. On a state standardized test, you are required to keep your responses in the area provided for each question. Sometimes that is plenty of work space and sometimes that is a few lines. Make sure you plan your response. If you will need more space than provided, consider writing in smaller letters or between the lines provided. You do not have to write only on the lines, but the key is to only use the space provided.

Today, you and your Guide will review the final response to the open-ended question. The student's answers are taken from a state standardized assessment in science. You and your Guide can review the scorer's comments and score in Section 2, page 303.

1. A group of fourth grade students in the Science Club constructed a weather station in the woods behind their school. They recorded the temperatures and amounts of precipitation during the days they were there.

Weather Observations

Day	High Temperature (°C)	Precipitation (centimeters per day)
Monday	26	1
Tuesday	20	3
Wednesday	22	0
Thursday	27	0
Friday	21	6
Saturday	28	2

- Explain how the Science Club collected data for the temperature.
- Explain how the Science Club collected data for precipitation.
- Identify another condition that the Science Club might include in describing the weather, and explain how information about this condition could be gathered.

The Science Club collected the data for temperature by probably using a thermometer. A thermometer measures the temperature in two ways by Celsius or Fahrenheit. They probably picked the same time every day to measure temperature so they could control variables. Because it's a science club, they probably have access to a rain gauge to collect data for precipitation. They probably had to choose a time each day to check the rain gauge and write the amount of precipitation in the gauge and then empty it out for the next day. Finally, they could measure another condition like wind speed with an anemometer. The Science Club can observe the anemometer for one minute and count how many times it spins in a minute. Each spin is a mile per hour of the wind.

Score:

Scorer Comments:

LESSON 102   SOCIAL STUDIES ACE

0:10

Last year, you took your first state standardized test in reading, writing, and math; some states also have a listening section for language arts. In fourth grade, you will take the entire test schedule above and you may have to complete a state standardized test in social studies. Not all states have a social studies test in fourth grade. Even if you won't complete a state standardized test for social studies, you should know how to use the ACE strategy to answer social studies questions for your formal assessments.

In fourth grade, you will concentrate on learning about your individual state history, the geography of the United States, our national government, and map skills. As you create study notes for social studies, make sure you focus on your community, city, and state. You and your Guide will practice completing a study sheet about your city and state below. This is not a full study sheet, but it will give you an idea about the skills and concepts you will need to study in fourth grade.

Study Notes

1. I live in the state of _____.

2. List all the states that border your state. _____

   _____

3. The capital of my state is _____.

4. Describe the symbols on your state flag and what they represent. _____

   _____

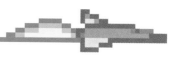

LESSON 103 — KNOW YOUR STATE

`0:15`

This year, you will learn a lot about the history of the United States and of your state. You will need to know about the Native Americans in your region and the European settlers in your state. You may learn about Pocahontas, John Smith, William Penn, Lewis and Clark, or countless other famous Americans that helped build your state. Before you and your Guide begin practicing ACE strategies, complete the remaining questions for the study notes you began in the previous lesson.

Study Notes

5. Make a timeline of four major events in your state's history.

6. List three important people in your state's history and describe what made them famous.

_____

_____

_____

7. List the features for which your state is known (mountain ranges, landforms, or bodies of water).

_____

_____

_____

LESSON 104

SOCIAL STUDIES CONCEPTS AND CONTENT: PART 1

`0:15`

It is important to build your knowledge of social studies content so that you can be prepared. There are five important content areas that you will study in fourth grade:

- geography
- history
- politics and citizenship
- economics
- behavioral sciences

Over the next two lessons, you and your Guide can use the charts provided to set up study notes for your weekly study time. All of the concepts and content in the charts can appear on questions for the state standardized test. As you complete each content area during the year, you can store your study notes in a folder and review them before your state standardized test.

Geography:
recognize latitude and longitude, direction, and scale
locate continents, oceans, mountain ranges, landforms, natural resources, cities, states, and national borders on a map or globe
describe ways people interact with land and communities that lead to change caused by human behavior
use data, charts, graphs, and maps to gather information about your community
identify weather patterns, seasons, floods, droughts, and the social and economic effects of these changes
distinguish between your local community and the state you are located in
list scientific and technological advances that have led to environmental changes (pollution, energy sources)

History:
examine artifacts, documents, letters, maps, text, paintings, and architecture to construct an understanding of the past
use a timeline to organize and/or sequence information in history
examine biographies, stories, narratives, and folk tales to understand people's lives and important historical events
compare and contrast current social, economic, cultural, and political events with historical events
identify the political value of freedom, democracy, and justice
explain the significance of national and state holidays
identify and describe important events and famous people in United States history
describe examples of cooperation, interdependence, and technological change among individuals, groups, and nations
compare past and present technologies that have been beneficial or harmful to people and the environment

101-120

 **LESSON 105**

SOCIAL STUDIES CONCEPTS AND CONTENT: PART 2

0:15

It is time to begin practicing open-ended response questions that may appear on your state standardized test. In the previous lesson, you and your Guide reviewed the geography and history concepts that you will need to know. Today, you will review the final three content areas. You and your Guide can reference this list to create study notes; this will help you focus on the important information.

Politics and Citizenship:

explain your responsibilities to family, peers, community, and country
identify the Declaration of Independence, the Constitution, and the Bill of Rights
recognize the three levels of government and explain the purpose of government for our society
explain civic responsibility and civic actions to improve the well being of your local community and society
demonstrate and explain how viewpoints of different groups and individuals affect a community

Economics:

identify and explain the role of money, banking, and savings
identify opportunity costs as they relate to limited economic resources and natural resources
identify goods and services that are part of a community, country, or global economy
relate human resources to business and industry that depend on a specialized work force
identify the economic roles of households, business, and government
describe the effects of reducing, reusing, and recycling on needs of people, business, and government

Behavioral Sciences:

describe the similarities and differences of families past and present
describe the ways in which ethnic culture influences daily lives of people (music, folk tales, art, language)
list group and institutional influences (laws, rules, peer pressure) on people, historic events, and cultures
distinguish among the values and beliefs of different groups and institutions
explain how the media influences opinions, choices, and decisions
list examples of influential citizens and their contributions to your community and state

101-120

LESSON 106 **GEOGRAPHY ACE**

`0:20`

In the previous lessons, you learned that social studies covers five different content areas that are interdependent. Each content area helps you understand the world in which you live and the roles that people, culture, politics, and resources have in the global economy and global markets. You will practice five ACE questions, one for each content area, to gain an understanding of the types of questions you may be asked on a state standardized test.

Most geography questions on state standardized tests will have a diagram, map, or image. In this example, you and your Guide will respond to the open-ended question below. When you get to the *E* section of the response, you may want to elaborate on the hemispheres created by the imaginary lines or the weather pattern between the Tropic lines. You and your Guide can review your answer in Section 2, page 304.

Sample Questions
Use the map to answer the question below.

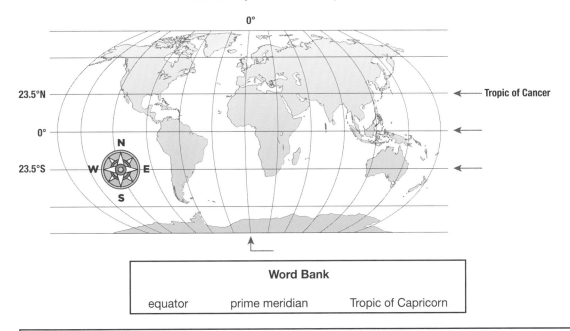

Word Bank

equator   prime meridian   Tropic of Capricorn

ACE

1. Mindy was given this map with only the Tropic of Cancer labeled. Label the map using the words in the word bank. Describe the significance of at least one of these imaginary lines.

    _____

    _____

    _____

    _____

    _____

    _____

101-120

LESSON 107 HISTORY ACE

In fourth grade, you learn about the history of your community, your state, and the United States. You will make comparisons of the way people lived many years ago and the way they live today. You and your Guide will have an opportunity to explore the many technological changes that have occurred throughout history, from the invention of the steam engine to the computer. There are many open-ended response questions that can be asked about history.

When you extend your thinking in the *E* section of your ACE response, you can try to think about text-to-self connections and text-to-world connections. This will help the scorer see that you can apply your knowledge of history and the role it plays in your life today.

You and your Guide will complete an open-ended response question in history. An answer key has been provided with possible responses in Section 2, page 305.

Sample Question
Use the image and passage provided to answer the following question.

Image Circa 1882: The Hawaiian Railroad was built from 1881 to 1883. It extended from the port of Mahukona to the Niulii plantation in the north Kohala district. It was bought out in 1899, and shut down in 1945. The terminus is now a county park.

Early drawbacks delayed the acceptance of railroads. The first rails, made of wood covered with a strip of iron, broke frequently under heavy carloads. Soft roadbeds and weak bridges added to the hazards. Still, promoters believed in the future of train travel. Engineers learned to build sturdier bridges and solid roadbeds. They replaced the wooden rail with a T-shaped cast-iron rail. Such improvements made railroad travel safer, faster, and more efficient. Soon, Americans looked hopefully to the railroads as they once had to the canal to ship goods and people.

ACE

1. Use evidence from the image or passage to respond to the following question. List two improvements the railroad industry had to make to replace canals as the most popular method of transporting goods and people.

_____

_____

_____

_____

_____

_____

LESSON 108

POLITICS AND CITIZENSHIP ACE

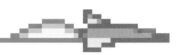

0:20

In fourth grade, you will learn about the rights and responsibilities of citizens in a community and the United States. The leaders of our country wrote the Constitution to form a government and set rules for how the new country would work; they also decided on the rights of the people.

In this example, the student does a great job of expanding or elaborating his response using his knowledge of social studies. The response expands his knowledge on the rights of the people by identifying the exact section of the Constitution that included the rights of all citizens. You and your Guide will read the student response and highlight the ACE strategy that the student used to earn a score of 4 (Advanced). As you grade the work, highlight the student response as follows:

A: Highlight the answer in RED.
C: Highlight cited evidence from the text in GREEN.
E: Highlight the student's explanation in BLUE.

You can check your answers in Section 2, page 306.

Sample Question
Use evidence from the image to answer the following question.

Freedom of Speech
An American citizen's right to say what he or she thinks about our country.

Freedom of Assembly
An American citizen's right to peacefully gather in groups.

Freedom of the Press
An American citizen's right to write and publish opinions about our country.

Freedom of Religion
An American citizen's right to practice his or her religion.

ACE

1. Robert wants to write an article for the school newspaper about including more choices on the lunch menu. Explain which freedom best gives Robert the right to express his opinion in the school paper.

    Robert has the right to write an article for the school newspaper because of his right under freedom of the press. He is publishing his opinion about the choices given in school lunches. The Bill of Rights was written into the Constitution to give every American ten rights as a citizen.

Score: 4

Scorer Comments: The student clearly made a connection between Robert's decision to write his opinion in the school newspaper and freedom of the press. He was able to articulate that Robert was giving an opinion about how he feels about school lunches. The student also clearly identified the Bill of Rights in his response.

LESSON 109 ECONOMICS ACE

0:20

In your social studies state standardized test, you will respond to questions about economics. Economics is the study of money, supply and demand, goods and services, needs and wants, resources, and business. You will begin to learn how all of these work together in a global economy. For instance, if you looked at the tag on your shirt, you may see that it was made in another country. But where did the cotton come from? Cotton is mostly produced in China, the United States, and India. That means that these countries share their goods and services with other countries so that clothing can be manufactured. When you answer open-ended response questions, you will want to use your knowledge of economics to extend your response.

You and your Guide will review a student's response to an open-ended response question. The student extended his answer based on his knowledge of needs and wants. Would you have made a different choice? You and your Guide will review the student's answer and decide the final score. You can check your answers in Section 2, page 307. To help with your scoring, highlight the student response as follows:

A: Highlight the answer in RED.
C: Highlight cited evidence from the text in GREEN.
E: Highlight the student's explanation in BLUE.

Sample Question
Use evidence from the graphic below to answer the following question.

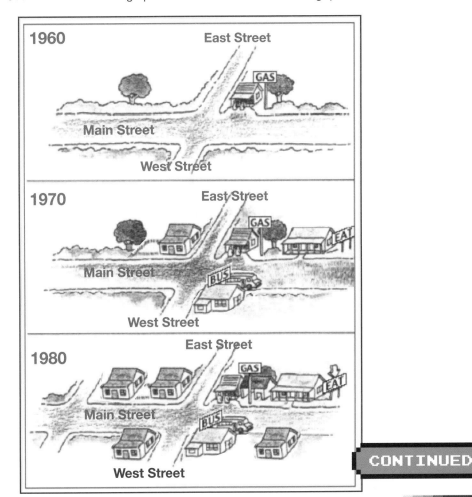

CONTINUED ->

101-120

ACE

1. Describe two changes shown in these pictures that occurred in the town between 1960 and 1980. Based on the pattern of changes from 1960 to 1980, evaluate what the town might look like in 2000.

The two changes the town made between 1960 and 1980 are that they added more houses for people to live in and a restaurant on Main Street. Based on the pattern in the pictures the town might look more like a city in 2000. I say this because when you increase a population, people are going to need more stores for groceries and house stuff. That means they will need stores to supply people with their wants and needs.

Score:

Scorer Comments:

LESSON 110   BEHAVIORAL SCIENCE ACE

0:20

Most state standardized assessments will require you to identify the influences other cultures have on life in the United States. You may have learned how Native Americans influenced our language or how different countries celebrate holidays. Learning about the influences of other cultures explains how we do some things in our society today. The state that you live in has been influenced by the past in its own unique way, which allows you to add your own unique experiences to the *E* section of your ACE response. When you complete your response about culture and society, the best strategy to use is to make a text-to-world or text-to-self connection. Your experience with the world around you will help you to elaborate your response based on your state's history.

Today, you and your Guide will complete your final open-ended response question in social studies. For this exercise, you will practice writing a good ACE response. You can see a list of possible responses for your ACE answer in Section 2, page 308.

Sample Question
Use evidence from the picture and explanation below to answer the following question.

The Canton waterfront is depicted from Honam Island where workers load a sampan with chests of tea.

ACE

1. Identify one type of transportation used by the people of the Asian community shown in this picture. Explain the importance of the river to the people of this Asian community.

    _____

    _____

    _____

    _____

101-120

LESSON 111

READING, WRITING, SPEAKING, AND LISTENING

You and your Guide will soon work on ACE strategies for language arts. On a state standardized test in language arts, you are tested on reading, writing, speaking, and listening skills. Questions require you to communicate an understanding of important information from a text or passage by focusing on the key concepts or main ideas. You have reviewed highlighting main ideas in a text, using the main ideas to summarize a passage, and summarizing details in your response. Summarizing is the best strategy to use when citing from the text; you use ideas from the text to support your answer. You learned to review your written response before moving to the next question. You can read directions, questions, and your response out loud in your head to make sure you understood and properly answered the question. All of these strategies are important to demonstrate in language arts because you are being tested on your skills in comprehending text.

During your language arts test, you will read many long passages that may include biographies, narratives, informative topics, directions, or stories. Before you begin reading passages, make sure you set your purpose; read the name of the passage and review any images or charts. This will help you decide if you are reading for information, for entertainment, or to learn how to perform a task. It will help you make connections to the text using your skills and knowledge. When you read a passage, you need to use your reading strategies to help with comprehension. Your brain will automatically try to make connections to information you already know; if that happens, take a few moments to think about what you are reading. Remember that state standardized assessments provide you plenty of time to do your best, so take advantage of every moment.

Discuss with your Guide: What types of strategies do you use after you read?

LESSON 112 CONSTRUCT YOUR RESPONSE

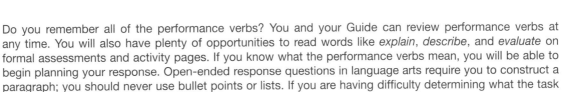

Do you remember all of the performance verbs? You and your Guide can review performance verbs at any time. You will also have plenty of opportunities to read words like *explain*, *describe*, and *evaluate* on formal assessments and activity pages. If you know what the performance verbs mean, you will be able to begin planning your response. Open-ended response questions in language arts require you to construct a paragraph; you should never use bullet points or lists. If you are having difficulty determining what the task is, go back and read the directions, questions, and passage carefully. The best strategy to use is to take your time and be sure that you understand the task you have to perform.

Review the following responses to an open-ended question; you will only see the *A* section of the ACE answer. Daryl's response is a list and Teddy's response uses an open restatement. Which response allows you to cite evidence from the text and explain the answer easily? If you said Teddy's, then you are correct. Can you explain to your Guide why Teddy's response is a better start to an ACE answer?

1. Describe the strategies Latasha used to teach Ella some manners so she didn't disturb Mrs. Okocho.

Daryl's response:

- Start puppy boot camp.
- Use teddy snacks.
- Take her for walks.

Teddy's response:

Latasha used many strategies to try to get Ella to have some manners so she didn't disturb Mrs. Okocho.

LESSON 113 BEGINNING, MIDDLE, END

`0:20`

In the next lesson, you will begin scoring and constructing language arts ACE responses. Before you begin, you will review three strategies you can use when you respond to open-ended questions. You already know the first strategy: restate the question. You learned how to use open and closed statements to begin your response. Restating the question helps organize your thinking and sets a clear path to your answer, evidence from the text, and your explanation.

The middle part of your response is the *C* section; **c**ite evidence from the text **c**oncisely to demonstrate your **c**omprehension of the **c**ontent. All of those *C*s should remind you that you will need to add details to your response, details that come directly from the text. In order to help you give as much detail as possible, using connection words is a good strategy that will help your *Cite* section come together. The following list does not contain all possible connection words, but it is a good start to help you organize your writing.

first, then, next, second, for example, now, after, afterward, finally, last, lastly

The ending of your response should **e**xtend, **e**xplain, or **e**laborate on your thinking. That means it should "explain your brain." In the *E* section of your response, you are trying to demonstrate a connection that you understood from the text or passage. You can have a text-to-text connection, a text-to-self connection, or a text-to-world connection. In your ending sentence, you can use the following words or phrases to tie all your thoughts together.

my evidence shows, therefore, I answered this way because, as a result, I remember, I learned, the example shows

When you think you have a good ACE response, make sure that you read your answer out loud in your head again to make sure it makes sense. You should also fix any noticeable mistakes in spelling, capitalization, grammar, and punctuation.

LESSON 114 | **LANGUAGE ARTS ACE**

`0:20`

Today, you and your Guide will practice writing an ACE response to a language arts question on a state standardized test. Use highlighting strategies to read the poem once all the way through. Take a few moments to think about the setting and message of the poem. When you write your explanation, think of a text-to-self or text-to world connection about how you or other families celebrate the holidays in December. Do you celebrate the holidays the same way? Do you celebrate a different holiday in December? You and your Guide can check your answer in Section 2, page 309. Check to see if you picked any of the responses from the answer key. Good luck!

Use evidence from the poem and your knowledge to answer the following question.

Christmas Memories
by Jason Fobes

Warm fall colors on the leaves of the trees,
gently blow away by a brush of the breeze.
The chill of the winter air comes rushing in,
Wondering where summer and fall has just been.

Gloves, hats, and boots are the required attire.
Families gather round by a warm cozy fire.
Stories and laughter are shared by us all,
Awaiting to lay eyes on the first snowfall.

Out through the window, eyes are a glaring.
Back in the kitchen, pies made with much caring.
Cinnamon and spice are the smells in our nose,
And the children gather round for a holiday pose.

Cider and eggnog, rich and overflowing.
Turkey and the fixings make a great showing.
Holiday dinners making our bellies so fat,
with a big "Season's Greetings!" on the porch welcome mat.

At the North Pole, Santa fills up his sleigh,
as all of the reindeer will help guide his way.
Elves working hard making all of the toys,
that soon will be given to the good girls and boys.

So snuggle up warm under your blankets in beds,
as Christmas dreams dance in the children's small heads.
Soon Santa arrives, so fall asleep fast,
Christmas will be here, FINALLY, AT LAST!!

He places the gifts under the bright Christmas tree.
Oh what a sight for the family to see!
Wrapping paper and ribbon make such a great mess,
the children shout loud, "This Christmas was best!"

Christmas Day carries on and things quiet down,
but one last hurrah, so listen around.
All through the streets, is a BIG sounding cheer,
Merry Christmas to all and a Happy New Year!!

CONTINUED ->

101-120

Mrs. Bertges read this poem to her class. After reading the poem, Eliana observed, "This poem doesn't begin in the month of December." Levi did not support Eliana's statement and thinks that the poem only talks about the month of December.

ACE

1. Evaluate both points of view and determine whose view you agree with. Use evidence from the text to support your answer.

    _____

    _____

    _____

    _____

    _____

LESSON 115

YOU GRADE A LANGUAGE ARTS ACE

0:20

In this lesson, you will read a student's response to an open-ended question. You and your Guide will evaluate the response for all sections of the ACE strategy. Read the passage through once and use your highlighting strategies to focus on the main ideas. Highlight the response using your ACE strategy. Did the student's response have *Answer*, *Cite*, and *Extend* sections? You and your Guide will decide on a score and give the student feedback. Decide what could have been done differently or better. You and your Guide can check the answers by turning to Section 2, page 310.

Life in New York City
by Jill Fisher

Have you ever visited a big city? If so, you probably noticed that cities are busy places. Close your eyes and picture a city. Think of all the ways a city can touch your senses. What did you imagine? Maybe you smelled the hotdogs cooking on every street corner. Perhaps you heard the loud horns of taxis and the wailing sirens of fire trucks. Or maybe you saw people everywhere, all of them in a hurry. In the city, there is something going on all of the time. In no American city is that more true than New York City.

New York City is an outstanding place to live. It is located in the state of New York. More people reside in New York City than in any other city in the United States. Over eight and a half million people call it home. New York City is an urban area, a community that has little open land and a lot of people. New York City has many fans and many nicknames. One of its nicknames is "the city that never sleeps." It earned that nickname because at any hour of the day, a person can find something fun to do there.

New York City is full of different cultures and places to visit. There are so many things to do. Many of the places are in easy walking distance. It would not take long to find a grocery store, bank, post office, or library. The city is filled with all sorts of entertainment. It is the home of two professional baseball teams, as well as a basketball team and a hockey team. Some of the most famous theaters in the world are in New York, on a long street called Broadway. You can find live music being played in town on any day of the week. In fact, many years ago New York City was nicknamed the Big Apple. Many believe it had to do with all the jazz musicians performing in the city.

The Big Apple has many other forms of entertainment as well. All kinds of museums can be found throughout the city. Often, there are festivals or parades on the busy streets. The city is full of beautiful sights as well, like skyscrapers, which are very tall buildings. It's true; you can always find something to do in New York City. Many visitors like to go to Ellis Island or take a ferry ride to see the Statue of Liberty. Others climb to the top of the Empire State Building. No matter what you like to do or how old you are, there is something for everyone to enjoy.

Use evidence from the text and your knowledge of language arts to answer the following question.

ACE

1. Identify the author's purpose of the passage. Evaluate the response and draw a conclusion on the author's feelings about visiting New York City.

   The author's purpose was to persuade the reader to visit New York City. "New York is an outstanding place to live." The author wants to live there. I don't want to live in New York City because it is too crowded and I might get lost and scared. The author may not have went to New York City and doesn't know what it would be like to live there. That is why I know that the author is trying to persuade.

101-120

Score:

Scorer Comments:

LESSON 116 · THE FINAL ACE

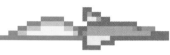

It is time to write your final ACE response. By now, you and your Guide should have a good understanding about answering open-ended response questions. You are ready for formal assessments and the state standardized tests. All you need to do now is put your test taking strategies to practice. You will need to spend a lot of time studying and learning the content. You can't study for a state standardized test; you just have to know the content and concepts for each subject. The time to study your skills is each week during your study times. You can prepare yourself for all tests by developing a complete understanding of the content and using good test taking strategies. Studying in small time blocks allows your mind to process the information you learn and allows you to make connections to concepts in all subjects.

You and your Guide can use this book to review all the strategies for effective test taking, including ACE responses. For this final assignment, complete the following open-ended response question and review the possible responses in Section 2, page 311.

Popcorn Explosion Causes Kernel Chaos in Local Neighborhood
by Summer Swauger

ORVILLE COUNTY—Neighbors had a huge mess to clean up following an explosion at the Poplar Popcorn Factory in Kettle Township. On Tuesday afternoon, the popping machine overflowed, causing two tons of popcorn to spill through the windows of the factory and out into the streets.

Mr. Stan Poplar, 54, and his wife Jan Poplar, 50, own the factory. They said the explosion happened because they were arguing about how many popcorn kernels to pop.

"I thought we had enough," Mrs. Poplar said, "but Mr. Poplar thought we should make more than usual."

"But we were so busy arguing," Mrs. Poplar said, "that neither of us closed the chute. We didn't notice that the kernels were still spilling into the machine."

One witness, a hair stylist who was working at Sally's Salon across the street, said she could hear loud popping noises coming from the factory.

Chief Terrence D. Higgins, head of the Kettle Township Police Department, was among the first on the scene.

"In all my years as a law officer, I've never seen anything like this," he stated. "It is a good thing that no one was hurt."

Chief Higgins said that despite the mess, there was no real damage to the factory. Now Kettle Township residents just have to figure out how to clean up all the popcorn. The manager of the local grocery store was helping with the cleanup effort.

Kettle Township Mayor William Jones is offering residents of surrounding towns free popcorn for the entire week if they are willing to help with the cleanup.

"All in all," the mayor said, "this hasn't been a total disaster. The entire community is working together. The factory wasn't damaged, and Mr. Poplar has since 'buttered' things over with his wife." The Poplars said that they will continue popcorn production as soon as the mess is cleaned up. The factory, located at the corner of Canola Street and Lincoln Avenue, was originally built in 1968. It was originally a jelly bean factory that was run by Mrs. Kelly Green. The Poplars bought the factory in 2000 and turned it into the Poplar Popcorn Factory. The factory currently produces about two tons of popcorn per month, or 24 tons a year. It is the largest popcorn factory in Orville County.

Use evidence from the news article and your knowledge to answer the following question.

ACE

1. Trace through the events that caused the popcorn explosion. Explain at least one effect the explosion had on Kettle Township and decide if it was a negative consequence or a positive consequence.

_____

_____

_____

_____

_____

_____

_____

_____

BEEP
WHY IS THIS PAGE
BLANK?
BEEP

SEE THOSE SCISSORS? THAT MEANS YOU CAN CUT ALONG THE DOTTED LINE AND USE THIS PAGE LATER!

LESSON 117　ACE CHECKLIST

0:05

Congratulations! You have completed all the lessons for answering open-ended response questions. It is time for you to practice these strategies for the rest of the school year. You and your Guide can practice these strategies on your activity pages, Scan It! activities, formal assessments, and during your study time. You will be well prepared for your state standardized assessment in math, language arts, science, and social studies. Below is a checklist you can cut out and post somewhere near your work space so that you can remember the ACE strategy when you are constructing responses.

ACE
STRATEGY CHECKLIST

- ☐ Read all directions.
- ☐ Read the question and highlight the performance verbs.
- ☐ Read the passage once through or review charts, graphs, and images for information.
- ☐ Highlight main ideas.
- ☐ Write an *A*, *C*, and *E* on the right-hand corner of your response area.

Answer

- ☐ Determine how many tasks you need to provide an answer for.
- ☐ Write a restatement of the task using an open or closed restatement to begin your answer.
- ☐ Review your response to make sure you answered the question/task.

Cite

- ☐ Use evidence from the text to support the *Answer* section.
- ☐ Cite multiple details from the passage or cite information from the chart or graph.
- ☐ MATH ONLY: Compute your answer using numbers from the question. In math, your *Cite* will come before your *Answer*.
- ☐ Review details to make sure the evidence cited supports the answer and demonstrates understanding of the passage, math solution, chart, or graph.
- ☐ Make sure you cited enough evidence from the text.

Explanation

- ☐ Check that every part of the question is answered and is cited for supporting details.
- ☐ Include a connection (text, self, or world) to the text, graph, chart, or image that supports your answer and evidence.
- ☐ MATH ONLY: Use math words and vocabulary to demonstrate a step-by-step process of your procedure.
- ☐ Review your response to make sure that there are no inaccurate or unrelated details.

101-120

LESSON 118

MULTIPLE CHOICE STRATEGY REVIEW

0:10

Today, you and your Guide will review and discuss good test taking strategies for multiple choice questions. Every state standardized assessment has multiple choice questions for all subjects: math, science, social studies, and language arts. The multiple choice sections of the tests are the biggest sections. This checklist will help you remember how to approach every multiple choice section. You may have this memorized, but a reminder is important.

Before You Begin

☐ Read all directions.

☐ Read the passage once through or review charts, graphs, and images for information.

☐ Highlight any main ideas or important information.

Multiple Choice Questions

☐ Have a blank sheet of paper available to help with the strategies.

☐ Cover all answer choices and read the question through once.

☐ Highlight the performance verbs to help you understand the task.

☐ Read the question with each answer choice.

☐ Eliminate answers that don't make sense or do not provide an appropriate response.

☐ Review or reread the text, passage, graph, chart, or diagram to help you solve or locate the correct answer.

☐ Select the correct answer choice by completely filling in the appropriate bubble.

☐ Check your work.
  • Is the information in the text?
  • Did you use addition to check your subtraction problem?
  • Did you use multiplication to check your division problem?
  • Did you carry over in the appropriate place value?
  • When you solved for subtraction, did you regroup in the appropriate place value?

LESSON 119

WORDS HAVE CLUES: REVIEW

`0:15`

All the clues and information you need to answer every question are provided for you on a state standardized test. State standardized tests are not taken to provide a hardship; you take the test to make sure you learned the required fourth grade content. This will help you achieve success in fifth grade. The state can assess your learning by providing you with the information you need to answer a question using evidence from the text and your own knowledge and learning.

There are some questions that really test your comprehension skills by adding negative words. Earlier you learned how to turn negative questions into positive statements to make a task clear. Words like *not*, *except*, *least*, and *least likely* in a question are called negative words because you are required to select the answer that is most wrong.

Another tip is to look for words in answer choices that could never be correct because they are definitive; they can never be changed. For example, if you say, "All dogs are big," that is a definitive statement. That means that there are no small dogs. You know this statement is not true. Sometimes test questions have responses with definitive statements. Most of the time these answers can be eliminated because they don't allow you to interpret or solve for an answer.

Can you or your Guide think of other definitive words? Review the list below and add at least three more choices to the box. You can check your answers in Section 2, page 312.

Definitive Words
always never all impossible

LESSON 120   POSITIVE WORDS: REVIEW

You and your Guide have been reviewing the strategies you learned in this book. In Lesson 119, you learned about looking for definitive words in a question or response that would most likely eliminate an answer choice. On the other hand, there are also "true words" that are used as clues to make the answer choice the most likely correct answer. True words are the opposite of definitive words because they don't group all things into one category. For example, you might state, "Some dogs are big", which would make the statement true because some dogs are big, some dogs are medium, and some dogs are small. For example, read the following question.

1. Determine which answer choice is true.
   - All dogs do tricks for their owners.
   - Dogs only eat dog food.
   - Dogs never chew shoes.
   - Many dogs are man's best friend.

In this question, there are three definitive answer choices and one statement with a true word. You will come across similar questions and answer choices on your state standardized tests. For this example, you would eliminate the first three choices because they would always have to be true, and the definitive words *all*, *only*, and *never* make each statement completely false.

Can you or your Guide think of other true words? Review the list below and add at least three more choices to the box. You can check your answers in Section 2, page 312.

True Words
some may maybe could

LESSON 121

STATE STANDARDIZED TESTS

0:10

State standardized testing is required in all fifty states. States receive money from the federal government if they can show evidence of learning. Each year, a state must demonstrate that its schools are meeting yearly progress goals in teaching students the basic math, reading, writing, science, and social studies skills they need to be successful learners for life. Adequate Yearly Progress (AYP) is a measurement that allows the federal government to determine how well each state is meeting the academic goals and standards it established for its schools. No matter what state you live in, you will take a state standardized test beginning in third grade. Can you find your test on this list?

State	Test name
Alabama	Alabama High School Graduation Exam (AHSGE)
	Alabama Reading and Mathematics Test (ARMT)
Alaska	High School Graduation Qualifying Examination (HSGQE)
	Standards-Based Assessment (SBA)
Arizona	Arizona's Instrument to Measure Standards (AIMS)
Arkansas	Augmented Benchmark Examinations
California	Standardized Testing and Reporting (STAR)
Colorado	Colorado Student Assessment Program (CSAP)
Connecticut	Connecticut Academic Performance Test (CAPT)
Delaware	Delaware Comprehensive Assessment System (DCAS)
District of Columbia	DC Comprehensive Assessment System (DC-CAS)
Florida	Florida Comprehensive Assessment Test (FCAT)
Georgia	Criterion-Referenced Competency Tests (CRCT)
Hawaii	Hawaii State Assessment (HAS)
Idaho	Idaho Standards Achievement Test (ISAT)
Illinois	Illinois Standards Achievement Test (ISAT)
Indiana	Indiana Statewide Testing for Educational Progress-Plus (ISTEP)
Iowa	Iowa Test of Basic Skills (ITBS)
Kansas	Kansas Mathematics Assessment Kansas Reading Assessment Kansas Writing Assessment Kansas Science Assessment Kansas History, Government, Economics, and Geography Assessment
Kentucky	Commonwealth Accountability Testing System (CATS)
Louisiana	Louisiana Educational Assessment Program (LEAP)
Maine	Maine Educational Assessment (MEA)
Maryland	Maryland State Assessment (MSA)

Massachusetts	Massachusetts Comprehensive Assessment System (MCAS)
Michigan	Michigan Educational Assessment Program (MEAP)
Minnesota	Minnesota Comprehensive Assessments—Series II (MCA-II)
Mississippi	Mississippi Curriculum Test (MCT)
Missouri	Missouri Assessment Program (MAP)
Montana	Montana Comprehensive Assessment System (MONTCAS)
Nebraska	Nebraska State Accountability Testing (NESA)
Nevada	Nevada Proficiency Examination Program (NPEP)
New Hampshire	New England Common Assessment Program (NECAP)
New Jersey	New Jersey Assessment of Skills and Knowledge (NJASK)
New Mexico	New Mexico Standards-Based Assessment (NMSBA)
New York	Regents Examinations (REGENTS)
North Carolina	North Carolina End of Grade Tests (EOGs)
North Dakota	North Dakota State Assessment
Ohio	Ohio Achievement Assessment (OAA)
Oklahoma	Oklahoma Core Curriculum Tests (OCCT)
Oregon	Oregon Assessment of Knowledge and Skills (OAKS)
Pennsylvania	Pennsylvania System of School Assessment (PSSA)
Rhode Island	New England Common Assessment Program (NECAP)
South Carolina	Palmetto Assessment of State Standards (PASS)
South Dakota	South Dakota State Test of Educational Progress (DSTEP)
Tennessee	Tennessee Comprehensive Assessment Program (TCAP)
Texas	State of Texas Assessments of Academic Readiness (STAAR)
Utah	Iowa Test of Basic Skills (ITBS)
Vermont	New England Common Assessment Program (NECAP)
Virginia	Standards of Learning (SOL)
Washington	Washington Assessment of Student Learning (WASL)
West Virginia	West Virginia Educational Standards Test (WESTEST)
Wisconsin	Wisconsin Knowledge and Concepts Examination (WKCE)
Wyoming	Proficiency Assessments for Wyoming Students (PAWS)

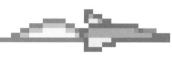

LESSON 122 — THE WEEK BEFORE YOUR TEST

121-140

The time leading up to your state standardized tests can be very stressful. You are probably preparing for your test at school and at home. You have to be sure of one thing: that you are very prepared to take this test because you have spent almost an entire year learning all the concepts and content. That is really all you can do to study for this test. You are being tested on all that you have learned in fourth grade. It is important that you don't try to cram a bunch of extra study time in for this test; you have to trust that you have all the knowledge you need. Have you completed all your homework? Have you asked questions in school? Have you created a schedule with set study times? Have you read for pleasure? If you answered *yes* to all of these questions, then you are prepared for this test.

There are several strategies you can use to help prepare you mentally. You can relax and relieve yourself of stress leading up to the test. Below are several ideas that you can use to help relax. You and your Guide should choose the strategies that will work best for both of you.

T-Minus 7 Days
State Standardized Test
Preparation Strategies

☐ Set a bedtime that will allow you to get at least eight hours of sleep each night.
- Research shows that well-rested students have a better attention span and concentration skills.

☐ Eat well-balanced meals; stay away from excessive sweets.
- Sugary diets only give you energy for short spans of time. Well-balanced meals will allow your body to give you just the right amount of energy all day to help you concentrate.

☐ Review or study only formal assessments, Scan It! activities, or spelling tests.
- You can't study an entire year's content in one week; it will only overwhelm and stress you.

☐ Read for enjoyment only.
- Reading for enjoyment reduces stress and relaxes your mind.

☐ Try to exercise or get some extra outside playtime the week prior to your test.
- Exercise is energy for the mind and body; an exercised body is a relaxed mind.

☐ Express your anxiety with your Guide.
- Take some time to talk about your nervousness and worries. You will feel better if you share your worries with someone else and not keep them inside.

☐ Stay healthy.
- You will need an entire week to prepare your body and mind; avoid running yourself down the week prior to the test.

☐ Allow yourself to relax.
- You are prepared for this test. There is nothing you can do in one week, so allow yourself downtime to relax your mind.

LESSON 123

WHAT, WHERE, WHEN, WHY, HOW

0:20

121-140

It is important that you and your Guide spend time preparing for your school's testing days. You should mark the days on your monthly planning calendar so you know the exact date. Each state sets a testing schedule prior to beginning a new school year. Generally, state standardized tests are administered between January and June; most states schedule March, April, and May for testing dates.

You may have questions that you and your Guide can talk about before your test. The more you talk about the test, the less anxiety you will have. Below are some questions to think about along with any you may already have. Don't be afraid to ask questions that could help you prepare yourself mentally for your state standardized tests.

What	What subject am I completing first? What is included in that section (multiple choice, extended response, writing prompts)? What accommodations is the school preparing to maximize the quiet time? What do I need to be successful? What types of questions will I be able to ask during the test? What if I need to go to the bathroom? What if I need to take a break or get a drink? What happens if all my pencils break?
Where	Where will I be completing my state standardized assessment? Where will my teacher be during the test? Where will I eat lunch? Where do I go if I need a break? Where will my test go after I am finished?
When	When are the exact dates and times for my test? When will we have breaks? When will I get the results of my test? When are the make-up dates for testing?
Why	Why do I need to take this test? Why don't they wait until the end of the year?
How	How will I know how much time is left? How will I finish my exam if I am absent? How many hours a day will I be testing? How much time will I be given to complete each section?

LESSON 124 — THE NIGHT BEFORE

121-140

0:15

By the time you come to the night before your state standardized assessment, you should be relaxed. Did you adjust your bedtime schedule and stay away from sweets for the entire week before the test? If you did, you may have noticed that your body is enjoying good rest and you may feel more alert. That is because your mind and body are not stressed. When you are stressed, your body produces a lot of energy and that can make you feel tired all the time.

Have you ever heard of the phrase "My mind is racing?" That means that you have a lot on your mind. That is why good rest, good food, and spending time with your Guide talking about the test are important. If you haven't adjusted your schedule, it's not too late to prepare yourself.

You and your Guide can adjust the following sample checklist to fit your needs; however, it is important to set some type of schedule or routine so you know exactly what to expect on the day of the test.

State Standardized Test Day
Checklist

The Day Before

☐ Have one final discussion with your Guide to make sure all your questions are answered.

☐ Eat a good healthful dinner; try to stay away from sweets.

☐ Set your alarm for an early start.

☐ Read a book of your choosing for fifteen minutes; no schoolwork.

☐ Go to bed between 8:00 p.m. and 9:00 p.m.

The Morning of Your Test

☐ Wake up and follow your morning routine.

☐ Choose comfortable clothing for the day; if you think you might be cold, grab a jacket or sweater.

☐ Eat a good breakfast (oatmeal, eggs, toast, breakfast bar, or shake); try to stay away from sweets.

☐ Pack a small snack just in case you need some energy.

☐ Arrive at school on time.

LESSON 125

I'M AT MY TEST SITE, NOW WHAT?

121-140

0:20

When you arrive for your test, you may notice that everyone is a little on edge; teachers are getting last-minute instructions and some students are a little nervous. This is no time to panic. You just have to remind yourself that you are prepared. You have prepared all year to take this test. You completed all your schoolwork, you have managed your study time, and you have practiced good test taking strategies. This is your time to relax and talk to yourself about all the strategies you will use. You need to focus your attention on the skills and strategies you do know:

- I will read all the directions before I begin any work.
- I will listen to all instructions and directions from the teacher.
- I will read passages or review charts, graphs, or diagrams through before I read any questions.
- I will highlight performance verbs.
- I will eliminate answers that don't make sense.
- I will use the ACE strategy for all open-ended response questions.
- I will construct great ACE answers.

The morning of your test is time to focus your mind on what you need to do; quiet time so you can think will help you begin the test stress free. Try not to do any strenuous physical activity during the test or get into conversations that will get you nervous. It is time to relax and feel confident that you will do well. You are ready to begin!

Discuss with your Guide: What other strategies can you add to the list above?

121-140

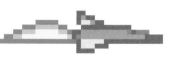

LESSON 126 — FILL IN THE BUBBLES

0:20

On the day you take a standardized test, your first task will be to write your name on the test. You may remember from third grade that this doesn't mean that you write your name on a blank line. The multiple choice section of your test may be graded by a computer that reads the bubbles filled in with a No. 2 pencil. This means that you have to write your name in a specific way.

Below is a sample of how you may be asked to write your name. In the spaces provided for your last name, you will write your last name, with one letter in each box. You will notice that there is also a place for your first name. You will write your full first name (not your nickname) in the spaces that begin under the heading *First Name*. Write one letter in each box. Then you will have to fill in each bubble that has the correct letter to match the letter in each box. When you have completed filling in the bubbles, make sure you check your name one more time. If you do not fill in the bubbles correctly, the computer grading your test may spell your name incorrectly. If you need to erase a bubble, make sure you completely erase it and fill in the correct bubble completely.

Last Name: A N D E R S O N

First Name: M A R I S A

Use the sample as an example of the correct way to write your name on the state standardized test. Practice writing your name on the test booklet cover and fill in the correct bubble for each letter in the box.

Last Name

First Name

121-140

LESSON 127   **BUBBLES ARE IMPORTANT**

0:20

Throughout this book, you have practiced multiple choice assessment questions with four choices that have a bubble next to them. Depending on your state standardized test, you will see different style bubbles. Some bubbles have a circle with a letter in it like the example below.

Some states add four more bubble responses to the group above. The bubbles have two sets of alternating letters so students can keep track of which set of bubbles go along with each test. The *E* is skipped so students can't confuse the *E* and *F*.

Some provide a separate answer sheet and others include the bubbles below the questions, such as in this book. Whichever bubble type, remember to fill in the bubble completely. Half-filled bubbles may result in the computer missing your answer. The following bubbles are not filled in correctly.

All of your response bubbles should be filled in completely with your No. 2 pencil. The example below is how all your bubbles should look when you have completed your state standardized test.

LESSON 128   3,2,1 BLAST OFF!

121-140

It's test time! What do you do now? First, take a deep breath and clear your mind of any doubt. You are ready. State standardized tests are not scary; you can't fail them. This is a test for you to demonstrate your skills and knowledge. It allows the school to prove it taught you the skills you needed to learn in fourth grade. Your teacher will guide you through the test and explain all the instructions you have to follow. You will begin by filling in your name on the test booklet, and then you will listen to directions and practice a few test questions. This process is meant to calm you down and let you work in the test booklet. You can also ask questions, get scratch paper, make sure all your pencils are sharpened, and get comfortable in your workspace.

When you first open the test booklet, you will notice that there are symbols and directions on the bottom right-hand side. These are important symbols because they tell you when to move on and when to stop. You will review what these signs mean in the next lesson. The symbols you will see may look like this:

This symbol lets you know what page to stop working on; it may signify the end of a section.

or

This symbol lets you know that you can turn the page and continue working.

Discuss with your Guide: What do you think you need to do for each sign?

_____

_____

LESSON 129   MORE THAN A STOP SIGN

This symbol is more than just a stop sign that tells you that you have reached the end of a section or a time period; it also tells you that you have time to check your work. Most state standardized tests are designed to give you plenty of time to spare. It is up to you to use that time wisely and not just take a break or put your head down. You can't move forward in the test booklet, but you can look back through the section you have just completed. Remember, only look through the section you are working on. When you get to this symbol, use the following strategies.

- ☐ Put your pencil down and take a few moments to think about the section you just worked on.
  - Did you feel confident?
  - Is there anything you got stuck on?
- ☐ Go back to all passages, charts, and graphs and read them again. Don't look at any of the questions that accompany the passage.
  - Read for pleasure.
  - Try to read for comprehension only.
  - Pause between each review and think about what you have just read or reviewed.
- ☐ Go back to the questions that accompany the passages, charts, and graphs.
  - Check your work using the same multiple choice strategies you used the first time.
  - Act like you are answering the questions for the first time.
- ☐ Review all other test questions using the same multiple choice strategies you used the first time.
- ☐ MATH ONLY: Check your math computation.
  - Did you check your subtraction by adding the difference to the subtrahend?
    - ***minuend – subtrahend = difference***
  - Did you check your division by multiplying the divisor and the quotient?
    - ***dividend ÷ divisor = quotient***
- ☐ Review all other multiple choice questions using the same strategies you used the first time.

LESSON 130

MATH STRATEGY REVIEW

0:20

In lesson 129, you were given a list of strategies to use when you get to a stop sign in your test booklet. When you are completing your math state standardized assessment, you may have to do a lot of your computations on scratch paper. It is important to organize your scratch paper wisely so that you can go back through and review your work. You can draw a grid on your paper using horizontal and vertical lines and use each box to solve a problem. For example:

1. 1 120 x 5 600	7.	8.	11.
15.	23.	31.	32.

This will allow you to review your work when you get to a stop sign. In the checklist in Lesson 129, you saw the following:

☐ MATH ONLY: Check your math computation.

- Did you check your subtraction by adding the difference to the subtrahend?
  - *minuend – subtrahend = difference*
- Did you check your division by multiplying the divisor and the quotient?
  - *dividend ÷ divisor = quotient*

In the next lesson, you will review how to check your math problems.

Discuss with your Guide: How do you check addition and multiplication problems to make sure your computation is correct?

_____

_____

LESSON 131 CHECKING YOUR WORK

0:20

121-140

You learned that when you get to a stop sign, you will not be allowed to move to the next section of your state standardized test. This is done to make sure that all students are working on the same section of the test. This is a rule for state standardized testing that all schools must follow because it prevents students from giving answers to other students. State standardized tests are supposed to test a student's skills and knowledge, so they try to prevent sharing answers or ideas by keeping all students on the same section of the test booklet.

The stop sign tells you that you can check your work. In math, you should go back through all your computations and check that you were able to compute the correct answer. It is easy to make a mistake in your computation; you may have missed a carry over or a regrouping in your work that leads to a careless error. You will have time to check for that.

Most fourth graders make errors in subtraction and division on state standardized tests. That is because you are working with larger numbers. Below you will see an example of a student's scratch paper.

In the division problem, the student solves the problem and then checks his work by using the quotient and divisor as factors to find the product. The product should equal the dividend.

In the subtraction problem, the student solves the problem and then checks his work by using the difference and subtrahend as addends to find the sum. The sum should be equal to the minuend.

Division:	Subtraction:
dividend ÷ divisor = quotient	minuend − subtrahend = difference

Division:
$$\text{dividend} \div \text{divisor} = \text{quotient}$$

Check your work:
$$\begin{array}{r} \text{quotient} \\ \times \quad \text{divisor} \\ \hline \text{dividend} \end{array}$$

Subtraction:
$$\text{minuend} - \text{subtrahend} = \text{difference}$$

Check your work:
$$\begin{array}{r} \text{difference} \\ + \quad \text{subtrahend} \\ \hline \text{minuend} \end{array}$$

1. $448 \div 8 =$

$$\begin{array}{r} 56 \\ 8\overline{)448} \\ 40\downarrow \\ \hline 48 \\ 48 \\ \hline 0 \end{array}$$

Check your work:
$$\begin{array}{r} 4 \\ 56 \\ \times \quad 8 \\ \hline 448 \end{array}$$

2. $70,008 - 21,765 =$

$$\begin{array}{r} {}^{6}\;{}^{9}\;{}^{9} \\ 70,008 \\ - 21,765 \\ \hline 48,243 \end{array}$$

Check your work:
$$\begin{array}{r} {}^{1}\;{}^{1}\;{}^{1} \\ 48,243 \\ + 21,765 \\ \hline 70,008 \end{array}$$

Discuss with your Guide: Do you have a different way to check your math work?

_____

_____

LESSON 132   TEST DAY GUESS?

0:20

121-140

It is important to go into every testing day positive and confident in your skills. You have been preparing for this test all year by being a responsible learner. What happens if you come to a question that you don't understand? First, don't panic! Second, don't panic! This may be the time to use an educated guess. An educated guess is when you use the knowledge that you do have about a concept or content area and try to determine the answer through reasoning. For example, look at the question below:

1. In math, ones are the first place value in a whole number. The larger the number, the more zeros you will see separated by commas when the number is written in standard form. Using your knowledge of math, identify the **largest** number:

    ○   googolplexian

    ○   billion

    ○   trillion

    ○   googol

You may not know the answer and you won't have access to the Internet, you can't ask the teacher for any explanations, and you can't wait until the next testing day to go back in the book to change your answer. It is time to just answer the question. It is important to mention that state standardized tests don't penalize you for wrong answers; you won't go from a grade of 100 to 95 because you missed a question. That is not how state standardized tests work. You are being tested on your knowledge, but we will review that later in this book.

What do you do? Use your knowledge of math. You know that a billion is a number followed by nine zeros, and a trillion is a number followed by twelve zero. So what are a googol and a googolplexian? Are those really numbers? If you just don't know, all you can do is take an educated guess. Don't worry about it; you just need to guess and move on to the next question. In other words, don't let one question make you get stuck. There are plenty of other questions that need your attention. Do you want to know the answer to the question? The largest number is a googolplexian. You and your Guide can look it up on the Internet.

LESSON 133 ONE LAST TEST TIP

121-140

0:10

We have come to the end of test preparation and test tips because you truly have all the information you need to be successful. There is one more tip that you and your Guide need to know. This lesson is more for your Guide than it is for you. If you don't mind, let your Guide read this one alone.

You may be wondering what you do each day of state standardized testing. Your student will probably be tired, concerned, cranky, or just plain exhausted. This behavior is normal. Your student is using all his energy and concentration on doing well on this test. Most states give state standardized tests over a three- to five-day period; that is a lot for a fourth grader. Below are some tips that can help your student have a positive experience with his state standardized test.

Guide Tips

- ☐ Allow your student a small snack when he comes home; he's used a lot of energy on the test.
  - • Make sure you have plenty of healthful snacks for test days.
- ☐ Spend no more than fifteen (15) minutes discussing the testing day with your student.
  - • Let your student lead the conversation.
  - • Avoid asking how well he may have performed.
  - • Give him an opportunity to share questions and anxiety.
- ☐ Plan to serve a well-balanced meal with a minimal amount of sweets if the next day is a testing day.
  - • You can have your student plan the meals for the week.
  - • You may want to plan special meals.
- ☐ Minimize the amount of school work your student is responsible to complete.
  - • Some schools don't assign homework during testing week.
- ☐ Increase your student's physical activity since he has been sitting for extended periods of time all week.
  - • Plan trips to the park.
  - • Get him to his activities and practices; don't allow him to skip out on these.
  - • Plan something special.
- ☐ Make sure he is getting plenty of sleep.
  - • Ask him to read for pleasure before bed.
  - • Gently ask if he got all his questions asked from the earlier conversation; don't let him go to sleep with something on his mind.

LESSON 134 — IT'S OVER! WHAT NOW?

121-140

On the last day of your state standardized test, you may experience a lot of emotions. You may feel relief that your school days will finally return to normal or you may have questions about what happens to the test when you are finished. These feelings are normal; you probably will have so many questions in your head that you don't know where to begin asking. Mostly, you may be thinking about what happens for the rest of the school year. That answer is simple; you resume your regular schedule. You have plenty of math, science, social studies, and language arts left to learn in fourth grade to prepare you for fifth grade. Most importantly, you have to continue practicing the same strategies that you have learned throughout this book. From this point on, you have to evaluate your entire experience completing the state standardized test and set some new goals. Over the next several lessons, you will work on using your state standardized test to set goals for fifth grade. If you have not completed your state standardized test, plan on referring back to these lessons at a later date.

What types of questions might you have at the end of your testing schedule? A possible answer has been provided to get you started.

When do I get my score?

_____

_____

_____

_____

LESSON 135 PREPARING NEW GOALS

0:20

After you complete your standardized test, you and your Guide should spend some time reflecting and evaluating your test experience. To become a consistent learner, you should always take time to think about what you learned, what you still need to learn, and how you learn.

You read that correctly: how you learn! Knowing how you learn is very important, especially when you are setting goals for fifth grade. When you know how you learn best, you and your Guide can plan to outline your schedule to give you time to use strategies that work best for you. For example, if you learn best by doing a hands-on activity and you use your kitchen table to complete your math work using counters, then dinnertime is not the best study time for your schedule.

After you have completed your state standardized test, you and your Guide should fill out the following form to help you begin the process of practicing the strategies you learned in this book and evaluating what subject content and concepts you need to improve upon.

Post-Test Evaluation

Overall Experience:			
Language Arts	☺	😐	☹
Math	☺	😐	☹
Science	☺	😐	☹
Social Studies	☺	😐	☹
Explain:			

**Strategies I Used
(check all that apply)**

- ☐ I created a weekly study schedule.
- ☐ I created a monthly calendar.
- ☐ I created study notes to review.

- ☐ I read all the directions before I began working.
- ☐ I read the passage once all the way through.
- ☐ I read the passage and highlighted main ideas.
- ☐ I read each question and highlighted performance verbs.
- ☐ I paused after reading questions to think about my answer.
- ☐ I read multiple choice questions with each answer; I read the question four times.
- ☐ I used the process of elimination on my multiple choice questions.
- ☐ I turned negative statements into positive statements.
- ☐ I reviewed all my work when I got to a stop sign.
- ☐ I read the passages all the way through when I got to the stop sign.
- ☐ I checked all my math work in division and subtraction with multiplication and addition.

I need more practice with the following strategies:

Which strategy did I like best? Why?

I had the most difficulty with questions about (e.g., food webs, weather, measurement):

I need to improve on my knowledge of (history, multiplication, scientific method, reading comprehension) for fifth grade:

I learned best when I:

LESSON 136 — NEW GOALS

After you have completed your state standardized tests and evaluated your experience, it is time to set new goals. Your new goals should focus on two areas. The first area is practicing the strategies you learned in fourth grade and this book, and the second area is what you want to learn better in fifth grade. For example, if John struggled in math all year and didn't feel confident about how he performed on the math standardized assessment, then John's goal might be to improve in math. State standardized tests let you know what you have to improve. You have to be reflective and honest when you complete your post-test evaluation; your new goals depend on it. When you set reasonable goals based on an honest assessment of your knowledge and skills, then you have a better chance of success.

When you set goals for learning, you want to make them reasonable. You will not learn everything you need to know about a subject in one grade. Goals are like the rungs on a ladder; you have to put your foot in one rung at a time and pull yourself up. You have to break your goals down into smaller parts. Look at the two groups of goals below. On one side are goals that are too difficult to achieve by the end of fifth grade, and on the other side are goals that are reasonable with a high chance of success.

Hard-To-Reach Goals	Successful Goal Statements
I want to learn everything about outer space.	I want to learn why Mars is red and Saturn has rings.
I want to score 100% on all my formal assessments.	I want to practice using the process of elimination on formal assessments.
I want to read an eighth grade novel.	I want to read every evening before bed for thirty minutes.
I want to score a 4 (Advanced) on my fifth grade state standardized assessment.	I want to create study notes one night a week and review study notes two days a week.

Discuss with your Guide: Successful goal statements help you meet hard-to-reach goals. Explain to your Guide why learning about one planet at a time will help you learn about outer space.

LESSON 137 — SETTING GOALS

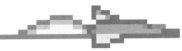

0:20

After you and your Guide spend time reviewing your performance on the state standardized assessments, it is time to set goals for the remainder of your fourth grade year and for fifth grade. There are many goals that you can set. You may want a new bike, you may want to start playing a sport, or you may want to join a club. Those are all great goals; however, the goals that you set after completing the state standardized assessments are learning goals, improvement goals, or other goals that will help you be a great student. Think about the lessons you learned from your state standardized tests. Did you need more practice on test taking strategies? Do you want to improve a strategy that worked well for you? Did you miss a question because you didn't know the content? Those are the types of questions you need to ask yourself. This takes time, so don't think you have to set all these goals today. You can start with one or two goals and post them in your workspace or on the refrigerator. Then you can add to it and use it to remind yourself that you are working towards these goals.

Review the example goal statement below. This student has goals that he can achieve and he can measure his progress. Notice that the student also lists ways to help him achieve each goal in small chunks. It is important to think about a goal as a process that is broken up into smaller parts, and each part leads to achieving the goal.

Oscar's Goals		
I want to...	**I can do this by...**	**Steps completed for my goal**
have a better understanding of long division.	<ul><li>knowing all my multiplication facts up to 12.</li><li>learning how to check my work.</li><li>using graph paper to line up my numbers.</li><li>creating study notes with detailed instructions that I can use when I practice.</li></ul>	<ul><li>I practiced every night and learned my multiplication facts through 12.</li></ul>
get better at using the ACE strategy.	<ul><li>figuring out how to write a good restatement.</li><li>learning to summarize passages in my writing.</li><li>practicing reading every night.</li></ul>	<ul><li>I have been reading every night for thirty days.</li></ul>

Discuss with your Guide: Should goals come with due dates?

_____

_____

LESSON 138   NO LIMITS

Do goals need to have time limits? That is a difficult question because some goals have to have time limits. Let's say that your goal was to learn the names of all eight planets for the test on Friday. It won't help if you memorize them all the Saturday after the test. That specific goal has to have a time limit.

As a fourth grade student, you may want to think about goals that you can work on over a long period of time. This way you can break your long-term goals into short-term tasks. If you wanted to get good at the ACE strategy, then think about all the things that you struggled with on your fourth grade assessment. Maybe it's reading comprehension or summarizing that you had the most difficulty with. Those two things will help you get better at the ACE strategy so you want to master those skills first. By the time you get to your fifth grade state standardized test, you will be a little better at using the ACE strategy. You can plan on getting a little better every year until you don't have to think about the *Answer*, *Cite*, *Extend* in your answer because your brain automatically completes the process.

You can write your goals at any time after this lesson. You may need time to think about it and talk it over with your Guide; however, let's practice writing one goal. List the steps you need to complete to help you with your goal. You will not have to complete the third column because you wouldn't have worked on this goal yet.

My Goal		
I want to...	**I can do this by...**	**Steps completed for my goal**

LESSON 139   WHAT ABOUT MY SCORE?

121-140

At this point, you and your Guide may be asking the following:

- Where are my scores?
- What do they mean?
- What do the results tell me about my learning ability?
- Why are testing skills important?

The last question is difficult to answer because you have to figure out why testing skills are important to you. You may feel that practicing test taking strategies helps you organize your study time or that knowing good strategies helps you feel confident when taking tests. You may even want a career that will require a lot of school, so you want to be prepared. This book is a great start to understanding how to be a good learner. You can practice all you learned in this book and research new strategies to help you with the many other tests you will take in middle school and high school.

Now, it's time to answer the questions about your state standardized test. The first question is easy to answer; you will receive your test scores at the end of June or with your last report card. State standardized tests are given between February and May in order to give the state time to score your results. Each state has thousands of students in its school system that are all required to complete the tests. Be patient, your results are coming soon. In the meantime, it is important that you go back to being a typical fourth grade student with lots of studying and schoolwork to complete.

LESSON 140

0:10

PERFORMANCE LEVEL: READING

Most states have a four-point performance level that is used to describe your achievement level on the state standardized tests. The four points are like a rubric; each state lists the criteria that you need to demonstrate for each level. Not all states use the same terms. The table below provides a general description of each performance level and the descriptors used to identify each level. Each state is different but this example should help you understand the four points that you will see on your report.

Reading	1	2	3	4
Criteria/ Academic Standard	You are able to read most grade level material to yourself (stories, books, novels, how-to guides). You do not fully understand the content to draw meaning.	You are able to read most grade level material to yourself (stories, books, novels, how-to guides). You are able to understand most of the content.	You are able to read at grade level material to yourself (stories, books, novels, how-to guides). You are able to understand the content and concepts completely.	You are able to read at or beyond grade level material to yourself (stories, books, novels, how-to guides). You are able to understand the content and concepts completely and draw meaning from the selection to other material.
Descriptors (varies by state)	Below Basic, Standard Not Met, Not Proficient, Novice, Below Standard, Minimal Performance, Limited Performance	Basic, Below Standard, Partially Proficient, Partial Mastery, Approaches Standard	Proficient, Standard, Mastery, Meets Standard	Advanced, Commended Performance, Distinguished, Exceeds Standard, Accelerated

Discuss with your Guide: What is an academic standard?

_____

_____

PERFORMANCE LEVEL:
MATH

0:15

Earlier, you learned about setting large goals and breaking them down into smaller tasks to achieve success. An academic standard is a goal set by your state that describes the complete skills you should have by the end of fourth grade. An academic standard is then broken down into content standards (language arts, math, science, social studies) that describe what you need to know and be able to do in each subject to meet the academic standard. Finally, each subject is broken down into performance standards to describe how you will show that you meet the standard. For example:

- **Academic Standard**: Students will understand numbers, number systems, and number relationships.
  - **Content Standard**: Students will apply number patterns and relationships to count and compare values of whole numbers and simple fractions and decimals.
    - **Performance Standard**: Students will use models and/or words to represent quantities as decimals, fractions, or mixed numbers.

141-160

Math	1	2	3	4
Criteria/ Academic Standard	You are working consistently on grade level in most mathematical tasks. You demonstrate some problem solving strategies.	You are working on grade level in all mathematical tasks. You perform consistently and accurately. You demonstrate accurate problem solving strategies.	You are working on grade level in all mathematical tasks. You perform consistently and accurately. You demonstrate effective problem solving strategies.	You are working on or above grade level in all mathematical tasks. You always perform consistently and accurately. You demonstrate multiple problem solving strategies effectively.
Descriptors (varies by state)	Below Basic, Standard Not Met, Not Proficient, Novice, Below Standard, Minimal Performance, Limited Performance	Basic, Below Standard, Partially Proficient, Partial Mastery, Approaches Standard	Proficient, Standard, Mastery, Meets Standard	Advanced, Commended Performance, Distinguished, Exceeds Standard, Accelerated

LESSON 142

PERFORMANCE LEVEL: SCIENCE

0:15

141-160

Now that you know that an academic standard is a goal set by your state, you should begin to understand why states use standardized tests to figure out what you need to learn. The state is required to show the federal government that you are learning what the state said you will learn. All of your lessons, videos, activities, Scan It! activities, and formal assessments are part of the curriculum that your Guide uses to help you demonstrate that you can perform at the academic standard set by your state. Each day, your Guide uses the curriculum to plan your lessons and daily learning objectives. These lessons are the smallest pieces that are used over time to help you reach the highest level of an academic standard. It is similar to all the steps you will use to achieve your academic goals. Think of when you were a baby; you had to learn to hold yourself up with your arms before you could learn to crawl. Then you had to build up your leg strength to learn to walk. After that, you were able to run, climb, and ride a bike. That is how the curriculum works—it teaches you to hold yourself up so you can learn bigger concepts.

Science	1	2	3	4
Criteria/ Academic Standard	You are working on grade level in science. You demonstrate limited content knowledge to apply scientific processes and connections.	You are working on grade level in science. You demonstrate sufficient content knowledge to apply scientific processes and connections.	You are working on grade level in science. You demonstrate well-developed content knowledge to apply scientific processes and connections.	You are working on or above grade level in science. You demonstrate highly-developed content knowledge to apply scientific processes and connections.
Descriptors (varies by state)	Below Basic, Standard Not Met, Not Proficient, Novice, Below Standard, Minimal Performance, Limited Performance	Basic, Below Standard, Partially Proficient, Partial Mastery, Approaches Standard	Proficient, Standard, Mastery, Meets Standard	Advanced, Commended Performance, Distinguished, Exceeds Standard, Accelerated

LESSON 143

PERFORMANCE LEVEL: SOCIAL STUDIES

0:15

Performance levels are an indication of how well you have learned the knowledge and skills taught in the curriculum. From the moment you finish your fourth grade standardized assessments, you are learning skills that you will need for fifth grade. That is why you are setting goals for fifth grade and are encouraged to keep working on your test strategies. Looking at the chart below, the numbers and the descriptors are your performance levels. You want to try to achieve the highest performance levels, so keep that in mind when you are setting your performance goals.

Social Studies	1	2	3	4
Criteria/ Academic Standard	You are working on grade level material in social studies. You demonstrate limited ability to gather evidence to process and apply information presented in the curriculum.	You are working on grade level material in social studies. You sufficiently demonstrate the ability to gather evidence to process and apply information presented in the curriculum.	You are working on grade level material in social studies. You usually demonstrate the ability to gather evidence to process and apply information presented in the curriculum.	You are working on or above grade level material in social studies. You consistently demonstrate the ability to gather evidence to process and apply information presented in the curriculum.
Descriptors (varies by state)	Below Basic, Standard Not Met, Not Proficient, Novice, Below Standard, Minimal Performance, Limited Performance	Basic, Below Standard, Partially Proficient, Partial Mastery, Approaches Standard	Proficient, Standard, Mastery, Meets Standard	Advanced, Commended Performance, Distinguished, Exceeds Standard, Accelerated

141-160

LESSON 144

CATEGORIES:
LANGUAGE ARTS

`0:20`

When you get your report, the first place you will want to look is at your performance level in each subject. It is natural to want to know how you performed. However, the overall score in a subject doesn't tell the entire story. Within each subject, your state lists the categories in which you were tested and how well you performed in each. The categories listed and how they are scored vary by state. Some states give you the number of questions asked within a category and how many you answered correctly. Some states use a performance level explanation to show how well you performed in each category. It is difficult to give an example that reflects all states' reports and categories; therefore, the sample below will help you understand what to look for but may not match your state's report.

Reading Scores			
Performance Level: Advanced			
	Student Points	**Total Points**	**Strength**
Reading Comprehension	12	15	High
Thinking Skills	16	20	High
Use of Literary Information	7	12	High
Analysis of Fiction and Nonfiction text	6	8	Medium

Each state measures how well you did in each section based on the difficulty of the tasks. So the points earned to the total points may be a bit confusing. In the score above, the student should set a goal to improve his understanding of the difference between fiction and nonfiction texts. He may choose to achieve this goal by increasing the amount of time he spends reading for pleasure or by reading an equal amount of fiction and nonfiction books.

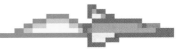

LESSON 145   CATEGORIES: MATH

0:15

In the reading score in Lesson 144, you were given categories with no descriptions to let you know what skills were actually being tested. Some states will mail or attach a separate report to your Guide so he can interpret the scores for you. These reports are designed to help you determine the areas that you need to improve. It is important that you spend time with your Guide understanding what each category means and what concepts you need to improve upon in each subject. This will help you organize your study time to concentrate on the categories with which you have the most difficulty. It will help you be a better learner in each subject.

Math Scores			
Performance Level: Advanced			
	Student Points	**Total Points**	**Strength**
Number, Number Sense, and Operations Compare numbers and match fractions to pictures. Add, subtract, multiply, and divide whole numbers. Use place values to solve problems. Count money and make change.	12	15	High
Measurement Tell time, read thermometers, and identify units of measure (inch, meter, pound). Measure and estimate length, weight, area, and volume. Draw slopes with given measurements.	8	11	Medium
Geometry and Spatial Sense Describe two-dimensional shapes and three-dimensional objects by their properties. Find points on a grid. Draw lines that divide objects into two identical parts.	10	13	Medium
Patterns, Functions, and Algebra Describe and extend patterns. Write and solve number sentences.	18	20	High
Data Analysis and Probability Read, construct, and interpret bar and picture graphs. Understand different displays of data. Find the mode.	14	14	High

Discuss with your Guide: Look at the example above and decide which categories the student needs to improve.

LESSON 146

**CATEGORIES:
SCIENCE**

141-160

0:15

When you read your report and review your performance, you may wonder how the points earned is calculated for a grade and how you earned your performance level. Each state has a complicated scoring procedure to determine performance level. This information is not important for you to know. When you and your Guide review your report, make sure you focus on the categories and the strength. Those two columns will help you understand on which categories you need to focus your studies. For example, the student below is having difficulty in physical science. Physical science is the study of common properties, forms, and changes in matter and energy. He needs to develop a better understanding of these topics. If he made a study sheet for physical science, he may want to spend time reviewing the study notes and adding information to it. This could be one of his goals.

Science Scores			
Performance Level: Proficient			
	Student Points	**Total Points**	**Strength**
Scientific Investigation and the Nature of Science	28	35	Medium
Biological Science/Life Science	8	10	High
Physical Science	7	12	Low
Earth and Space Science	14	18	Medium

 **LESSON 147**

0:20

CATEGORIES:
SOCIAL STUDIES

141-160

Remember, not all states have a social studies standardized test in fourth grade. Most states begin testing social studies skills in fifth grade. The categories listed below represent some of the concepts in which you will be tested in social studies.

This is the final report that you receive on your state standardized test report. Once you and your Guide have reviewed the results, set some goals based on the categories in which you need improvement. Discuss your feelings about your results with your Guide. If you didn't score well, your goals will help you score better on the fifth grade assessments. The categories on standardized tests do not change from fourth to fifth grade. If you struggled in a category in fourth grade and don't work to improve it, you may find that your fifth grade report looks similar.

Social Studies Scores			
Performance Level: Proficient			
	Student Points	**Total Points**	**Strength**
Culture and History of World Communities	4	4	High
Location and Geographic Characteristics	8	12	Medium
Meeting Basic Needs and Wants	7	9	High
Governments	8	8	High
Early Inhabitants and European Encounter	3	7	Low
Colonial Life	3	7	Low
Government: Local, State, and National	14	15	High

Discuss with your Guide: What types of concepts would a fourth grade student learn in the category *Colonial Life*?

_____

_____

LESSON 148 — ONE FINAL NOTE

0:05

You have completed 147 lessons on state standardized testing. You should have a good understanding of successful test taking skills. Your work is not done, though. In Section 3, there are four practice exams—one in each subject area. The practice exams contain questions that assess the categories you read about in the previous lessons. Over the next ten lessons, you will complete some of the practice assessments. Your Guide will help you use the strategies you reviewed in this book. It is important that you do all the work using your own knowledge. Your Guide's job is to prompt you to use the multiple choice strategies, ACE strategy, and reading comprehension strategies you learned. You need to answer the questions as if you are really taking a standardized test. This will give you extra practice with your Guide's help.

Discuss with your Guide: Plan out your strategies for completing the practice questions. What strategies will you need your Guide to help you with? (circle one)

Highlighting Main Ideas

Multiple-Choice Strategies

ACE Strategy

Identifying Performance Verbs

LESSON 149 — LANGUAGE ARTS: SECTION 1 QUESTIONS 1-10

0:20

Today, you will turn to Section 3 of this book. You and your Guide will complete the first ten questions. Your Guide will help you practice the multiple choice strategies you learned earlier in this book. You may want to review the strategies first. Before you begin, read through the following instructions.

Instructions

✓ You will work for fifteen minutes. It is fine if you do not complete all ten questions. The key is to practice strategies.
✓ Try to work through the questions by yourself. Your Guide can help you with highlighting if necessary.
✓ Check your answers using the answer key in Section 4.

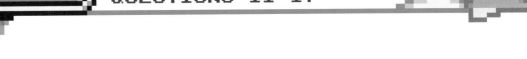

LESSON 150

LANGUAGE ARTS: SECTION 1
QUESTIONS 11–17

Today, you will complete questions 11 – 17 in the language arts practice exam. Turn to Section 3. You and your Guide will work through all the questions using the strategies you have learned. Read through the following instructions before you begin.

Instructions

✓ You will work for fifteen minutes. It is fine if you do not complete all seven questions. The key is to practice strategies.
✓ Try to work through the questions by yourself. Your Guide can help you with highlighting if necessary.
✓ Check your answers using the answer key in Section 4.

141-160

LESSON 151

LANGUAGE ARTS:
SECTION 2

It's time to practice answering constructed response questions. Section 2 of the practice language arts exam contains questions in which you will need to use the ACE strategy. You can write an *A*, *C*, and *E* on the right-hand side of your response area to remind you of each task. Your Guide's responsibility is to help you remember how to use the ACE strategy, but you should try to complete the responses on your own. Remember to make connections to the text in your *Explanation* section. Read through the instructions below before you begin.

Instructions

✓ You will work for fifteen minutes. It is fine if you do not complete all the constructed response questions. The key is to practice strategies.
✓ Try to work through the questions by yourself. Your Guide can help you with highlighting if necessary.
✓ Check your answers using the answer key in Section 4.

LESSON 152   MATH: SECTION 1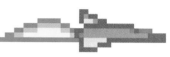

0:20

141-160

Today, you will practice your math skills using the practice exam in Section 3. You will only complete the first section. You will need to have scratch paper to compute some of the answers. Make sure you check your math before you select a response. Your Guide's responsibility is to help you remember your multiple choice test strategies, such as reading each response with the question. That means you will read the question four times and check to see if each response makes sense. This allows you to quickly eliminate answers that don't make sense. You can use mental math to help you make a quick decision, too. Read through the instructions before you begin.

Instructions

✓ You will work for fifteen minutes. It is fine if you do not complete the multiple choice questions. The key is to practice strategies.
✓ Try to work through the questions by yourself. Your Guide can help you with highlighting if necessary.
✓ Check your answers using the answer key in Section 4.

LESSON 153   MATH: SECTION 2

0:20

The math practice section that you will complete today contains "show your work" tasks. You will demonstrate your skills in mathematical computation. That means you have to show how you solve the math problems. You will complete all your work in the space provided below the question. You can use scratch paper to help check your answers, or if you have extra space, you can use *check your answers* in the test booklet. Your Guide's responsibility today is to help you remember the strategies for checking your subtraction and division. Remember, you use addition and multiplication to check your work. Read through the following instructions before you begin.

Instructions

✓ You will work for fifteen minutes. It is fine if you do not complete all of the questions. The key is to practice strategies.
✓ Try to work through the questions by yourself. Your Guide can help you with highlighting if necessary.
✓ Check your answers using the answer key in Section 4.

 **MATH: SECTION 3**

0:20

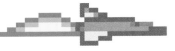

141-160

Before you begin the third section of the math practice exam, you will read the instructions below. Though you may have noticed the instructions have all been similar so far, you should still read through all instructions. In an earlier lesson, you completed an activity on following directions. Instructions and directions change on state standardized tests, so even if you think you read them before, there may be a slight difference. Do you notice the differences in the instructions below?

Turn to Section 3 and practice responding to constructed response math problems. Before you begin, read the following instructions:

Instructions

✓ You will work for fourteen minutes. You will only need to respond to one constructed response question. The key is to practice strategies.
✓ Try to work through the question by yourself. Your Guide can help you with highlighting if necessary.
✓ Check your answers using the answer key in Section 4.

LESSON 155 **SCIENCE: SECTION 1**

0:20

You have been working on sample standardized tests for six lessons. For some states, that is the number of days you will be testing in fourth grade. How is your Guide holding up? Take a moment to reflect on how much work you put into preparing for state standardized tests. You should be proud of yourself for all the work you have done this year to learn test taking strategies.

Today, you will work on multiple choice questions in science. It is fine if you are not able to finish all of the questions; you should focus on using your multiple choice strategies. Remember, it is helpful to have a blank piece of scratch paper to cover the responses as you read each question through.

Instructions

✓ You will work for fifteen minutes. Answer only five of the multiple choice questions. The key is to practice strategies.
✓ Try to work through the questions by yourself. Your Guide can help you with highlighting if necessary.
✓ Check your answers using the answer key in Section 4.

LESSON 156 SCIENCE: SECTION 2

0:20

141-160

Constructed response questions take time. You have to think through the process; review charts, graphs, or diagrams, and extend your knowledge of science concepts. In science, making text-to-self and text-to-world connections are the best ways to complete the explanation part of the ACE strategy because science is the study of the world around you. On most science state standardized tests, the constructed response section usually has one question followed by two or three constructed responses that ask you to apply a science concept, and an open-ended response question that requires you to extend your brief constructed responses. Today, you will complete the second section of the practice exam in science.

Instructions

✓ You will work on two or three brief constructed response questions and only one open-ended (extended constructed response) question.
✓ Try to work through the questions by yourself. Your Guide can help you with highlighting if necessary.
✓ Check your answers using the answer key in Section 4.

LESSON 157 SOCIAL STUDIES: SECTION 1

0:20

The final practice exam in Section 3 is for social studies. The first section of this exam requires you to demonstrate your knowledge of different social studies concepts: culture, government, geography, and early American history. Your Guide's responsibility is to help you work through each question using the multiple choice strategies you learned in this book. Read the following instructions before you begin.

Instructions

✓ You will work for fifteen minutes. Try to answer between five and ten questions. The key is to practice strategies.
✓ Try to work through the questions by yourself. Your Guide can help you with highlighting if necessary.
✓ Check your answers using the answer key in Section 4.

LESSON 158

SOCIAL STUDIES: SECTION 2

`0:20`

Today is the last day of practice questions. In the second section of the social studies practice exam, you are required to respond to short answer questions. Short answer questions are sometimes called brief constructed responses. Choose one brief constructed response question with your Guide and complete the tasks required. Read through the following instructions before you begin.

Instructions

✓ You will work on one brief constructed response question. Your Guide's responsibility is to help you remember the concepts you learned in social studies.
✓ Try to talk the problem through with your Guide using evidence from the text and your knowledge of social studies. If you need help highlighting, your Guide can help you.
✓ Check your answers using the answer key in Section 4.

LESSON 159

WHAT NOW?

`0:20`

Congratulations, you have completed all the lessons on test taking strategies. You must be very excited. You have learned many new skills. You should be proud of yourself for completing all of the lessons. You and your Guide will spend time reviewing your opinions and feelings about this book. Discuss and answer the following questions with your Guide.

1. What did you learn?

_____

_____

2. What did you enjoy?

_____

_____

3. What skills do you still need to practice?

_____

_____

4. Which skill helped you the most?

_____

_____

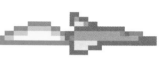

LESSON 160 — INDEPENDENT PRACTICE

0:10

141-160

Today is the last lesson in this book. It is time for you and your Guide to complete all the practice exams in Section 3. You don't have to complete them all at once. Go at your own pace. Take your time and practice the skills you learned about being an effective test taker. You and your Guide should focus on your knowledge of concepts, the content of each subject area, and the skills you use to respond to each question. After you have finished each practice exam, review the answers with your Guide in Section 4. Don't forget that you have other items on your "To Do" list. You and your Guide should set time aside to complete some of the following items.

- ☐ Practice Test Taking Strategies
- ☐ Set Goals
- ☐ Create a Reading List
- ☐ Review Study Notes

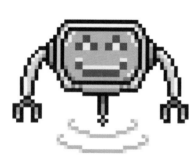

BEEP
YOU ARE DOING
GREAT!
BEEP

KEEP PRACTICING!

THERE ARE STILL A LOT OF QUESTIONS LEFT TO ANSWER.

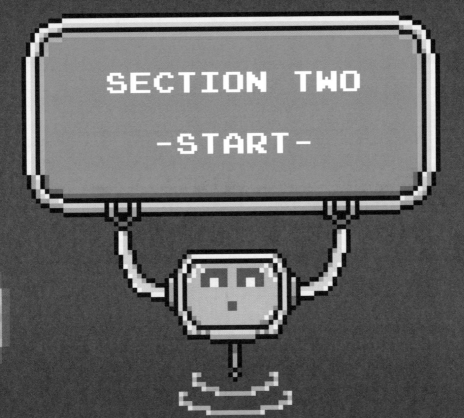

SECTION TWO

-START-

BEEP
DID YOU FINISH
SECTION 1?
CONGRATULATIONS!
BEEP

STOP! THIS
IS AN ANSWER
SECTION.
COMPLETE YOUR
WORK BEFORE
YOU CHECK
ANSWERS!

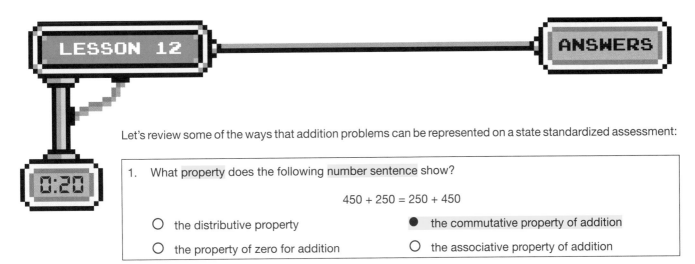

LESSON 12   **ANSWERS**

0:20

Let's review some of the ways that addition problems can be represented on a state standardized assessment:

1. What property does the following number sentence show?

450 + 250 = 250 + 450

○ the distributive property   ● the commutative property of addition

○ the property of zero for addition   ○ the associative property of addition

There are four properties of math in addition: the associative, the commutative, the identity, and the distributive. The property of zero for addition can automatically be eliminated as a possible answer because it is not worded correctly. When you answer multiple choice questions, you should eliminate the choices that are definitely incorrect, so you only have two or three possible answers.

We are looking at the commutative property. The commutative property states that when two numbers are added, the sum is the same regardless of the order of the addends. When you add 450 to 250, you will get the same answer as when you add 250 to 450. The best way to think about the commutative property is to think about ways in which people commute to work. Some people drive themselves to work and at the end of the day commute back home by changing the direction that they traveled in the morning. They are going from home to work and from work to home. That is what makes them commuters. The commutative property is the same thing; the numbers are changing places but they are still the same numbers.

2. What is the sum of 53,370 and 19,656?

○ 46,326   ● 73,026

○ 82,409   ○ 61,291

In this problem, the first thing you want to do is eliminate answers using mental math. The first addend can be rounded down to 50,000 and the second addend can be rounded up to 20,000. This will tell you that the sum will be about 70,000. Using this strategy, you can immediately eliminate 46,326 and 61,291 because they are not close to 70,000. This leaves you two possible answers.

A good strategy for answering addition questions is to use graph paper in order to line up the addends from right (ones) to left (ten thousands). In this question, 73,026 is the correct answer.

1	1	1		
5	3,	3	7	0
1	9,	6	5	6
7	**3,**	**0**	**2**	**6**

3. What is 9,236 in **expanded form**?

○ 9,000 + 200 + 36   ○ 9,000 + 200 + 360

● 9,000 + 200 + 30 + 6   ○ 9,000 + 200 + 300 + 6

When you write a number in expanded form, you start from left to right and represent the digit by its place value. In this example, the 9 is in the thousands place (9,000), the 2 is in the hundreds place (200), the three is in the tens place (30), and the 6 is in the ones place (6). Once you have the place values defined in your head, you will have to represent them as an addition problem without the sum. In this problem, the correct answer is 9,000 + 200 + 30 + 6.

---

4. Allison bought 2 comic books for $5.36 each and a bookmark for $1.59. What is the total amount of money she paid?

   ◯ $ 8.54   ◯ $ 6.95

   ◯ $ 8.95   ● $12.31

You are asked to find the total of the given addends. In math language, the word *total* means exactly the same thing as the word *sum*. It is very important that you take your time with problems that give you one addend but want you to use it more than once. In this problem, there are two comic books for $5.36 each. That means that you will have two addends that are the same: $5.36 and $5.36. You will also have $1.59 as an addend.

If you apply the same mental math strategy as above, you can round down $5.36 to $5.00. $5.00 + $5.00 is $10.00. You can round up $1.59 to $2.00 and add that to the total of $10.00. The answer will be about $12.00. If you remembered that $5.36 needed to be added twice, you could have eliminated all the other answer choices using mental math.

---

5. Casey, Tyler, and Nicole each put $8.00 into a jar to start their car washing business. On Saturday, they washed 2 cars. They collected $6.00 for each car washed. On Sunday, they washed just one car and collected $10.00. How much money was in the jar at the end of the weekend? Show all your work. Explain your work using words.

At the end of the weekend the jar had $46.00.

Casey, Tyler, and Nicole had $24.00 to start their car washing business.

   $ 8.00
   $ 8.00
   $ 8.00
   $24.00

On Saturday they made $12.00.

   $ 6.00
   $ 6.00
   $12.00

On Sunday they made only $10.00. If I add all these totals together, it will give the total in the jar at the end of the weekend.

   Total
   $24.00
   $12.00
   $10.00
   $46.00

You are asked to provide an extended response. This is where the ACE strategy comes in. The first thing you have to do is read the question carefully and search for the question you have to answer.

The question is highlighted in green above. The first sentence in your answer will restate the question and provide an answer.

At the end of the weekend the jar had _____.

Now you can figure out how to answer the question. Casey, Tyler, and Nicole each put in $8.00 to start their business. So in the box you will have to show how much money was in the jar in the beginning. Make sure you use the space provided in the answer to show and label your work. You will need to explain each step you use to solve the problem and use the text to support your thinking. At the end of the problem, don't forget to go back to the answer and fill in the correct amount.

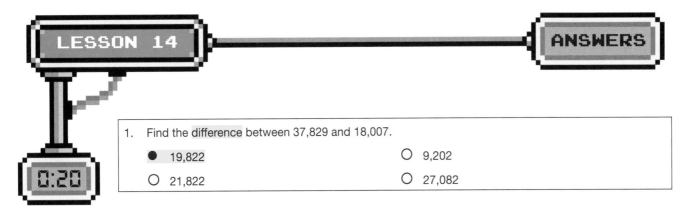

LESSON 14

ANSWERS

0:20

1. Find the difference between 37,829 and 18,007.

   ● 19,822

   ○ 9,202

   ○ 21,822

   ○ 27,082

You are asked to find the difference between two numbers. You should automatically know that you are subtracting. The first strategy you want to use is estimating using mental math. The subtrahend is 37,829. You can round this up to 40,000. The minuend is 18,007. You can round this up to 20,000. If you subtract the two numbers, you will find that the answer will be about 20,000. Using this strategy, you can eliminate 9,202 and 27,082. This leaves you with two possible answers.

The next step is to use scratch graph paper to write your numbers and line up the digits from right to left. Don't forget about regrouping (More on top? No need to stop! More on the floor? Go next door and get ten more! Numbers the same? Zero's the game.).

The final step is to check your answer. In this problem, you can use the difference (19,822) and add it to the minuend (18,007) to see if it equals the subtrahend (the top number). Checking your work does not take a lot of time. You will feel better knowing that you are correct and don't have to go back and check your work at the end of the test when the question has been out of your head for a long time.

2	17			
3	7	8	2	9
1	8	0	0	7
1	**9**	**8**	**2**	**2**

Check your work				
1				
1	9	8	2	2
1	8	0	0	7
3	**7**	**8**	**2**	**9**

2. Find the quotient if the divisor is 8 and the dividend is 96.

   ○ 13

   ○ 14

   ● 12

   ○ 15

This word problem is a simple division question. The words *quotient*, *divisor*, and *dividend* should let you know that you will divide. The tricky part of this question is the vocabulary. You have to know that a *quotient* is the answer, the *dividend* is the number that will be divided, and the *divisor* is what you will divide by. That is why sometimes you will hear your teacher ask, "What is 96 divided by 8?" It is the same question said in a different way.

There are many strategies you can use in division, such as multiples, repeated subtraction, skip counting, or drawing pictures. In class you will be allowed to use tiles or some other manipulative; however, on a test you will not be able to use this strategy. There are several ways to write division problems. For example, 96 ÷ 8, 96/8, and 8⟌96 are all ways to write this problem. Once you have identified that you must solve a division problem, choose the strategy that works best for you.

Possible Strategy: skip counting using a multiplication table, where the first row represents the divisor

1	2	3	4	5	6	7	8	9	10	11	**12**
8	16	24	32	40	48	56	64	72	80	88	**96**

Possible Strategy: long division

```
      12
 8 )96
   - 8↓
     16
   - 16
      0
```

Don't forget to check your answer using multiplication. You can use the divisor (8) and multiply by the quotient (12).

---

3. Mr. Ford wrote these number problems on the board:

$$11 \div 1 = 11$$

$$11 \times 1 = 11$$

Write a different sign (+, −, x, ÷) in each box above that would give the same answer for both number problems. Then write the answers to the problems on the lines. Use your knowledge of properties of math to support your answer.

This problem has a lot of keywords that you will have to figure out before you can solve it. First, you have to figure out what is the question and what is the answer. Then the question asks you to support your answer. Remember that to support means to give facts or examples to justify your answer. *Support* is a performance verb, which means you have to use the ACE strategy to help answer your question.

You are given the hint that you can support your answer using properties of math. This is also the solution to the problem. Your answer should be the ÷ and x symbols. The key to this question is that both word problems need to have the same answer. You can support your answer using the identity property of multiplication. Remember to restate the question. Your answer may read: *I used the division and multiplication sign because they both gave me the same answer to each number problem. I knew this was the answer because the identity property of multiplication says that any factor/number multiplied by 1 says its name (is the same number).*

---

4. There are 117 donuts in the display case at Todd's Bakery. The bakery sells powdered, glazed, and jelly donuts. If there are 26 powdered donuts and 38 glazed donuts in the display case, how many *jelly* donuts are in the display case?

This question does not use any performance verbs, so you will not use the ACE strategy. You are asked to determine how many jelly donuts are in the display case. You are given the total donuts and how many donuts are powdered and glazed.

The first step is to add the number of powdered and glazed donuts (26 + 38 = 64). Then you need to decide how you will get the number of jelly donuts. You have the total number of donuts and the sum of two types of donuts. This means that in order to find out how many jelly donuts you have, you will subtract the number of powdered and glazed donuts from the total donuts. You should use scratch graph paper to line up your numbers from right (ones) to left (hundreds).

0	11	
̶1̶	̶1̶	7
	6	4
	5	3

When you have finished solving your subtraction problem, you will need to check your answer using addition. You can use the difference (53) and add the total number of powered and glazed donuts (64). 53 + 64 = 117. You can then write your answer by restating the question: *The total number of jelly donuts in the display case is 53.*

5. Casey and Holli have been saving pennies. Casey has 433 pennies, and Holli has 142 pennies. How many more pennies does Casey have than Holli? Show all your work.

This word problem is trying to see if you can decide what kind of math you will need to solve the problem. You are given two numbers, representing pennies, and are asked how many more Casey has than Holli. You are asked to show all your math work. This is not a performance verb that will require you to use the ACE strategy. Your answer will be simple math. Make sure you still take the time to check your answer using addition (291 + 142 = 433). This is all you will need to show in the box under the question.

3	13	
4	3	3
1	4	2
2	9	1

6. Adam wants to give 27 baseball cards to 3 of his friends. He gives the same number of baseball cards to each friend. How many baseball cards does Adam give to each friend? Show all your work.

This word problem is trying to see if you can decide what kind of math you will need to solve the problem. You are given two numbers that represent a dividend and a divisor. The word problem gives you a clue by saying each friend got the same number. You will also have to show all your work. This is not a performance verb that will require you to use the ACE strategy. Your answer will be simple division.

There are many strategies you can use in division, such as multiples, repeated subtraction, skip counting, or drawing pictures. One strategy you can use is drawing a picture:

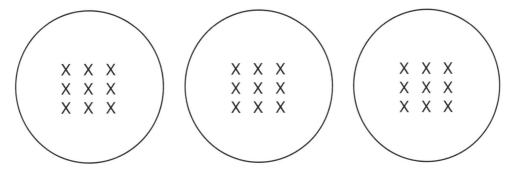

The important point to remember when you are solving simple math questions is to show the steps you took to solve the problem in your head. You have learned all your math facts up to 12. You also have learned how to multiply with two- and three-digit numbers. You need to demonstrate your skills using the strategies you learned to solve division problems. Don't forget to check your work using multiplication (9 x 3 = 27).

LESSON 16

ANSWERS

0:20

biome	An area classified by the climate, soil, animals, and plants living there. Land biomes include tundra, coniferous forests, deciduous forests, chaparrals, grasslands, and deserts. Aquatic biomes include lakes, rivers, wetlands, estuaries, intertidal zones, coral reefs, oceans, and ocean floors.
energy	the ability to do work
matter	any solid, liquid, or gas that has mass and takes up space
organism	any living thing (Examples: plants and animals)
producer	any organism that can produce its own food (Examples: green plants and trees)
consumer	any organism that gets its energy by eating other organisms (Example: humans, sharks, and cows)
herbivore	a consumer that only eats plants (Examples: deer, bees, and butterflies)
carnivore	a consumer that only eats animals (Examples: lions, tigers, and snakes)
omnivore	a consumer that eats both plants and animals (Example: bears, pigs, and skunks)
decomposer	any organism that breaks down dead organic matter and returns nutrients to the environment (Examples: worms, mold, and fungus)
food web	a system of the flow of food made by a food chain
food chain	a group of organisms that transfer energy from a primary source (Example: Plants are eaten by crickets, which are eaten by frogs.)
ecosystem	a community of living things (organisms) that interact with their environment
biotic	an ecosystem's living parts (Examples: plants and animals)
abiotic	an ecosystem's nonliving parts (Examples: soil, temperature, and climate)

LESSON 17

ANSWERS

0:20

Look at the green highlights below. These are instructions for a group of questions that you will have to answer in your state standardized assessment in science. The important pieces of information to understand are how many questions you will have to answer and what you need to know to answer them.

Base your answers to questions 1 through 3 on the water cycle diagram below and on your knowledge of science. Letters A, B, and C represent three processes in the water cycle.

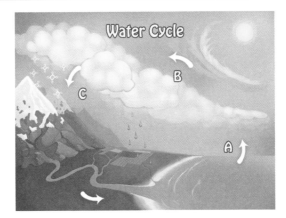

You are asked to identify processes of the water cycle from a picture. The performance verb *identify* means to list or name. In these questions, you will name the **processes** in the water cycle that are represented by a letter. These types of extended response questions are called closed-ended questions because they don't ask you to explain your thinking. Your thinking is explained by being able to look at the picture and identify what processes are taking place. You will have to completely think out all the things you learned about the water cycle. You probably did an experiment in science about condensation and making it rain in an empty soda bottle. As you can see, all the explaining goes on in your brain and your only task is to **identify** what is going on in the picture. If you keep excellent notes in your Science Lab Journal and take the time to write out an explanation for experiments and key vocabulary words, you would be able to study the water cycle during your study time.

1. Identify process **A**. _____

In this process, you have an arrow pointing up from the ocean floor to process B. Evaporation is when water from a water source makes its way up to the clouds in the form of water vapor. So water evaporates from liquid to gas. You can identify/list either the word *evaporation* or *evaporate* in your answer. If you forgot the vocabulary word *evaporate,* you could have identified the process of liquid turning into gas and that would have been acceptable on a state standardized assessment. The key is to know what you are identifying. Remember to always try to answer every question—even if you forgot the exact word. Sometimes you can explain your brain and it will show that you know the process, but may have forgotten the word.

2. Identify process **B**. _____

In this process, the B is on the end of the clouds. You can use the words *condensation* or *condense* to explain this process. If you forget the word *condensation,* you can also explain the process of water turning back into liquid to form clouds. At the very least, you are identifying the process and not leaving the answer blank.

3. Identify two forms of precipitation that return water to the earth's surface in process **C**. _____ and _____.

The following question has many answers. They give you the definition of process C in the question; it is precipitation that returns water to the earth's surface. Scientists observe the world around them every day. You are a living organism that is part of an ecosystem. You make observations about the world around you. When you answer this question, think about the environment you live in. Does it rain, hail, and drizzle? Do you live in a climate where it snows, sleets, or gets freezing rain? The water cycle is something that happens all around you every day. Make sure that you spend time discussing the world around you with your Guide. It is a good strategy to study and write out notes, but it is a better strategy to use those notes to have great discussions with your Guide or friends and practice what you learn.

Base your answers to questions 4 and 5 on this diagram of a food chain.

In these questions, you are asked to look at a food chain and answer two questions. As you prepare to answer this question, think about what you learned about organisms, adaptations, food webs, and food chains. Knowing what information you have to concentrate on is an important strategy in test taking. You have to focus your brain on the one question that is in front of you. For instance, you no longer have to think about the water cycle from the question above because you already finished answering that question. Refocus your brain on this question only.

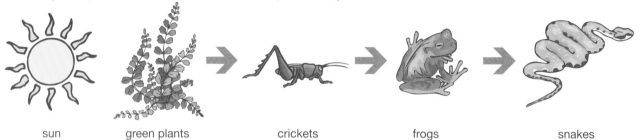

| sun | green plants | crickets | frogs | snakes |

(Organisms not drawn to scale)

4. Identify a predator in this food chain. _____

This question uses the performance verb *identify*. That means you can give a list or name one predator in this food chain. When you answer closed-ended questions on a state standardized test, you need to explain your answer only to yourself. That means you have to remember what you learned from your science labs and explain what you see. In this example, you should know that a predator is an animal that hunts or preys on another animal. In this food chain, the plant can be eliminated because it is not an animal. The cricket can be eliminated because it can only eat the plant. You can choose the frog because it eats the crickets or you can choose the snake because it preys on the frogs.

5. Explain why the population of crickets might decrease if the number of frogs increases.
   _____
   _____
   _____

Question 5 is an open-ended extended response question because you are required to explain what you know about food chains. In this example, you are asked one closed-ended question and one open-ended question. The performance verb *explain* means to make the correct answer clear by giving the reasons how and why. The question asks you to explain why the cricket population might decrease if the frog population increases. You will have to remember what happens in an ecosystem that increases its population of an organism and how that affects other parts of the ecosystem. Don't forget to use evidence from the picture to support your answer. Here is an example of a good explanation:

Restate to **answer** the question: *If the population of frogs increases, the cricket population might decrease because there would be more frogs to feed.*

Cite from the picture: *In this food chain frogs only eat crickets, so more frogs will need to eat more crickets.*

Explain your thinking: *This would happen because there would be fewer crickets to have babies so the population would decrease.*

LESSON 20

ANSWERS

0:20

You may have noticed the theme of these questions: energy. You and your Guide can create a study sheet for energy. You can include vocabulary and facts about energy, how the world around you uses energy, or how you can see different types of energy being used. That is one good strategy to use for study sheets; however, when you review these questions, work on the strategies you learned about being a good test taker. Remember, eliminate wrong answers, understand what the question is asking you to know, and read each answer in the question.

---

1. You would need _____ energy to cut a piece of wood into smaller pieces with a saw.

   ○ light   ○ sound

   ○ heat   ● mechanical

You are asked about the energy that can cut a piece of wood with a saw. Did you put that mental image in your head? Carpenters cut wood into smaller pieces all the time. The first step is to read the question and put each possible answer into the empty space. For example, you would need _light_ energy to cut a piece of wood into smaller pieces with a saw.

After you read each answer, your next step is to eliminate the sources of energy that don't make sense. You could automatically delete _light_ energy as a possible answer because a saw going through wood does get hot, it makes loud noises, and saws are either powered by machine or by a carpenter. You now have three possible answers.

The next step is to think about what you know about energy and apply it to the question. A saw does not produce sound to cut through wood and it does not generate heat that will cut wood. A saw uses mechanical energy because it uses motion to do the work. _Mechanical_ energy is the correct answer.

---

2. To conduct electricity, the best material to use is _____.

   ● metal   ○ glass

   ○ wood   ○ plastic

You are asked what is the best material to conduct electricity. Did you put that mental image in your head? Remember that Ben Franklin conducted energy with a kite and a key. First, read the question and put each possible answer into the empty space.

After you read each answer, your next step is to eliminate the materials that don't make sense. In this instance, you could automatically delete **wood**, **glass**, and **plastic** because they are all insulators. They don't conduct electricity; instead, they can be used to insulate (protect) you from coming into direct contact with electrical currents. Metals are called conductors and are the best material used if you want to conduct electricity. A good study sheet will have all these facts for you to study.

---

3. Which energy transformation occurs when a person hits a xylophone with a mallet?

   ○ electrical to light   ○ light to mechanical

   ○ sound to electrical   ● mechanical to sound

You are asked to think about energy transferring from one object to another, like a drumstick hitting a drum. Did you put that mental image in your head? First, read the question with each response.

Eliminate incorrect answer(s). *Light* and *electrical* do not make sense. You can't get light or electricity from a mallet in your hand hitting a xylophone. You should have eliminated all choices that have light or electrical in them.

Have you figured it out? You eliminated three answers. A mallet uses mechanical energy to produce sound when it hits the keys of a xylophone. Mechanical energy is transformed to sound energy when the two make contact with each other.

---

4. John went out on a cold winter day and rubbed his hands together. The heat that warmed his hands was produced by
    _____.

    ● friction   ○ gravity

    ○ light   ○ magnetism

You are asked what produces heat when two hands are rubbed together. Did you put that mental image in your head? Have you ever been outside playing in the snow and warmed your hands by rubbing them together?

After you read each answer, your next step is to eliminate the ones that don't make sense. In this instance, you could automatically delete **light** as a possible answer. That's because rubbing your hands together does not produce light. You now have three possible answers.

The next step is to think about what you know about the transfer of heat to hands. When two objects rub against each other, they slow down because of friction. Friction between two objects causes heat to be produced. *Friction* is the correct answer. What other objects produce friction?

---

5. A magnet and a metal object will have the strongest magnetic attraction when the distance between them is _____.

    ● 5 centimeters   ○ 10 centimeters

    ○ 15 centimeters   ○ 20 centimeters

You are asked at which distance the attraction of a metal object to a magnet would be the strongest. You have probably worked with magnets many times. Did metal objects go to the magnet faster when you got farther away from the magnet, or did they attach to the magnet faster when you got closer?

Your experiment should show that metal objects attach to a magnet faster the closer you get. In this answer, the shortest distance you can hold the magnet is 5 centimeters. All other answers can be eliminated because they are larger than 5.

LESSON 22

ANSWERS

0:20

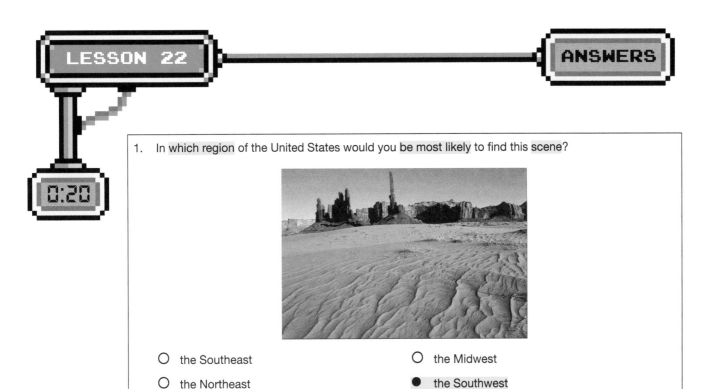

1. In which region of the United States would you be most likely to find this scene?

○ the Southeast

○ the Midwest

○ the Northeast

● the Southwest

This question is taken from the geography theme: regions. You are asked what area of the United States is best represented by the image. The clues in the sentence are the words *which region* and *most likely.*

In the picture, you can see a cactus, the sun, and an empty and desolate land region. If you guessed that you are looking at a desert region, then you are correct. The cactus is the best clue for picking out the region. Through the process of elimination, you probably know that cacti do not grow in the Northeast or the Southeast of the United States. The two answer choices left are possible places where cacti may grow, but the best location for a cactus to grow is in the deserts of Arizona, which is located in the Southwest region. If you chose the *Southwest* as the most likely place to find a cactus, you are correct.

2. Which of these would have been commonly found in early American cities, but **not** in modern cities?

● horse-drawn carriages

○ paved highways

○ large factories

○ traffic lights

When you answer a question with the word *not* in it, you should take a few extra moments to understand what the question is really asking. You are asked to identify the choice that would ordinarily be found in an early American city.

Use the process of elimination to take out the choices that don't make sense. Make a connection between the themes of geography of location, movement, and human environment interaction as they relate to early American cities. Would you find large factories or traffic lights in an early American city? Those answers don't make sense because cars weren't manufactured until 1893, so traffic lights wouldn't have existed and the factories that made cars wouldn't have been invented.

That leaves you with the choices *paved highways* and *horse-drawn carriages.* The question asks you to think about things that were *commonly found* in early American cities. There may have been some cities with paved highways, but there would definitely have been horse-drawn carriages in all cities. The best answer to this question is *horse-drawn carriages.*

3. How did the steamboat change transportation?

- ○ River travel became slower than ever.
- ● People could travel both upstream and downstream.
- ○ Less cargo could be carried on the rivers.
- ○ Land travel became easier and cheaper.

You are asked about the invention of steamboats and how they changed transportation. From this unit, you would have learned that traveling by boat was not a new invention. Early Americans came to North America by boat and settled along the eastern coast of what is now the United States. The steamboat was the first boat powered by an engine that used steam. Therefore, the steamboat had power that didn't need the currents or sails to help it move across water. You can make a connection to the themes of geography of movement and human environment interaction to think about this answer. Early Americans used waterways to move goods quickly from one city to another.

The first step is to eliminate the answers that don't make sense. The answer *River travel became slower than ever* doesn't make sense. Steamboats used engines to move the boat faster. This answer can be eliminated. That leaves you with three possible answers.

Read each of the three remaining answers carefully. People were able to travel to other cities to sell their agricultural goods quickly and then get back to their farms to produce more goods. *People could travel both upstream and downstream* is the best answer because steamboats were big boats for traveling and didn't have any impact on movement by land.

4. What term best describes this kind of community?

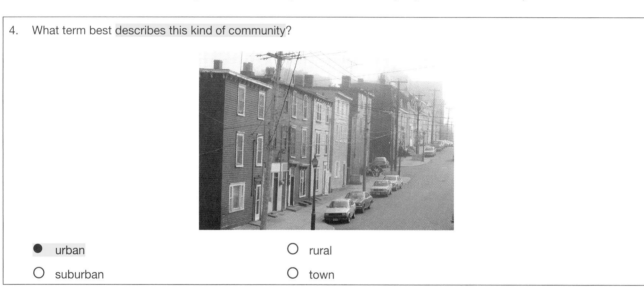

- ● urban
- ○ suburban
- ○ rural
- ○ town

You are asked to recall information about the geography theme of human environment interaction. You are asked to look at a picture and identify (name using evidence from the image) what the picture represents. You have learned that there are three types of communities: urban, suburban, and rural. In this question, the answer *town* can be eliminated because it is not a description of a type of community. A town can be located in any one of these communities.

This question is an example of a fact that you just need to know based on the context of the picture. Suburban communities are located outside of big cities and are usually defined by lots of homes and small shops. A rural community is a large area of land usually used for agriculture. Factories, traffic, and lots of buildings located together in an area is an example of an urban community. The picture represents an urban community.

5. Which city can be located on the map using these coordinates?

Latitude: 40 degrees south, Longitude: 20 degrees east

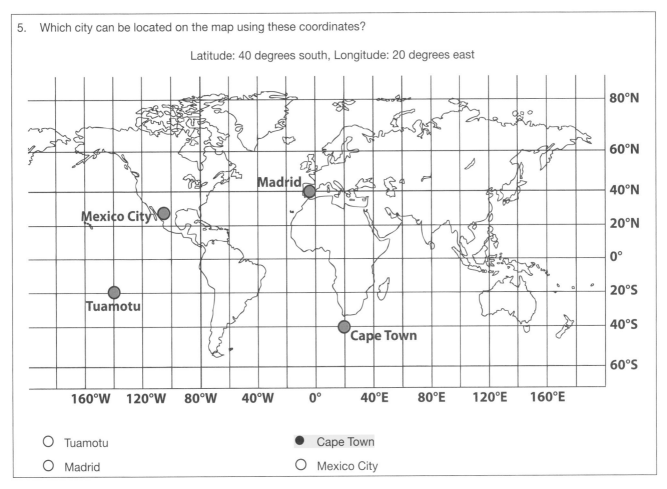

○ Tuamotu ● Cape Town

○ Madrid ○ Mexico City

This question is taken from the geography theme of location. You are asked to demonstrate the use of longitude and latitude to locate a place on a map. You will have to remember which lines represent longitude and which lines represent latitude. You can remember latitude by associating it with the word *lateral*. The word *lateral* means extending side to side. A lateral pass in football is a side pass to a receiver. Word association is a great study technique you can use for any subject. On the other hand, the word *longitude* can be thought of by the first syllable: *long*. The lines of longitude are long from top to bottom. The lines on the globe going from the North Pole to the South Pole are the lines of longitude. If you find the degree for each line of latitude and longitude, you will find the coordinates point to Cape Town.

LESSON 23   ANSWERS

0:20

It is important to know about the planet we live on. Our planet has an abundance of natural resources that only grow in certain regions of the world. You will learn how to locate places on Earth, about the climate in various regions, and how humans interact with their environment. Completing study notes will help you organize what you need to learn and help you make connections between the different main topics that make up geography.

1. The western part of the Northwest is along the _____.

   ● Pacific Ocean   ○ Atlantic Ocean

   ○ Rocky Mountains   ○ Gulf of Mexico

You are asked to identify an area west of the Northwest. The states in the Northwest of the United States are Colorado, North Dakota, Washington, Idaho, South Dakota, Wyoming, Montana, Utah, and Oregon. Oregon and Washington have coastal areas.

After you have a conversation in your head, the first step is to see if you can eliminate one of the choices. The Rocky Mountains are located east of the Northwest. Since it is not the farthest point west, you can eliminate it as an answer. You are left with three choices. The Atlantic Ocean is located to the northeast and the Gulf of Mexico is located to the southeast. If you chose the *Pacific Ocean*, you are correct.

2. The hilly areas between flat lands and mountains are called _____.

   ○ plains   ● highlands

   ○ coasts   ○ plateaus

The main clue is the reference to hilly areas. Hilly areas or a range of low mountains are usually between flat lands and mountains. You can eliminate two choices: *plains* and *coasts*. The plains are grassy flat lands and the coast is the area of land near water. That leaves you with two choices.

These types of questions contain answers that you just need to know by studying the landforms in the context of a text or story or by memorizing the vocabulary words. These types of facts work best in a study sheet. A plateau is an area of land that is flat but raised above the adjoining surface. If you chose *highlands* as your answer, you are correct.

3. The northern and southern halves of Earth are called the _____.

   ○ prime meridian   ● hemispheres

   ○ fault   ○ axis

The main clue is the word *halves*. If you cut the planet in half, what are the two halves called? This question is a fact that you have to memorize or read about in an informational text. You can eliminate the answer choice *fault* because it doesn't have any relationship to half of the planet. You are left with three choices.

The prime meridian is the imaginary line that divides the Eastern and Western Hemispheres, and the axis is the imaginary line that goes through the North and South Poles. The word *hemisphere* means half of a sphere. Earth's shape can be thought of as a sphere and the imaginary line that divides the Northern and Southern Hemispheres of Earth is the equator. If you chose *hemispheres* as your answer, then you are correct.

4. A map that shows about how many people live in an area is a _____.

    ○ climate map   ○ weather map

    ● population map   ○ physical map

When you study geography, you will learn about different types of maps and what they are used for. There are climate maps, population maps, economic maps, physical maps, political maps, road maps, and topographical maps. This question gives you a clue about the type of map that you would need to select. You need to select the type of map that would show how many people live in an area. Weather and climate maps do not show people. A physical map tells you about mountains, grasslands, and desert regions. If you chose *population map*, then you are correct.

5. Identify the two lines that divide Earth into hemispheres.

    The performance verb *identify* means to name or list. In this question, you need to list the names of the imaginary lines that divide Earth into hemispheres. Your answer should be:

    1. equator
    2. prime meridian

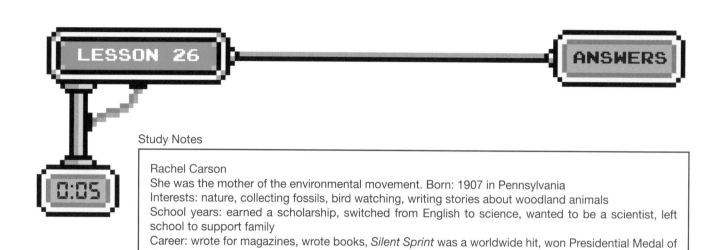

LESSON 26

ANSWERS

0:05

Study Notes

Rachel Carson
She was the mother of the environmental movement. Born: 1907 in Pennsylvania
Interests: nature, collecting fossils, bird watching, writing stories about woodland animals
School years: earned a scholarship, switched from English to science, wanted to be a scientist, left school to support family
Career: wrote for magazines, wrote books, *Silent Sprint* was a worldwide hit, won Presidential Medal of Freedom

LESSON 27

ANSWERS

0:05

Many know Rachel Carson as the mother of the environmental movement. She was born in rural Pennsylvania in 1907. There she showed an early interest in nature. As a girl, Carson collected fossils. She went bird watching. She also loved to write stories about woodland animals.

Carson's family was very poor, but she earned a scholarship for college. She studied English at first, but after one year, Carson changed her focus to science. She wished to become a **scientist.** She did very well, but there was trouble back at home. Over the years, Carson's family farmland had been ruined by factories. Carson's family moved in with her. Soon, she had to drop out of school to care for them. Distressed, she began to write for comfort. Magazines paid for her stories and articles. In this way, Carson supported her family.

Her articles became popular, so Carson began to write books. Her third book, *Silent Spring*, is her most famous. It warned about the effects of pollution on wildlife. She had seen these effects at her ruined family farm. The book was a worldwide hit. It inspired millions to care for the environment. Sadly, soon after the book was published, Rachel Carson died at age 56. After her passing, she was honored with the Presidential Medal of Freedom.

It is important for you to use highlighters as little as possible so that the main ideas and supporting details stand out from the rest of the passage. Highlighters are used to draw your attention to keywords that provide supporting details to a passage.

---

1. When Rachel was a child, what were her interests in nature?

   ○ factories

   ● writing about woodland animals

   ○ reading magazines

   ○ science experiments

The key to this question is the word *child*. When you complete the language arts state standardized assessment, you should always go back to the text to check your answers. You will need to locate the section of the text that explains what Rachel did when she was young. In the text it says, "There she showed an early interest in nature. As a girl, Carson collected fossils. She went bird watching. She also loved to write stories about woodland animals." The correct answer is *writing about woodland animals* because it comes directly from the text.

---

2. Why did Rachel drop out of college?

   ○ Rachel did not have good grades.

   ○ Rachel no longer wanted to become a scientist.

   ● Rachel needed to care for her parents.

   ○ Rachel's parents' farm burned down.

It is very important to know the exact question that you need to answer. This question wants you to give the reason that Rachel had to leave school. Another strategy that is very important in language arts assessments is to read all the answer choices before you select one. This question shows four answers that are all good reasons for Rachel dropping out of school. The text states, "Soon, she had to drop out of school to care for them." The word *them* may be a little confusing because it does not identify who that may be in the sentence. Make sure you read the sentences before and after to identify that *them* refers to Rachel's parents.

3. Why was Rachel Carson's third book, *Silent Spring*, so famous?

   ○ Rachel died and it then became a bestseller.

   ● Rachel wrote about the effects of pollution.

   ○ Rachel talked about the effects of her family farm.

   ○ Rachel was awarded the Presidential Medal of Freedom.

The answers listed to language arts questions can all be verified in the text. The longer the text, the greater the care you have to take in searching for clues to the answer. Read the question and the answers carefully. In this question, you are asked why Rachel's book was famous. If you scan the highlighted text in the passage, then you will be able to locate *Silent Spring* because it is highlighted. Read the sentence before and after this sentence, "It warned about the effects of pollution on wildlife." You will need to use this strategy to make sure you have the exact evidence to answer the question. If you selected *Rachel wrote about the effects on pollution*, then you are correct.

4. What does the term *scientist* mean?

   ○ person that takes care of wild animals

   ○ person that warns against environmental dangers

   ○ person having expert knowledge of natural science

   ● all of the above

This question cannot be answered directly from the text. You need to use what you learned about scientists. Scientists are people that study the world around them. In this question, you will have to use context clues to help you figure out your answer. In the text, Rachel wanted to be a scientist. She also wrote about the effects of pollution on wildlife and on her family's farm. In this question, you have a choice called *all of the above*. That means that all the answer choices could identify the job a scientist would do. When you have questions like this on a state standardized test, you must be sure that all choices are possible answers. *All of the above* is the correct answer.

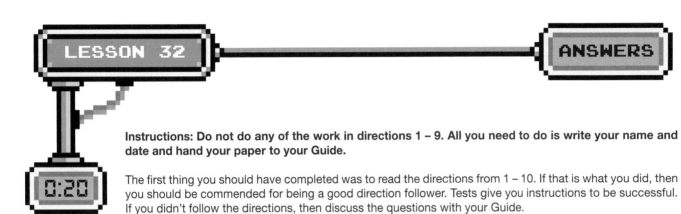

LESSON 32

ANSWERS

0:20

Instructions: Do not do any of the work in directions 1 – 9. All you need to do is write your name and date and hand your paper to your Guide.

The first thing you should have completed was to read the directions from 1 – 10. If that is what you did, then you should be commended for being a good direction follower. Tests give you instructions to be successful. If you didn't follow the directions, then discuss the questions with your Guide.

Were the directions easy to follow?

Discussion: The directions were long but the first and tenth were the most important directions.

Did you read all the directions first before you started working?

Discussion: It is natural to want to begin working right away. However, it is more important that you understand exactly what is expected of you.

Now that you have completed this activity, do you have a better understanding of the importance of following directions?

Discussion: Directions are like clues; they tell you what you need to do to be successful in your task. Think about directions for a school project or a book report. If you miss some of what you are supposed to include, then you have not completed all of the requirements. Listening to and reading directions are the most important tasks to complete before beginning any quiz.

What did you learn?

Discussion: It is important to have a clear mind when you begin a test. A clear direction to achieving success begins with knowing what is expected of you.

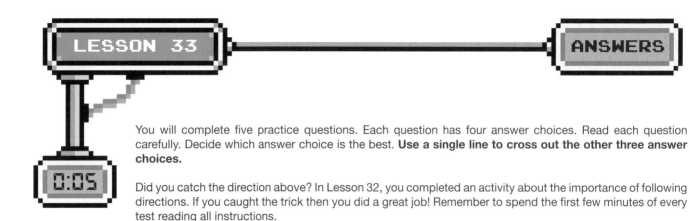

LESSON 33   ANSWERS

0:05

You will complete five practice questions. Each question has four answer choices. Read each question carefully. Decide which answer choice is the best. **Use a single line to cross out the other three answer choices.**

Did you catch the direction above? In Lesson 32, you completed an activity about the importance of following directions. If you caught the trick then you did a great job! Remember to spend the first few minutes of every test reading all instructions.

1. Terry went outside at 9:00 a.m. on a sunny morning and looked at his shadow. He went back out at 10:00 a.m., 11:00 a.m., and noon. Which answer **best describes** the length of Terry's shadow?

   ⊖ His shadow did not change.

   ● It was shorter each time Terry looked.

   ⊖ It was longer each time Terry looked.

   ⊖ It was shorter at 9:00 a.m. than it was at 11:00 a.m.

Your shadow is created when your body blocks the sun's light. The length of your shadow depends on how high the sun is in the sky. You can eliminate the answer *His shadow did not change*, because the statement is not possible. In the early morning sky, the sun is nearer the horizon so your shadow is long. At noon, your shadow is directly overhead so your shadow is at its shortest. In this question, the 9:00 a.m. sun will be closer to the horizon than the 11:00 a.m. sun. This question asked you to choose the best **description** of what happens to Terry's shadow. *It was shorter each time Terry looked* is the correct answer.

2. The primary energy source in all living communities is _____.

   ● the sun

   ⊖ the animals

   ⊖ the plants

   ⊖ the soil

When you were studying ecosystems, biomes, and food chains, you learned that any living organism that can produce its own food (photosynthesis) is a producer. The sun is the primary energy source because it provides a source of food for producers, and those producers provide a food source for herbivores, organisms that eat plants, which are then an energy source for carnivores, organisms that eat other animals. *The sun* is the correct answer.

3. When light hits a dark object, most of the light is _____.

   ● absorbed

   ⊖ reflected

   ⊖ diffused

   ⊖ refracted

This question is difficult because it requires you to know the definition of each term and how it relates to light. In science, you learned that when light hits water the light refracts. When light is diffused, it is spreads out (bends) or scatters due to a white surface. These two choices can be eliminated because both water and white objects do not answer what happens when light hits a dark object. That leaves you with two choices, *absorbed* and *reflected*. When light reflects, it bounces off an object; for instance, light hits a glass mirror and you see your reflection. However, when light hits a dark surface or object, the light is absorbed into that object. You may have noticed that dark clothing in the summer makes you warmer than light-colored clothing. *Absorbed* is the correct answer.

4. Which statement **best** describes the relationship between a lion and a gazelle?

○ The lion is the consumer, and the gazelle is the producer.

○ The lion is the prey, and the gazelle is the consumer.

○ The lion is the predator, and the gazelle is the decomposer.

● The lion is the predator, and the gazelle is the prey.

You are asked to choose the best description of the relationship between a lion and a gazelle. You will need to remember all that you learned about food chains, producers, consumers, and decomposers. You will also need to know the difference between a predator, an organism that hunts for its food, and a prey, an organism that is hunted. The trick to this question is to know that a lion is a consumer and a predator, and a gazelle is a consumer and a prey. As you read each answer, eliminate any choice that does not identify a lion or gazelle properly. That leaves only one answer choice that best describes the relationship between a lion and gazelle: *The lion is the predator, and the gazelle is the prey*.

5. A ball is thrown up into the air. Which force causes the ball to fall to the ground?

○ friction

○ magnetism

● gravity

○ electricity

There is an old saying that you may have heard or even used: "What goes up must come down." Gravity is the force that keeps us from floating into outer space. The gravitational pull of the earth attracts objects. Gravity keeps the air around us and is responsible for ocean tides. *Electricity* and *friction* can be eliminated because they do not describe an object that is pulled toward another object. *Gravity* is the correct answer.

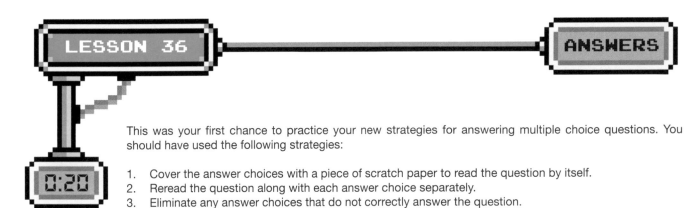

This was your first chance to practice your new strategies for answering multiple choice questions. You should have used the following strategies:

1. Cover the answer choices with a piece of scratch paper to read the question by itself.
2. Reread the question along with each answer choice separately.
3. Eliminate any answer choices that do not correctly answer the question.

Practice Test

1. Choose the sentence that uses **to**, **too**, or **two** correctly.	
○ Amanda likes to dance and she likes to read, **two**.	○ Todd always wanted **too** be a doctor.
● If Jim had **to** make a choice, he would rather play the drums than the clarinet.	○ Lydia hopes **too** help animals when she finishes veterinary school.

When you read this question, you may have realized that the only difficulty you were going to have is in comparing the words *to* and *too*. Very seldom do fourth graders confuse the word *two* for *to* or *too*. Two is a number (2). So any sentence that references something numeric would use the word *two*. The word *too* means also or in excess. You can think of the word *too* as having an extra *o* because you have to add something more to something. The word *to* begins a prepositional phrase (*We went to the movies*) or an infinitive (*We like to watch movies*). In this question, you can eliminate the sentence with the word *two* because it doesn't represent a number. That leaves you with three choices. Although the sentences with the word *too* are infinitives, they are not being used to add to the sentence. *If Jim had to make a choice, he would rather play the drums than the clarinet* is the correct answer.

2. Choose the sentence that uses **there**, **they're**, or **their** correctly.	
○ The baseball team was well prepared for **they're** game.	● **Their** boots are by the front door.
○ Can you hand me that book over **their** on the floor?	○ **There** studying science.

The first thing you may have noticed about this question is the contraction *they're*. If you read the sentence and replace the contraction with the words *they are*, you would quickly be able to figure out that the sentence does not make sense and can be eliminated. The word *their* is a possessive pronoun which means that the noun following belongs to the subject in the sentence. (Examples: their house, their books, their school) If you read each sentence and apply these rules, you could decide if the words *there*, *they're*, or *their* are being used correctly. *Their boots are by the front door* is the correct answer.

3. Choose the sentence that is written **correctly**.	
○ Yes you may open your test booklet.	○ Timothy, on the other hand likes baseball.
● The temperature outside, I think, is perfect.	○ He believes, that going to school is important.

You have to choose the sentence that is grammatically correct. You will practice this almost every day in fourth grade. The lessons you learned about grammar will make great study sheets because there are many rules you will have to know. You can discuss the conventions of grammar with your Guide to develop understanding for this question. Here are the corrected sentences:

Yes, you may open your test booklet.
Timothy, on the other hand, likes baseball.
He believes that going to school is important.

The temperature outside, I think, is perfect is the correct answer.

4.	Which of these is an example of alliteration?	
○ wonderful pancakes	● marvelous milkshakes
○ huge feet	○ glass houses

In this question, the keyword is *alliteration*. This type of question can be difficult because there are no context clues and you have to know what alliteration means. Alliteration is the repetition of an initial consonant sound in two or more neighboring words. There are three answer choices that can be eliminated because they do not have words that have repeating consonant sounds. *Marvelous milkshakes* is the correct answer.

5.	Which of these is an example of an idiom?	
○ The moon is like a light of fire in the sky.	○ The bees buzzed, the horses neighed, and the dog woofed when the farmer went into the barn.
○ The lizard laughed at the silly snake.	● He thought the test was a piece of cake.

This question requires you to know what the keyword *idiom* means. An idiom is language that is specific to a group of people. You may use idioms every day. *I'm so hungry I can eat a horse* and *I can hear you as clear as a bell* are examples of idioms you and your friends would understand. However, in other countries they would have their own idioms and may not understand your idioms. In this question, you are presented with four choices of figurative language. You will need to know how to pick out figurative language, so this may be a good time to create a study sheet.

Simile: The moon is like a light of fire in the sky.
Personification: The lizard laughed at the silly snake.
Onomatopoeia: The bees buzzed, the horses neighed, and the dog woofed when the farmer went into the barn.

If you chose *He thought the test was a piece of cake*, then you knew the definition of an idiom. Great work!

LESSON 37

ANSWERS

0:05

When you change a negative question into a positive statement, you need to focus on the task you are supposed to do. The choices provided are examples of rephrasing the question in your head so you understand what you are supposed to answer. That is what is meant by a positive statement—you are changing the question so you can identify what you need to do or know.

1.   All of the following are supporting details for the story **except**:

Choose the statement that does not explain a supporting detail for the story.

2.   According to the passage, which statement about Athena's dog is **not** false?

Which statement about Athena's dog is true?

3.   Mimi is planning a vegetable garden. Mimi is **least likely** to grow:

Mimi would not choose to grow which type of plant in her garden?

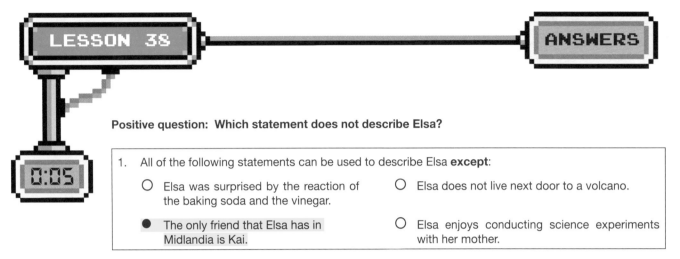

LESSON 38 — ANSWERS — 0:05

Positive question: Which statement does not describe Elsa?

1. All of the following statements can be used to describe Elsa **except**:

    ○ Elsa was surprised by the reaction of the baking soda and the vinegar.

    ● The only friend that Elsa has in Midlandia is Kai.

    ○ Elsa does not live next door to a volcano.

    ○ Elsa enjoys conducting science experiments with her mother.

The first step you should have taken is to cover the answer choices with a piece of scratch paper. Read the question and write out the question as a positive statement to identify the task that you are supposed to complete. It is often difficult when a question asks you to think about the types of answers you don't want and doesn't explain what answer you do want. That is why we call rewriting the question a positive statement; it positively tells you what the question is asking.

The second step was to read the new question with the answer choices, eliminate answers that you know are not correct, and select the best answer choice. *The only friend that Elsa has in Midlandia is Kai* is the correct answer. In the passage, the author states that Elsa liked everyone in Midlandia and went to visit Beaker whenever she went to Midlandia.

Positive question: Which example is not an onomatopoeia?

2. All of the following are examples of onomatopoeia **except**:

    ○ woof, meow

    ○ bang, clink

    ○ tick, tock

    ● massive mountains

This question is difficult because the positive statement above has a *not* in it. This is still considered a positive statement because it identifies the task you need to do. You are looking at each answer and deciding if it is an example of onomatopoeia; the correct answer will not be an example of onomatopoeia.

Using the process of elimination is difficult with these questions because you need to know what onomatopoeia means without context clues; therefore, go through each answer choice and make a decision about which choice best answers the question. Onomatopoeia is a technique an author uses to describe the sound of an object or an action. Woof and meow are sounds a dog and a cat make, so these are great examples of onomatopoeia. Bang and clink are sounds that pots and pans, silverware, or dishes might make. Tick tock is a sound that analogue clocks may make as the second hand moves around the face. In this question, *massive mountains* is an example of alliteration. Alliteration is the repeating of the same initial consonant sound in adjoining words.

Positive question: Which example is an onomatopoeia?

3. The author uses many examples of onomatopoeia in this passage. All of the following are **not** examples of onomatopoeia **except**:

● Her boot heels clicked as she trotted over to greet the kids.

○ "Foam started shooting everywhere!"

○ "You could toast marshmallows whenever you wanted!"

○ Beaker was a scientist, much like Elsa's mom.

When turned into a positive statement, this question is similar to the previous one; however, in this question you are looking for the choice that is an onomatopoeia. After you had covered the answers and rewrote the question into a positive statement, you should have read the new question with each answer choice. In the first answer choice, *boot heels clicked* is an example of the sound a shoe makes when you are walking on pavement. That is a great example of onomatopoeia. Even though you have an answer that makes sense, don't stop checking the other answers. This allows you to check your work and make absolutely certain that you have the correct answer. This is a mistake that many fourth graders make on a state standardized assessment. The first answer seems to be the best answer, so all the other answers remain unchecked. Read through the remaining answer choices; they are clearly not good examples of onomatopoeia, which makes the first choice the best choice. Now when you move on from this question, you can be confident that you have the correct choice and have checked your work.

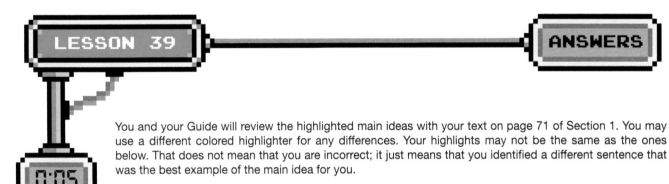

LESSON 39

ANSWERS

0:05

You and your Guide will review the highlighted main ideas with your text on page 71 of Section 1. You may use a different colored highlighter for any differences. Your highlights may not be the same as the ones below. That does not mean that you are incorrect; it just means that you identified a different sentence that was the best example of the main idea for you.

The Importance of Protecting Endangered Species
by Nicole Costlow

The word *extinction* is a scary term. It means that a species of plant or animal has been eliminated from existence on the earth forever. Extinction is a very real threat to thousands of plants and animal species. Sadly, many species face extinction because of human actions. It is important not only to understand how our actions affect wildlife, but also to understand why humans should protect endangered species.

Awareness of endangered species began to grow in 1973 when government leaders passed the Endangered Species Act. This act is enforced by the US Fish and Wildlife Service. This act protects species that fall into two main categories: endangered and threatened. A species becomes *endangered* when it is very close to extinction. A *threatened* species is one that is not yet endangered, but is likely to become so soon. As of 2011, there were 1,383 endangered or threatened species of plants and animals in the United States alone.

Many animals are placed on the endangered or threatened list because humans are destroying their habitats, or where they live. In states like California and Utah, the habitat of the desert tortoise is shrinking due to the construction of new homes. Not only are desert tortoises losing their habitat, but many are killed by the heavy machinery used to build the new homes. Scientists estimate that only about one hundred thousand desert tortoises remain in the wild.

Another species that has suffered due to human interaction and development is the brown bear, commonly known as the grizzly bear. As the bears' natural, wooded habitat changes and disappears, they are forced into areas where humans live in order to find new food sources. When this happens, grizzlies are often shot and killed to keep humans safe. Also, during hunting season, hunters often mistake brown bears for black bears and kill them for sport. Today, brown bears are listed as a threatened species.

Global warming, or climate change, is another serious threat to endangered species. Scientists have found that our planet's temperature is rising. Most believe that this is due to gases released from the fuels many humans use in their daily lives. These gases get trapped in the earth's atmosphere and cause the planet's temperature to become warmer over time. The rising temperatures cause ice to melt in places like the Arctic. This process has caused creatures such as polar bears to be considered threatened animals under the Endangered Species Act.

Polar bears depend on the natural sea ice in the Arctic for their habitat and for hunting. Without it, they will have fewer places to find food and will have to swim father distances to find a resting place. Scientists estimate that there are only about twenty-five thousand polar bears left in the wild. Two-thirds of that population may vanish within the next fifty years if Arctic temperatures continue to rise. That equals more than sixteen thousand polar bears that may be lost due to global warming.

The world's tiger population has suffered some of the greatest loss at the hands of humans. At one time, there were nine different types of tigers in the world. Over the past seventy years, three of those species have become extinct. Today, only a little more than three thousand tigers remain in the wild. The tiger population is shrinking for several reasons. Many were hunted for their fur; others lost their habitat as the human population expanded in countries such as India and China. Luckily for the tiger, organizations such as the World Wildlife Fund have begun efforts to save the species. Their goal is to double the world population of tigers by the year 2022.

There are many reasons why it is important for humans to help save endangered species from extinction. Our own survival may depend on it. Our planet is made up of many different ecosystems. Ecosystems are specific areas of living organisms that all depend on each other for survival. If one species in a particular ecosystem becomes extinct, all of the other living things in that ecosystem will be affected by the loss.

To understand how the extinction of a species can impact humans, it is important to think small. For example, in a forest ecosystem, a certain type of moss growing on a tree could provide shelter for hundreds of insects. Those insects leave their home in the moss to eat certain types of plants in the same forest. While feeding on those plants, the insects pollinate other plants in the forest that feed deer in the area. Humans who live near the forest use the deer as a food source. If the species of moss becomes extinct, the insects have no shelter and eventually die off. This harms the plants, which are no longer being pollinated and cannot grow. Without a plant supply, the deer are forced to move away to find another food source. Once the deer are gone, the humans in the area must find another source of meat for their meals. With the loss of just one species in an environment—even something as small as moss—the entire ecosystem could change forever.

In addition to saving endangered animal species, science has also proven that endangered plants could be extremely valuable to humans. Many medicines commonly used today contain substances from plants, including antibiotics and pain medications. In addition, medicines used to treat serious diseases, such as cancer, have come from plants. Today, there are 794 species of plants listed as endangered or threatened under the Endangered Species Act. Even if only a few of these species become extinct, scientists will lose the chance to study them. They could miss out on finding cures and treatments for diseases that affect people all over the world.

It is very important to understand how our actions on the planet affect the natural world around us. Once extinct, a species, whether beautiful or valuable, is gone forever. When we allow a plant or animal to become extinct, we are not just hurting nature; we could be hurting ourselves.

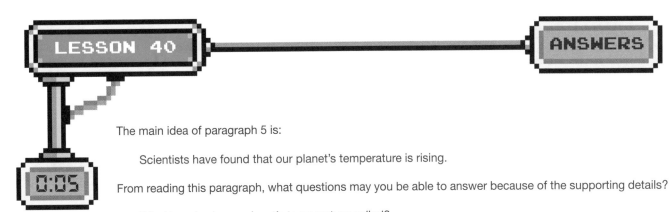

The main idea of paragraph 5 is:

Scientists have found that our planet's temperature is rising.

From reading this paragraph, what questions may you be able to answer because of the supporting details?

- What is a rise in our planet's temperature called?
- How are the gases affecting our planet?
- What does the rise in temperature do to our environment?
- Name a species affected by global warming.
- How is that species affected?

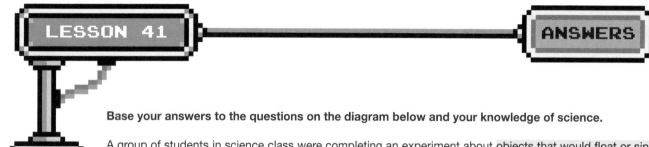

LESSON 41

ANSWERS

0:20

Base your answers to the questions on the diagram below and your knowledge of science.

A group of students in science class were completing an experiment about objects that would float or sink. They had four objects to test. The students dropped a steel nail and a steel spoon into a bucket of water and watched them sink to the bottom of the bucket. They had two experiments left.

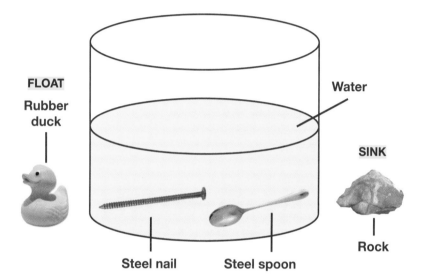

FLOAT
Rubber duck

Water

SINK

Steel nail   **Steel spoon**

Rock

Objects that float displace water, and objects that sink are dense so gravity makes them sink.

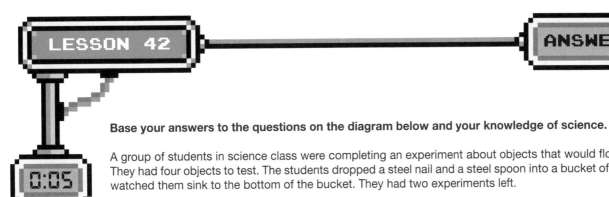

LESSON 42

ANSWERS

0:05

Base your answers to the questions on the diagram below and your knowledge of science.

A group of students in science class were completing an experiment about objects that would float or sink. They had four objects to test. The students dropped a steel nail and a steel spoon into a bucket of water and watched them sink to the bottom of the bucket. They had two experiments left.

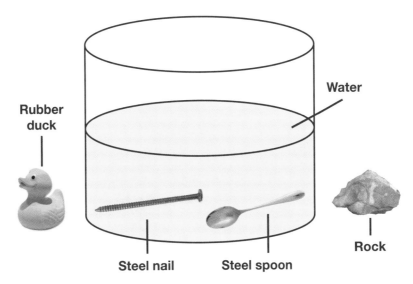

Water

Rubber duck

Steel nail   **Steel spoon**

Rock

Practice Questions

The following questions only have three answer choices.

1. When the rock is placed in the bucket, the water level will _____.

    ○ decrease   ○ remain the same

    ● increase

Using your knowledge of science, you know that whenever an object with a dense mass is placed in water it will sink. An object that sinks moves the water out of the way and takes up space. The space that is taken up by the object will cause the water level in the bucket to increase.

2. The group places the rock in the bucket. Which property can be used to best describe the reason the rock sinks?

    ○ texture   ○ color

    ● density

For this question and the next question, you need to have a good understanding of the science behind whether an object will sink or float. The color of an object does not cause an object to sink or float; therefore, that answer can be eliminated. When an object is placed in water, it will either sink or float. The object may even partially sink. That is because water is being displaced by the mass of the object. Rocks can be dense objects. Dense objects have more mass than objects like the rubber duck so they would displace the water and sink.

3. The group places the rubber duck in the bucket. Which property can be used to best describe the reason the duck floats?

   ● mass   ○ color

   ○ texture

The duck has two properties that allow it to float: mass and shape. In the examples above, the steel nail and the steel spoon sank to the bottom of the bucket. However, there are many boats made out of steel that float. This is because the shape of a boat allows air to remain in the bottom of the boat (hull), which helps it stay afloat. The mass of an object is based on the amount of matter the object contains. The rubber duck's mass and its shape help it float.

LESSON 43

ANSWERS

0:05

Four friends have savings accounts. Each friend adds the same amount of dollars to his or her savings account each month. The table below shows the total amount of money each student has at the end of the month.

Savings Accounts

Month	Account Balance (in dollars)			
	Jason (+3)	Corey	Tyler	Brianne
January	$38.00	$34.00	$32.00	$35.00
February	$41.00	$38.00	$38.00	$40.00
March	$44.00	$42.00	$44.00	$45.00
	$47.00	$46.00	$50.00	$50.00
	$50.00	$50.00	$56.00	$55.00
	$53.00	$54.00	$62.00	$60.00

1. Write the number pattern next to each friend's name that is added to that friend's savings account each month.

You will need to look at each friend's savings account and determine how much money is being added to the account balance each month. This is simply a number pattern. In the question, you were informed that the amount will be the same each month. If you look at Corey's balance ($34.00, $38.00, $42.00), you will be able to determine that his balance goes up by $4.00 every month; therefore, the number pattern is +4. Once you have filled in all of the number patterns next to each name, make sure to check your work and review it again to make sure you are correct.

2. Extend the chart for each friend three more months.

You are asked to extend the number pattern by three numbers. It is uncommon to be asked to extend it more than this because these test questions are not meant to be time consuming. If you look at Corey's March balance of $42.00 and his pattern of +4, you would be able to extend the pattern from $42.00. The new amounts will be $46.00, $50.00, and $54.00.

3. Circle the name of the friend who has the most money at the end of the sixth month and circle the amount.

Tyler did not start out with the most money, but he is adding +6 to his total each month; this is more than any other friend. Jason started with the most, but he only added +3. So in March, he and Tyler had the same amount of money. But when you extend it out, Tyler begins to accumulate the most money by the end of the sixth month. You would circle Tyler's name and the $62.00.

LESSON 44

ANSWERS

0:05

List the three strategies to answering multiple choice questions:

Step 1: Cover the answer choices and read the question.

Step 2: Read the question with each answer choice.

Step 3: Eliminate all incorrect answer choices.

Four friends have savings accounts. Each friend adds the same amount of dollars to his or her savings account each month. The table below shows the total amount of money each student has at the end of the month.

Savings Accounts

Month	Account Balance (in dollars)			
	Jason (+3)	Corey (+4)	Tyler (+6)	Brianne (+5)
January	$38.00	$34.00	$32.00	$35.00
February	$41.00	$38.00	$38.00	$40.00
March	$44.00	$42.00	$44.00	$45.00
	$47.00	$46.00	$50.00	$50.00
	$50.00	$50.00	$56.00	$55.00

Practice Questions

1. If each friend continues saving the same amount of dollars each month, who will have the **most** money at the end of the fifth month?

    ○ Corey   ● Tyler

    ○ Brianne   ○ Jason

You are asked to extend out the monthly account balance for each friend's savings account. You will often have questions like this when you see a table that shows a pattern. This is the reason why you spend time interpreting the data before answering a question. In this question, you will be able to see the highlighted word in the question: *Who will have the most money at the end of the fifth month?* Tyler had the largest increase in savings in the fifth month even though he didn't begin with the most money.

2. Which pattern is the same as Corey's?

    ○ 71, 77, 83, 89 **(+6)**   ○ 10, 15, 20, 25 **(+5)**

    ○ 33, 36, 39, 42 **(+3)**   ● 23, 27, 31, 35 **(+4)**

This question is more difficult because you have to figure out the pattern in all four choices. A good strategy to use is to write the pattern next to the answer choices while you are reading the question with each answer choice. If you took the time to review and interpret the question, you can turn this into a simple matching question. Corey's pattern was to add $4.00 to his savings account each month. The answer choice *23, 27, 31, 35* has the same pattern as Corey's.

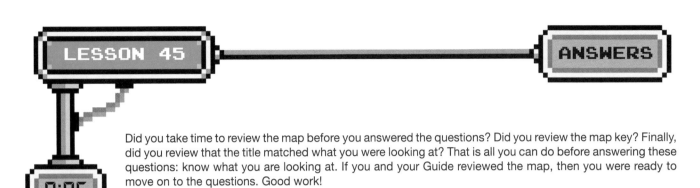

LESSON 45

ANSWERS

0:05

Did you take time to review the map before you answered the questions? Did you review the map key? Finally, did you review that the title matched what you were looking at? That is all you can do before answering these questions: know what you are looking at. If you and your Guide reviewed the map, then you were ready to move on to the questions. Good work!

Base your answers to the questions on the map below.

Rivers and Lakes of Pennsylvania

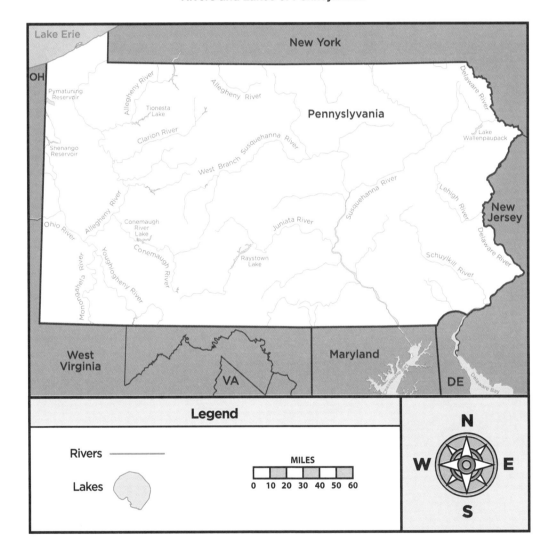

1. Which river forms a boundary between the states of Pennsylvania and New York?

   ● Delaware River   ○ Monongahela River

   ○ Susquehanna River   ○ Ohio River

You need to locate the boundary between the state of New York and Pennsylvania. A boundary is an imaginary line on a map that shows a political border between two landforms. You should be able to locate the border of New York and Pennsylvania that spans east to west. On the eastern boundary, you will see the border turns slightly south. In that area, the Delaware River forms a natural boundary between the two states. On one side of the Delaware River is the state of New York and on the other side is the state of Pennsylvania. The *Delaware River* is the correct answer.

2. Which Pennsylvania river flows into the Chesapeake Bay in Maryland?

   ○ Delaware River   ○ Ohio River

   ● Susquehanna River   ○ Allegheny River

For this question, you have to head south towards Maryland and locate the Chesapeake Bay. There are many rivers in Pennsylvania that flow into the Chesapeake Bay, but according to this map, they all flow into the Susquehanna River first. The *Susquehanna River* is the correct answer.

How did you do with grading this friendly letter? Below you will find highlighted text of all the errors that needed to be corrected. It was a well-written letter with few errors. Were you paying attention? The letter contained three punctuation errors and two spelling errors but was otherwise well written. Compare your grades to the teacher's grade and read the teacher's explanation of the student's work.

506 Memory Lane
Pittsburgh, PA 15232
August 10, 2010

Dear Amanda,

It feels like forever since school ended and we were able to see each other. I can't believe beleve I only saw you a few weeks ago because it feels like forever. My summer vacation has been amazing until this week; boredom has finally set in.

I went to visit my grandmother for a couple of weeks then we went on a family vacation to the beach. At my grandmother's, we went to an amusement park and the zoo. Most days we swam in her pool all day. I was very proud of myself because I learned to dive off a diving board. At the beach I played in the sand, went boogie boarding, and read lots of books. My tan looks great!

This is my first week back at home and there is nothing exciting going on. My mom is starting to buy me school clothes, a new book bag, and school supplies. Most days I just go out and ride my bike. That is definitely not as exciting as the first part of my summer.

I hope the summer time has been good for you, too. I can't wait to hear here about your summer vacation.

Your friend,
Elise

Grade:
Salutation and Closing: **3** This letter was very well written. Your opening and closing are well done and have the appropriate indenting.

Body of Letter: **3** The paragraphs and sentences in your letter are complete, well written, and have varied transition words. Your opening paragraph is a great explanation of what your letter is about and your closing paragraph sets the purpose for you writing. Great work!

Conventions of Writing: **2** You have a few errors in punctuation and spelling. These are called the conventions of writing because they measure your ability to use good grammar and sentence formation so the message of the letter represents what you wanted the reader to know. A good strategy for you to use would be to proofread your work before you make a final draft.

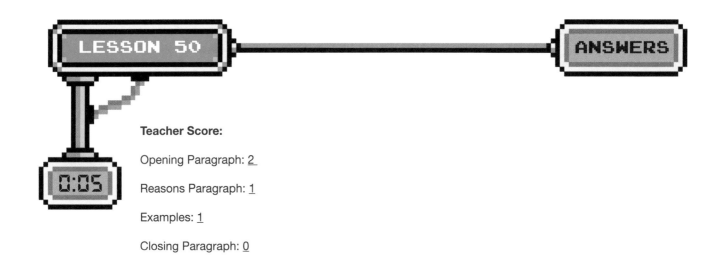

LESSON 50   ANSWERS

0:05

Teacher Score:

Opening Paragraph: 2

Reasons Paragraph: 1

Examples: 1

Closing Paragraph: 0

Conventions of Writing: 1

School Uniforms Should Not Be Required

Task: Opening Paragraph, Conventions of Writing

Some teachers say that uniforms are a great way for schoolwork to be a priority. I don't think that is true because kids are going to learn whatever they want. After thinking about the way I feel there is no way uniforms should be required in school.

This paragraph doesn't contain an attention-grabbing opinion statement. The reader doesn't know why the writer is stating this opinion. The opening paragraph task was given a 2 even though the student's opinion is clearly stated and easy to understand.

The following opening statement would have turned this score into a 3:

What if you went to school and looked like everybody else? I say no way! Recently, there has been a movement, by teachers and principals, to have schools require school uniforms for all students. Some teachers say that uniforms are a great way for schoolwork to be a priority. I don't think that is true because kids are going to learn whatever they want. After thinking about the way I feel there is no way uniforms should be required in school.

The opening sentence contains an attention-grabbing statement for the reader to think about. The closing sentence states the student's opinion.

Task: Reasons Paragraph, Examples, Conventions of Writing

My parents don't think that I what I wear is important or gets in the way of my schoolwork. However teachers feel that letting kids where the latest fashions causes many fights in school that interferes with class. I think my parents are right and your only going to get a grade that is for how smart you are and not for what clothes you wear. It must be the kid's that can't dress as nice as I do that are jealous. These are all the reasons that some teachers insist that school uniforms should be worn.

The Reasons Paragraph task was given a *1* because it only included one reason to support the opinion. Next, the Examples task was given a *1*; it did not fully support the reason. The teacher gave credit for the "voice" of the paragraph, even though the errors made the paragraph difficult to follow and the voice inconsistent. Finally, the Conventions of Writing task was given a *0* because the paragraph contained many errors in spelling, grammar, and punctuation. Please see the following corrections that needed to be made.

The paragraph cannot be corrected to be a *3*, but you need to see the errors in the Conventions of Writing task:

My parents don't think that ~~I~~ what I wear is important or gets in the way of my schoolwork. However, teachers feel that letting kids wear ~~where~~ the latest fashions causes many fights in school that interferes with class. <u>I think my parents are right,</u> ~~and your~~ <u>you're only going to get a grade that is for how smart you are and not for what clothes you wear</u>. It must be the kids ~~kid's~~ that can't dress as nice as I do that are jealous. These are all the reasons that some teachers insist that school uniforms should be worn.

In the Reasons Paragraph and the Examples tasks, you will need to provide a minimum of two reasons in your own paragraphs with examples. When you complete your writing, you should read the essay out loud in your head, sentence by sentence, to fix any grammatical, punctuation, and spelling errors. By doing this, you will certainly be able to earn a *2* or *3* in the Conventions of Writing task.

The following paragraphs could have been used to earn a *3* in the tasks mentioned above:

Some teachers feel that students pay too much attention discussing fashion during group activities. That was an actual opinion my teacher shared with the class. I couldn't disagree more. I think that any student that lets fashion interfere with schoolwork may not have the right friends. Paying attention in class and learning each subject make kids smarter. You can't get smarter because of clothes.

My parents don't think that what I wear gets in the way of my schoolwork. They enjoy buying me clothes that express my individuality. Every year my mother and I spend a lot of time planning out appropriate outfits for school. When I look nice then I feel confident and that helps me concentrate better in school.

Task: Closing Paragraph and Conventions of Writing

For all of these reasons and a ton more, no one should require schools to make students wear school uniforms.

The score issued for the Closing Paragraph was a *0* because it is not a paragraph. It is one sentence that restates the writer's opinion but doesn't clearly summarize his reasons. A paragraph is a group of sentences that explain one main topic or idea. Paragraphs contain an opening sentence, one or more detail sentences, and a closing sentence.

The following paragraphs could have been used to earn a *3* in the Closing Paragraph task:

I rest my case! It is clear to me that I'm not going to be smarter just because I wear a uniform to school. School uniforms will not help me make better friends either. For all of these reasons and a ton more, no one should require schools to make students wear school uniforms.

The following is the completed essay that would be scored a *3* for all tasks:

What if you went to school and looked like everybody else? I say no way! Recently, there has been a movement, by teachers and principals, to have schools require school uniforms for all students. Some teachers say that uniforms are a great way for schoolwork to be a priority. I don't think that is true because kids are going to learn whatever they want. After thinking about the way I feel there is no way uniforms should be required in school.

Some teachers feel that students pay too much attention discussing fashion during group activities. That was an actual opinion my teacher shared with the class. I couldn't disagree more. I think that any student that lets fashion interfere with schoolwork may not have the right friends. Paying attention in class and learning each subject make kids smarter. You can't get smarter because of clothes.

My parents don't think that what I wear gets in the way of my schoolwork. They enjoy buying me clothes that express my individuality. Every year my mother and I spend a lot of time planning out appropriate outfits for school. When I look nice then I feel confident and that helps me concentrate better in school.

I rest my case! It is clear to me that I'm not going to be smarter just because I wear a uniform to school. School uniforms will not help me make better friends either. For all of these reasons and a ton more, no one should require schools to make students wear school uniforms.

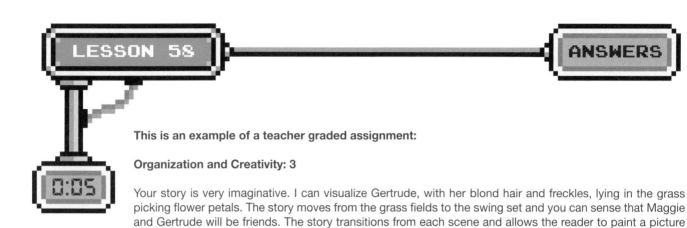

LESSON 58

ANSWERS

0:05

This is an example of a teacher graded assignment:

Organization and Creativity: 3

Your story is very imaginative. I can visualize Gertrude, with her blond hair and freckles, lying in the grass picking flower petals. The story moves from the grass fields to the swing set and you can sense that Maggie and Gertrude will be friends. The story transitions from each scene and allows the reader to paint a picture in his head.

Character(s): 3

As the narrator and main character, Maggie's personality through her thoughts and actions allows the reader to make a judgment about the character. Your use of actions, thoughts, and speech also allows the reader to get to know the character.

Setting: 3

As a reader I was able to picture Maggie observing Gertrude, the memory of Todd and Gregg laughing at Maggie, and the unfortunate incident at the swing sets. The use of vivid and descriptive details allows the reader to imagine a school playground.

Problem and Solution of the Story: 3

As you begin the story, a reader can quickly imagine Maggie's problem; she doesn't feel like Todd is a good choice because he has cooties. The story uses a nice transition towards solving Gertrude's problems with a cootie shot.

Conventions of Writing: 3

Your story is very well written. There is a variety of transitions with good punctuation. Also, there are no spelling or grammar errors.

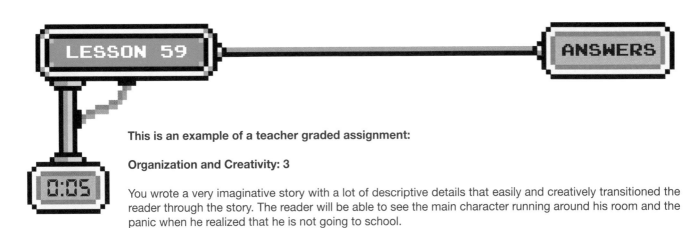

LESSON 59

ANSWERS

0:05

This is an example of a teacher graded assignment:

Organization and Creativity: 3

You wrote a very imaginative story with a lot of descriptive details that easily and creatively transitioned the reader through the story. The reader will be able to see the main character running around his room and the panic when he realized that he is not going to school.

Character(s): 2

Your main character is very clear. The reader will be able to get to know your main character through actions, speech, and thoughts; however, it is difficult to tell whether the main character is a girl or boy. In the second paragraph, the character is first introduced as just *she*, which could make it difficult for the reader to immediately figure out that it is the main character's mother.

Setting: 3

From the bedroom to the eating place, and from the car to the doctor's office, you did an excellent job of transitioning through different settings in the story. In the story, you wrote *She was standing there in her pajamas*, which made that setting difficult for the reader to figure out. In other settings, you used some descriptive words to describe the *frosty window*, the *snowy streets*, and the *cold table*, which let the reader picture a cold winter's day.

Problem and Solution of the Story: 3

Your story did an excellent job of creating a problem for the main character; he unexpectedly finds out he has to go to the doctor. My favorite part in your story takes place when the main character doesn't feel the shot he feared. Great work!

Conventions of Writing: 1

It is important that you take the time to read the final draft of your story out loud in your head or with your Guide. You have frequent errors in spelling, punctuation, and grammar.

Please review the story. Corrections to the original story are highlighted.

I Made It out Alive, Barely

I woke up and it was a day just like any other. I rolled out of bed to peek out of the frosty window, making sure no more snow had fallen. In ~~maine~~ Maine, it is always best to check for a snow day before getting ready. Seeing that I would have school today, I turned my back to the window and with a ready, set, go, I ran and dove onto my bed, bouncing off and landing with a crash on the other side. My clock read 6:45 a.m., I'm late! Why didn't my mom wake me up? I rushed around the room getting dressed, bouncing on one foot to get my last sock on, and I dashed out my door and down the ~~stares~~ stairs.

~~She~~ Mom was standing there in her pajamas and robe. She hadn't ~~brush~~ brushed her hair yet. She slid the pancakes from the skillet onto my plate~~.~~, ~~Seeing~~ seeing that I was confused because she was not ready to drive me to school yet. She smiled and pointed to the calendar, "You have a doctor appointment today, I'll drive you to school afterward." My heart dropped into my stomach as I took a huge gulp. I hated going to the doctor. I knew I was getting a shot. I sat nervously in my chair, barely able to eat as my mom went to get ready for the day.

We sat bundled up in the car, driving down the snowy street heading into town. Before I knew it, we had arrived at the office. I walked as slowly as I could toward the door, watching my breath turn into clouds that swept ~~pass~~ past my head. We walked in the door and I headed for the chairs as my mom went to check in at the counter. It's not fair, making me sit and wait. I could feel my nerves building up and my hands starting to shake. Shortly after my mom sat down, a nurse came out and said, "Bobby, you ready?" Here we go.

I sat on the cold table looking around at all the cartoon characters that were plastered on the walls. That's it, I couldn't take it anymore. I hopped ~~of~~ off the table and hid underneath it. Raising my head up to my mom I whispered, "They can't find me under here!" With a giggle, she told me to get back on the table and I reluctantly did. There was a knock on the door and the doctor came in and did the exam with ice cold hands. He finished and said the nurse would be in to give me my shot.

She came in carrying her tray with the needle and bandage on it. I looked at her panicked and she said with a smile, "Don't worry, it'll be over before you know it." I closed my eyes and started crying, I know it is going to hurt! She might as well just chop off my arm! Oh how awful it will feel, I won't be able to move my arms for days. "Okay, you're done," she said, "I told you it wouldn't be bad!" I looked down at the bandage on my arm, wondering if I actually got a shot.

LESSON 60

ANSWERS

0:05

This is an example of a teacher graded assignment.

Organization and Creativity: 1

Your story is creative. The reader can picture a girl's worst day out with her grandmother. The transitions throughout the story make it difficult to separate characters, events, settings, and other elements of the story. The lack of separate paragraphs makes the story difficult for the reader to transition through.

Character(s): 2

The narrator and her grandmother are the definite characters in your story. You do a nice job of describing the grandmother's appearance and the narrator's thoughts and actions. However, the reader is not given a chance to really get to know the narrator's appearance and can only picture the grandmother's appearance through her hat. You will need to add more descriptive and vivid words to help the reader picture the character's appearance, thoughts, and actions.

Setting: 1

Your story informs the reader where the story takes place but doesn't give any details of the setting beyond the location of a diner and a jukebox.

Problem and Solution of the Story: 1

Your story attempts to describe the main character's problem; the narrator clearly does not want to go to lunch with her grandmother and her grandmother's friends. The solution does not develop from events in the story. There is no transition through the story that leads to the narrator solving a problem; in fact, the reader cannot determine if the reader ended up enjoying the outing with her grandmother or finding a way to make the most of the situation.

Conventions of Writing: 0

Your story contains numerous errors in spelling, capitalization, punctuation, and grammar. The errors make the story difficult to follow for the reader. Your story will need to undergo major revisions in conventions and organization to fix the grammatical errors.

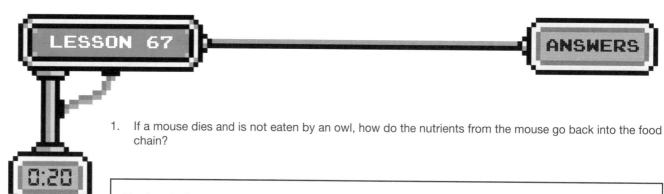

LESSON 67

ANSWERS

0:20

1. If a mouse dies and is not eaten by an owl, how do the nutrients from the mouse go back into the food chain?

Monique's Answer:

It lies on the ground and decomposes and that provides nutrients to the grass, plants, and trees.

How would you and your Guide restate the question? Provide your answer on the lines below.

When a mouse dies and is not eaten by an owl, the nutrients from the mouse go back into the food chain because the body decomposes into the soil.

When you restate your answer, you let the reader know that you understood that the mouse was the subject of the question, and that your knowledge of the science content led you to use the word *decomposes* to explain what provides nutrients to the food chain.

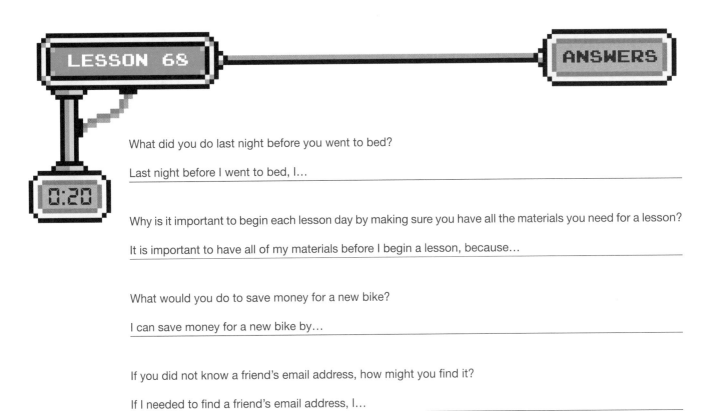

LESSON 68

ANSWERS

0:20

What did you do last night before you went to bed?

Last night before I went to bed, I...

_____

Why is it important to begin each lesson day by making sure you have all the materials you need for a lesson?

It is important to have all of my materials before I begin a lesson, because...

_____

What would you do to save money for a new bike?

I can save money for a new bike by...

_____

If you did not know a friend's email address, how might you find it?

If I needed to find a friend's email address, I...

_____

LESSON 70

ANSWERS

0:20

The following answers are samples. Your answer may not match the restatements below.

1. What two commands would you train your puppy to perform if you want it to be well behaved?

    Closed: I would teach my puppy to sit and stay to be well behaved.

    Open: If I wanted my dog to be well trained, the commands I would teach are...

2. What advice would you give a new pet owner who is having difficulty training his puppy?

    Closed: I would advise new pet owners to be patient if they are having difficulty training their puppy.

    Open: The advice I would give a new pet owner who is having difficulty train his puppy is...

3. How can seeds from plants and trees be dispersed?

    Closed: Wind and water can cause seeds from plants and trees to disperse.

    Open: Seeds from plants and trees can be dispersed by...

4. What is one responsibility of the judicial branch of the United States government?

    Closed: The judicial branch of the United States government judges whether federal, state, and local governments are acting within the law.

    Open: One responsibility of the judicial branch of the United States government is...

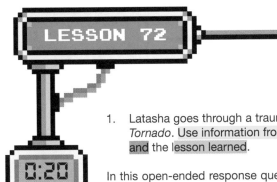

LESSON 72

`0:20`

ANSWERS

1. Latasha goes through a traumatic event but learns a very valuable lesson in *Latasha and the Little Red Tornado*. Use information from the passage and your own ideas or conclusions to describe the tragedy and the lesson learned.

In this open-ended response question, there are two tasks. You have to use information from the passage and your own ideas or conclusions to describe the tragedy that took place in the story. Then you have to use information from the passage and your own ideas or conclusion to describe the lesson that Latasha learned. The conjunction *and* will help you determine the tasks, and the conjunction *or* will help you decide how to provide an answer. You may need to review the lesson on performance verbs to help you determine what *describe* and *conclude* require for an answer.

You will have two restatements. The restatement you and your Guide wrote may or may not be similar to the restatements below.

The traumatic event that Lastasha goes through is… (open)
The lesson that Latasha learned from this terrible tragedy is… (open)

2. Explain why Latasha chose to go on a walk with Ella alone instead of having Ricky accompany them and identify the consequences of her choice. Use information from the story and your own ideas to support your answer.

This open-ended response question also has two tasks. First, you will need to explain why Latasha chose to walk Ella alone instead of with Ricky. The conjunction *instead of* requires you to describe Latasha's choice in your answer. Then, you have to identify the consequences of Latasha's actions. The conjunction *and* helps you identify the two tasks in the question.

The following are examples of restatements for the open-ended question above. The restatement you and your Guide wrote may or may not be similar to the restatements below.

Latasha chose to walk Ella without Ricky because she was angry with him for stealing her report. (closed)
The consequences of Latasha's choice were that Ella got away from her and was later hit by a car. (closed)

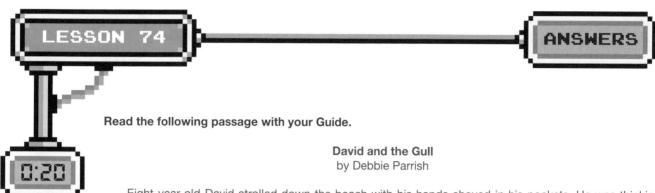

LESSON 74   ANSWERS

0:20

Read the following passage with your Guide.

David and the Gull
by Debbie Parrish

Eight-year-old David strolled down the beach with his hands shoved in his pockets. He was thinking and letting the sand drift through his toes as he went. David had just moved to the coast of North Carolina. His dad had gotten a new job in that community. While he was going to miss his friends, David had to admit that living near the Atlantic Ocean was going to be fun. As he walked, he kicked around a bent up can that was lying on the beach. When he got near the pier, David grew a bit tired. He sat down on a thick piece of driftwood that had washed up on the shore under the pier. David sat quietly, tossing the can he had been kicking from one hand to the other.

ACE: The following is an example of an answer to this question.

1. Identify how David feels about his move to North Carolina. Use evidence from the text to support your answer.

    David is both sad and excited about his move to North Carolina. David is sad because he will miss his friends. David is excited because living by the Atlantic Ocean will be fun.

LESSON 76

ANSWERS

0:20

Directions:
• Read a short passage with your Guide.
• Highlight the main idea in each paragraph.
• Read the questions provided at the end of the passage.
• Circle all the performance verbs.
• Do not answer the questions provided. You are preparing yourself to answer the questions.

Vacation to Disney World
by Brianne Kovacs

Every year families take vacations. Vacations are the best way to relax and create bonding experiences with the family. There are many destinations to choose from, but Disney World is the perfect option. Disney World offers attractions for all ages, affordable options, and endless family activities.

Disney World has all kinds of attractions and foods that we all can enjoy. They have thrilling roller coasters, slower rides, and water rides. Throughout the year, they have all kinds of parades, musical shows, and fireworks. Favorite Disney characters are available to have their picture taken with everyone. Along with all of this, Disney offers entertaining dining and shopping for its visitors.

Disney offers packages for a place to stay and tickets to their park. For adventurous families, they offer camps to stay at. Hotels are available to cater to families with lower incomes. For families that want nothing but the best or would like to experience luxury they, offer five-star hotel stays. Disney has family and group packages, too.

Disney is one of the best ways to ensure the family has fun while bonding. Thrilling rides can cause siblings to hug each other and admit they really do love one another, while long walks from ride to ride allow families time to talk and laugh together. Disney also offers individual activities for when members of the family need a short break from each other.

Disney is the best option for our family vacation. Disney provides fun and educational bonding experiences and affordable options for all types of families. Adults and children can appreciate the opportunities provided by a Disney vacation. At the end of the day, hearing, "You're the best, mom and dad," will make it all worth it.

1. Identify the purpose of this essay and interpret the author's opinion. Use evidence from the essay and your knowledge of persuasive essays to support your answer.

2. Conclude whether the author was able to persuade or dissuade your opinion. Use evidence from the persuasive essay to support your answer.

Do you remember what each circled performance verb means? You and your Guide should review the following table as a reminder.

Skill	Definition
analyze	to examine parts (of a story or a math problem) and see how they fit together
compare	to look at similarities and differences of parts
conclude	to reach an opinion or decision
contrast	to look at differences of two or more parts
construct	to make or create something out of parts
describe	to show/express in words what something is like
evaluate	to make a decision or judgment using your own words
explain	to make the correct answer clear by giving reasons (how and why)
formulate	to develop a new idea based on information already given
identify	to name or list using evidence from text
infer	to draw a conclusion beyond what is stated
interpret	to explain the meaning of
plan	to organize your answer
predict	to tell what could happen next
restate	to use your own words to state the question
review	to read your answer again out loud in your head to make sure it is well written
revise	to make changes to your answer to correct any grammar or spelling errors
summarize	to briefly state only the main points
support	to give facts or examples to justify your answer
trace	to describe a path or sequence

LESSON 77

ANSWERS

0:20

1. Identify the purpose of this of this essay and interpret the author's opinion. Use evidence from the essay and your knowledge of persuasive essays to support your answer.

Answer:
The author's purpose is to persuade the reader that going to Disney World is the perfect option for a vacation.

Cite:
In the essay, the author states that Disney World is the perfect option because it has all kinds of attractions that everyone can enjoy.

2. Conclude whether the author was able to persuade or dissuade your opinion. Use evidence from the persuasive essay to support your answer.

Answer:
The author was able to convince me that Disney would be a great place to take a vacation.

Cite:
The author stated that Disney was a great place for families to have bonding time and that is a very important part of keeping the love in a family.

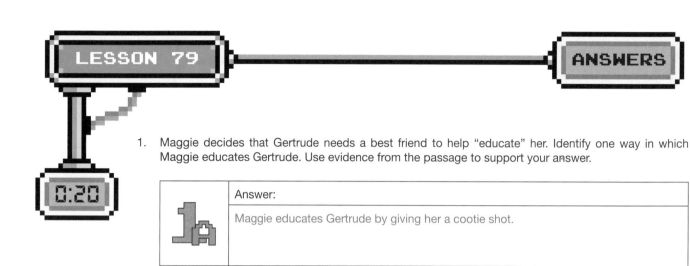

LESSON 79   **ANSWERS**

`0:20`

1. Maggie decides that Gertrude needs a best friend to help "educate" her. Identify one way in which Maggie educates Gertrude. Use evidence from the passage to support your answer.

1A	**Answer:** Maggie educates Gertrude by giving her a cootie shot.
2C	**Cite:** In the story, Gertrude is lying by herself in the grass pulling petals to see if Todd likes her but Maggie thinks boys have cooties and plans to save Gertrude.

The task of this question is for you to identify a way Gertrude is educated. The performance verb *identify* means to name or list using evidence from the text. The answer above uses a closed restatement to answer the question. Restatements should have part of the question in the sentence so that you can inform the reader what question you are answering. The explanation summarizes the part of the text that supports the answer.

2. In the story, Maggie injures Gregg while swinging on the swing set. Using evidence from the passage to support your answer, and your own personal knowledge, evaluate whether Maggie should have consequences for her actions.

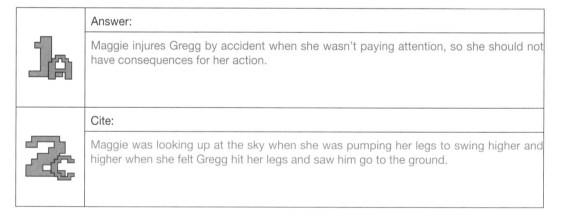

1A	**Answer:** Maggie injures Gregg by accident when she wasn't paying attention, so she should not have consequences for her action.
2C	**Cite:** Maggie was looking up at the sky when she was pumping her legs to swing higher and higher when she felt Gregg hit her legs and saw him go to the ground.

The task of this question is to evaluate whether Maggie should have consequences for kicking Gregg in the head. To *evaluate* means to make a decision or judgment using your own words. The same strategy is used to answer and cite this question. It is important to not copy any text from the passage directly. When you cite evidence from the text, it has to directly support the *A* part of the response. After you answer the question, the cite part of your response lets the scorer know what led you to give the answer that you wrote.

0:20

1. Amy's mother spends a lot of time explaining wild animals to her. Use evidence from the text to evaluate where Amy's mother was able to convince Amy that wild animals do not make good pets.

	Answer:
	Amy's mother was able to convince Amy that wild animals do not make good pets.

	Cite:
	Amy's mother explained how each animal has a habitat that is different than a human's habitat and it would unfair for the wild animal.

The task of this question is to evaluate whether Amy was convinced that wild animals do not make good pets. To *evaluate* means to make a decision or judgment using your own words. In the answer, your response is an opinion. You have to decide whether you were persuaded by Amy's mother explanation. In the student response, the student's opinion was that Amy's mother was able to convince Amy by explaining how each animal needs its own habitat.

Read the following sentence from the passage above.

"I need a pet," was Amy's glum reply.

2. Amy decides that she wants a pet but informs her mother that she "needs" a pet. Using evidence from the text and your knowledge of needs and wants, evaluate if Amy's statement is logical.

	Answer:
	Amy's statement that she needs a pet is not logical because a pet is not food, clothing, or shelter.

	Cite:
	In the text, Amy comes to the conclusion that she could live without a pet and really just wants one.

The task of this question is to evaluate whether Amy needs a pet. To *evaluate* means to make a decision or judgment using your own words. This question also asks you to use your knowledge of needs and wants. The difference between needs and wants is a concept that you may have learned in a previous grade but is very important to always remember. You may remember that needs are food, clothing, and shelter. This is a difficult one because the answer and the cite sections don't require the explanation above until you start learning about the *E* in ACE. Be patient, you are almost there.

LESSON 89

ANSWERS

0:20

Directions for the Open-Ended Questions

The following questions are open-ended questions. Remember to:

- read each question carefully and think about the answer.
- answer all the parts of the questions.
- show your work or explain your answers.

You can answer the questions by using words, tables, diagrams, or pictures.

Look at the map below.

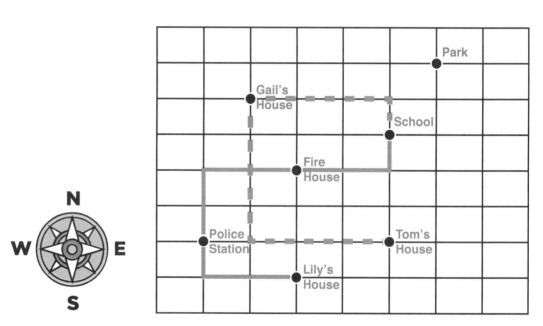

1. Lily left her house and followed this list of directions:

   1. Walk two blocks west.
   2. Walk three blocks north.
   3. Walk four blocks east.
   4. Walk one block north.

   Use the map to help you list all of the places Lily passed on her walk, including the place where she ended her walk.

2. After school, Gail is going to Tom's house to study for the big test. She wants to stop at home first to get her study notes.

   Make a list of directions that Gail can follow to walk from school to her house and then to Tom's house.

ACE

Student Work Area

1. Using the map, I determined that each square was one block that ended on the **+** between each block. I used a highlighter to trace the path Lily took using the compass rose to calculate my directions. When Lily leaves her house and follows the directions given to her, she passes the police station during the three blocks north and the fire house during her walk four blocks east. She ends her walk at the school after going one mile north.

2. 2. When I had to make directions for Gail to go home from school to grab her study notes and then to Tom's house, I had two choices. I could have sent Gail back to the school and then go south to Tom's house or I could have her walk south from her house. I chose to have Gail follow a new route. The list below is a set of directions that Gail needs to get to Tom's house.

Leave school and walk one block north.

Walk three blocks west; grab your study notes out of your house.

Leave your house and walk four blocks south.

Walk three blocks east; you are at Tom's house.

Score: 4

This student gave great responses to the open-ended response questions. He clearly answers the questions for each task. His extensions demonstrate a clear understanding of map concepts. He understands how to use a compass rose, and he extends his answer by describing a map key to identify what he considers one block. The only thing that could have made his response clearer was to point out that the map was missing a key element, the map key. He could have provided one by drawing a map key. Other than that, this student was able to answer the question and extend his answer.

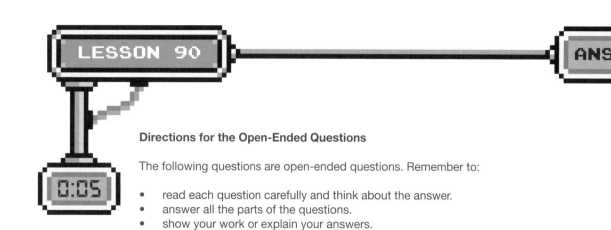

LESSON 90   ANSWERS

0:05

Directions for the Open-Ended Questions

The following questions are open-ended questions. Remember to:

• read each question carefully and think about the answer.
• answer all the parts of the questions.
• show your work or explain your answers.

You can answer the questions by using words, tables, diagrams, or pictures.

Pick a Plan

This month, Mr. Sadler's telephone bill included information about a new long distance plan being offered. The plans are listed below.

Current Plan	New Flat Rate Plan
Monthly service fee of $8.75	No monthly service fee
Plus $.09 for each call	$.30 for each call

Mr. Sadler generally makes fewer than 30 long distance calls each month. Which plan would you advise him to use to spend the least amount of money?

Show all your work. Explain in words how you found your answer. Tell why you took the steps you did to solve the problem.

Student Work Area

Possible Answers:
Appropriate answers could have a reasonable range.

Current Plan	New Flat Rate Plan
number of calls chosen by student x .09	number of calls chosen by student x .30
add monthly service fee of 8.75	
Reasonable price ranges: $8.84 – $11.45	Reasonable price ranges: $0.30 – $9.00

Possible starter restatements can include:
[Open] I would advise Mr. Sadler to choose (current plan or new flat rate plan)…
[Closed] In my computation, it is a better choice for Mr. Sadler to choose the (current plan or new flat rate plan).
The answer should also include a statement about the cost of the plan.

Cite/Compute:
The number of calls chosen by the student can range from 1 – 30 because the question states that Mr. Sadler makes less than 30 calls.
The student should demonstrate computational skills using decimals.
Computation in the Current Plan should include an additional $8.75 added to the multiplication problem.

Explanation:
A step-by-step explanation during calculations using math vocabulary words like *multiplication with decimals*, *factors*, *product*, *addition*, and *add-on*.

Plus:
The student should mention that the decimal has to be carried over two spots in the final product.
The student can mention that decimals are carried because money includes cents.
The student can make a text-to-world connection that talks about budgeting and saving money. He may also mention that the cost savings could be put into a savings account.
The student can make a text-to-self connection that includes what he might do with the cost savings.
The student can make a text-to-text connection about a story where a similar decision was made and what was done with the cost savings.

LESSON 91   ANSWERS

0:05

Directions for the Open-Ended Questions

The following questions are open-ended questions. Remember to:

• read each question carefully and think about the answer.
• answer all the parts of the questions.
• show your work or explain your answers.

You can answer the questions by using words, tables, diagrams, or pictures.

1.   Phyllis drew the following figures to make a pattern.

PART A

• Draw the next figure in the pattern. Use your knowledge of math patterns to describe the rule of the pattern in words.

PART B

Phyllis decided that she was going to try a new pattern using numbers to see if her classmate Aaron could find the missing numbers. Phyllis wrote the following pattern.

63, ___, 49, 42, 35, ___, ___, 14

Aaron wrote the following answer:

63, **56**, 49, 42, 35, **28**, **22**, 14

• Phyllis checks Aaron's work and finds an error. Evaluate Aaron's response and explain the error he made in the pattern. Demonstrate the correct number pattern, and describe the rule for the number pattern.

Student Work Area

Part A

Possible Answer(s):
The next figure in the pattern is ✖.

Possible Cite/Compute response(s):
The pattern is a smiley face, a down arrow, a smiley face, and an ✖.

Possible Explanations:
Student explanation should acknowledge that patterns repeat.
Student explanation should acknowledge that he needed to determine the symbol that marks the end of the pattern.

This pattern is a repeating pattern so I just had to figure out where the pattern begins again. In this example, the symbol ✖ ends the pattern before it begins again.

PART B

Possible Answer(s):
Aaron's error is the number 22.
Aaron uses – 6 in one of the numbers and gets a 22 instead of a 21.
Aaron doesn't follow the pattern of – 7.

Possible Cite/Compute response(s):
In this example, the rule is subtract 7 from each number.
In this example, the rule is to subtract 7 from the previous number.
In this example, all the numbers are multiples of 7.
In this example, all the numbers are divisible by 7.

Possible Explanations:
Student should acknowledge that Aaron made an error in calculation.
Student should acknowledge that the rule should be repeated for all numbers.

Aaron made a mistake in solving the math problem when he accidently subtracted 6 from the number 28. Aaron should apply the same rule for each number in the pattern.

LESSON 92   **ANSWERS**

0:05

Directions for the Open-Ended Questions

The following questions are open-ended questions. Remember to:

- read each question carefully and think about the answer.
- answer all the parts of the questions.
- show your work or explain your answers.

You can answer the questions by using words, tables, diagrams, or pictures.

Corin, Darryl, and Leeann collected 14 leaves for science class. Darryl has 5 leaves. Corin has fewer leaves than Darryl. Leeann has twice as many leaves as Corin.

Part A

Use the scratch paper and the counters (   ) provided to complete Part A.

In the table below, write the number of leaves that Corin and Leeann have.

LEAVES COLLECTED

Name	Leaves
Corin	3
Darryl	5
Leeann	6
Total	**14**

Part B

On the lines below, explain how you found your answer. Use words, symbols, or both in your explanation.

ACE

I started with 14 counters to represent the leaves and removed Darryl's five leaves. That was 14 − 5 = 9. I took the 9 counters and knew that Corin has fewer leaves than Darryl, which means that Corin has less than 5 leaves. So the answer is Leeann has to have 6 and Corin has to have 3.

Score: 2

Scorer Comments: The student answer is correct. The student also adequately cites evidence from the table to demonstrate that he comprehends that a total of 14 leaves were collected and that 5 are accounted for by Darryl. The explanation, however, is not sufficient to draw a conclusion about the student's process. The student shows some evidence of an explanation by checking his counter work using standard math. Further clarification would be needed to determine why the student chose to give Corin 3 leaves and Leeann 6.

LESSON 93

ANSWERS

0:05

Directions for the Open-Ended Questions

The following questions are open-ended questions. Remember to:

- read each question carefully and think about the answer.
- answer all the parts of the questions.
- show your work or explain your answers.

You can answer the questions by using words, tables, diagrams, or pictures.

Corin, Darryl, and Leeann collected 14 leaves for science class. Darryl has 5 leaves. Corin has fewer leaves than Darryl. Leeann has twice as many leaves as Corin.

Part A

Use the scratch paper and the counters (   ) provided to complete Part A.

In the table below, write the number of leaves that Corin and Leeann have.

LEAVES COLLECTED

Name	Leaves
Corin	3
Darryl	5
Leeann	6
Total	14

Part B

On the lines below, explain how you found your answer. Use words, symbols, or both in your explanation.

I started with 9 counters because I had to remove Darryl's 5 leaves from the 14 total leaves collected. I checked my work using math, 14 − 5 = 9. I knew that Corin had to have fewer leaves than Darryl, so I started with 4, that split the counters to 5 leaves for Leeann and 4 for Corin. I checked my math, 9 − 5 = 4. In the problem it says that Leeann has twice as many leaves as Corin but 5 is not twice as many as 4. I gave Corin 3 leaves and Leeann 6 leaves. Since 3 + 3 = 6, I knew that this was the correct answer. I checked my work, 3 + 5 + 6 = 14, and knew all the rules were followed.

Score: 4

Scorer Comments: The student answer is correct. The student clearly uses evidence from the text and his own knowledge to demonstrate comprehension of the problem. He uses logical steps to work through the problem and explains it clearly enough to be replicated by a reader.

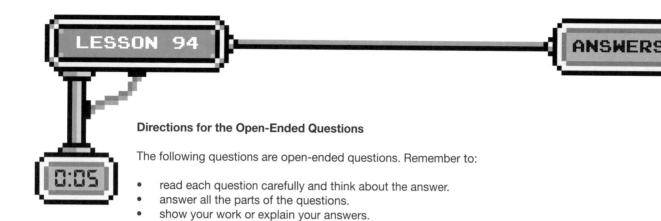

LESSON 94

ANSWERS

0:05

Directions for the Open-Ended Questions

The following questions are open-ended questions. Remember to:

- read each question carefully and think about the answer.
- answer all the parts of the questions.
- show your work or explain your answers.

You can answer the questions by using words, tables, diagrams, or pictures.

Students in fourth grade track their homework assignments on a bulletin board in each class. When 1,000 homework assignments have been completed, they will earn an extra hour of recess. The chart below shows how many homework assignments have currently been completed by each class.

Homework Assignments Completed

Mrs. Simpson	Mr. Givens	Ms. Lewis

Part A

Determine the number of homework assignments the three classes have currently completed. Show all your work.

	1	1	
	3	3	4
	2	5	5
+	3	1	7
	9	0	6

Part B

The students would like to know how many more homework assignments they need to complete to achieve their goal of 1,000. Using mental math, if you divided the remaining homework assignments among the three classes evenly, *about how many* would each class need to complete? Use words, symbols, and math to describe your answer.

ACE

Possible Answer(s):
Student needs to demonstrate understanding of mental math and use the following vocabulary: *about*, *approximately*, and *around*.
Student can round the approximate missing homework assignments up to 100.
Student can round the approximate missing homework assignments down to 90.
Student will approximate that each class can complete 30 homework assignments.

Possible Cite(s):
Student needs to demonstrate understanding that mental math requires no manual calculations.
Student needs to demonstrate comprehension of the concept of thirds, equal division, and rounding.

Possible Explanation(s):
Student can demonstrate understanding that approximates are not equal and some classes may accomplish more than others.
Student can demonstrate an understanding that mental math can be used to solve problems quickly.
Student can demonstrate an understanding of goals and teamwork.

LESSON 95

0:05

ANSWERS

Directions for the Open-Ended Questions

The following questions are open-ended questions. Remember to:

- read each question carefully and think about the answer.
- answer all the parts of the questions.
- show your work or explain your answers.

You can answer the questions by using words, tables, diagrams, or pictures.

1. Edythe made a banner for her sister Emme. She taped the tall edges of 10 pieces of paper together as shown below.

WELCOME   HOME   EMME!

Part A

Each piece of paper is 22 centimeters wide and 28 centimeters tall.

Solve for the perimeter of one piece of paper and show your work.

	1	2	
		2	2
		2	8
		2	2
		2	8
	1	0	0

The answer can have a varied process.

Part B

Edythe and Emme's father would like to hang the banner on a wall in the entryway of the house. He measures the space on the wall at 250 centimeters wide by 300 centimeters tall. Analyze the measurements of the wall to the total width and height of the banner to determine if the banner can hang in the entryway wall space. Use words or symbols to explain your work.

Possible Answer(s):
The banner will fit in the space provided.
The banner will definitely fit height-wise and just make it width-wise.
The student will define the width of the banner as 220 (22 x 10) centimeters wide and 28 centimeters tall.

Possible Citation(s):
Student will demonstrate an understanding that each paper is 22 inches wide and that there are 10 pieces.
Student can provide a labeled model drawing of the wall space and banner.
Student will demonstrate an understanding that height is related to tall, as width is related to wide.

Possible Explanation(s):
Students can describe the connection that height is not affected by the 10 pieces of paper and that it will always be 28 centimeters.
Students can describe that relative position of the banner to the space provided height-wise gives the father options for hanging the banner.
Students can acknowledge that centimeters are not a standard measurement for height of walls.

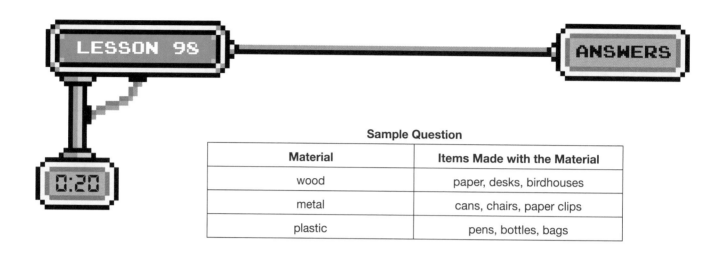

LESSON 98   ANSWERS

0:20

Sample Question

Material	Items Made with the Material
wood	paper, desks, birdhouses
metal	cans, chairs, paper clips
plastic	pens, bottles, bags

ACE

Part A

1. Identify and explain whether each material is a renewable or nonrenewable resource.

Possible Answer(s):

Wood is a renewable resource because it comes from trees and you can plant more trees.
Metal is a nonrenewable resource because once mined from the earth it is not easily replaced.
Plastic is a nonrenewable resource because it is manufactured from chemicals and is not easily replaced.

Part B

2. Describe one way to conserve nonrenewable resources.

Possible Answer(s):

One way to conserve nonrenewable resources is to… (open restatement)
recycle metals and plastics.
reuse containers.
reduce use of plastics.

Possible Cite(s):

In the examples from the chart, you can recycle the plastic bags and bottles in a recycling bin.
In the examples from the chart, you can use scrap pieces of wood to build birdhouses.
In the examples from the chart, you can refill old plastic water bottles with water from the faucet.

Possible Explanation(s):

Describe the impact on the earth's environment from pollution.
Explain the effects on a living organism's ecosystem.

LESSON 99

ANSWERS

0:05

1. A group of fourth grade students in the Science Club constructed a weather station in the woods behind their school. They recorded the temperatures and amounts of precipitation during the days they were there.

Weather Observations

Day	High Temperature (°C)	Precipitation (centimeters per day)
Monday	26	1
Tuesday	20	3
Wednesday	22	0
Thursday	27	0
Friday	21	6
Saturday	28	2

- Explain how the Science Club collected data for the temperature.
- Explain how the Science Club collected data for precipitation.
- Identify another condition that the Science Club might include in describing the weather, and explain how information about this condition could be gathered.

ACE

The Science Club collected the temperatures using Celsius instead of Fahrenheit all week. The Science Club then collected data for precipitation by collecting precipitation and measuring it in centimeters each day of the week. The Science Club could have also included the number of cloudy and sunny days as another condition and not included the partly sunny or cloudy days so it doesn't get confusing.

Score: 0

Scorer Comments: The student attempted to use appropriate restatements in his response, but unfortunately all three responses are inaccurate or incorrect.

LESSON 100

ANSWERS

0:05

1. A group of fourth grade students in the Science Club constructed a weather station in the woods behind their school. They recorded the temperatures and amounts of precipitation during the days they were there.

Weather Observations

Day	High Temperature (°C)	Precipitation (centimeters per day)
Monday	26	1
Tuesday	20	3
Wednesday	22	0
Thursday	27	0
Friday	21	6
Saturday	28	2

- Explain how the Science Club collected data for the temperature.
- Explain how the Science Club collected data for precipitation.
- Identify another condition that the Science Club might include in describing the weather, and explain how information about this condition could be gathered.

ACE

The Science Club collected data for the temperature by using a thermometer with Celsius degrees on it. The Science Club collected precipitation using a tool that had centimeters as a measurement. Another condition that the Science Club might include in describing the weather is the windy, cold, or raining conditions outside using words. They can gather this information by looking outside to see what the weather is like.

Score: 1

Scorer Comments: The student correctly identifies the tool that the Science Club can reasonably use to collect data, a thermometer. The student's use of a tool to describe the way precipitation is collected is vague and incorrect. No credit is given for that response. The student reasonably identified another weather condition that can be tracked by the Science Club; however, he did not explain or extend a reasonable tool or system that the Science Club could use to gather the data.

LESSON 101

ANSWERS

0:05

1. A group of fourth grade students in the Science Club constructed a weather station in the woods behind their school. They recorded the temperatures and amounts of precipitation during the days they were there.

Weather Observations

Day	High Temperature (°C)	Precipitation (centimeters per day)
Monday	26	1
Tuesday	20	3
Wednesday	22	0
Thursday	27	0
Friday	21	6
Saturday	28	2

- Explain how the Science Club collected data for the temperature.
- Explain how the Science Club collected data for precipitation.
- Identify another condition that the Science Club might include in describing the weather, and explain how information about this condition could be gathered.

ACE

The Science Club collected the data for temperature by probably using a thermometer. A thermometer measures the temperature in two ways by Celsius or Fahrenheit. They probably picked the same time every day to measure temperature so they could control variables. Because it's a science club, they probably have access to a rain gauge to collect data for precipitation. They probably had to choose a time each day to check the rain gauge and write the amount of precipitation in the gauge and then empty it out for the next day. Finally, they could measure another condition like wind speed with an anemometer. The Science Club can observe the anemometer for one minute and count how many times it spins in a minute. Each spin is a mile per hour of the wind.

Score: 4

Scorer Comments: This student clearly demonstrates comprehension of subject matter and task. His insightful extensions about knowing about controlling for variables during an experiment, the tool used to collect rain appropriately, and his knowledge of a tool to measure wind speed clearly connects his thinking to the real world.

LESSON 106

ANSWERS

0:20

Use the map to answer the question below.

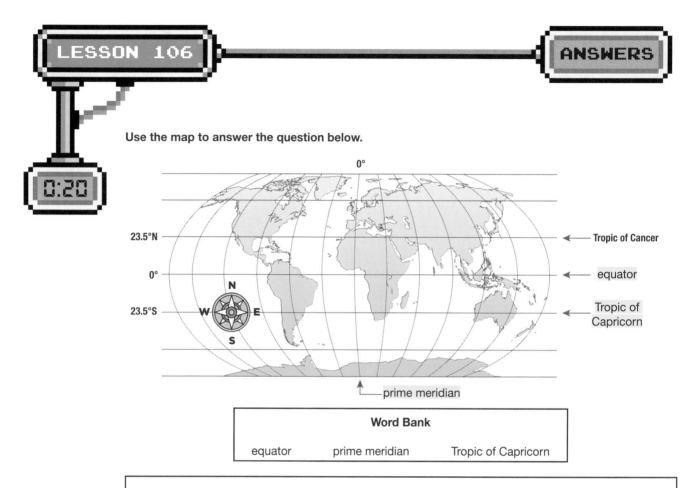

Word Bank		
equator	prime meridian	Tropic of Capricorn

ACE

1. Mindy was given this map with only the Tropic of Cancer labeled. Label the map using the words in the word bank. Describe the significance of at least one of these imaginary lines.

Possible Answer(s):
The significance of the (Tropic of Capricorn, Tropic of Cancer, equator, prime meridian) is… (open restatement)
divides Earth into halves.
shows Earth's axis.
divides Earth into hemispheres.
shows where the tropics are.
separates lines of latitude from north to south.
separates lines of longitude east to west.

Possible Cite(s):
The equator is at 0° latitude.
The prime meridian is at 0° longitude.
The Tropic of Capricorn is 23.5°S.
The Tropic of Cancer is 23.5°N.

Possible Explanation(s):
The area between both Tropic lines is where the rainforests and tropical islands are located.
Earth spins on an imaginary axis that goes directly through the North Pole and South Pole.
The equator and prime meridian split Earth into four hemispheres.
Every line of latitude below the equator is labeled south because it is in the Southern Hemisphere.

LESSON 107

ANSWERS

`0:05`

Use evidence from the image or passage to respond to the following question.

ACE

1. List two improvements the railroad industry had to make to replace canals as the most popular method of transporting goods and people.

Possible Answer(s):
Build sturdier bridges.
Build solid road beds.
Replace wooden rails with iron rails.
Make railroad travel safer.
Make railroad travel faster.
Make railroad travel more efficient.

Possible Cite(s):
Heavy carloads caused rails to break frequently.
Weak bridges added to the danger/hazard of railroad travel.
People were slow to accept railroads as transportation.

Possible Explanation(s):
Railroads made travel easier and faster.
You could connect to hillsides.
Goods and services were easier to transport.
Farmers could sell goods without spoiling or rotting.
People could travel and visit cities faster.

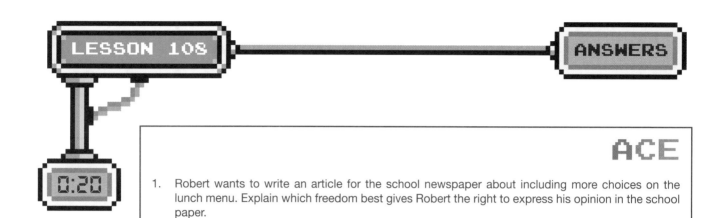

LESSON 108   **ANSWERS**

0:20

ACE

1. Robert wants to write an article for the school newspaper about including more choices on the lunch menu. Explain which freedom best gives Robert the right to express his opinion in the school paper.

Robert has the right to write an article for the school newspaper because of his right under freedom of the press. He is publishing his opinion about the choices given in school lunches. The Bill of Rights was written into the Constitution to give every American ten rights as a citizen.

Score: 4

Scorer Explanation: The student clearly made a connection between Robert's decision to write his opinion in the school newspaper and freedom of the press. He was able to articulate that Robert was giving an opinion about how he feels about school lunches. The student also clearly identified the Bill of Rights in his response.

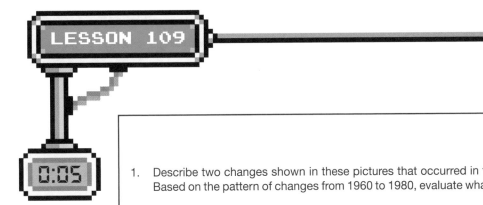

LESSON 109   ANSWERS

0:05

ACE

1. Describe two changes shown in these pictures that occurred in the town between 1960 and 1980. Based on the pattern of changes from 1960 to 1980, evaluate what the town might look like in 2000?

The two changes the town made between 1960 and 1980 are that they added more houses for people to live in and a restaurant on Main Street. Based on the pattern in the pictures, the town might look more like a city in 2000. I say this because when you increase a population, people are going to need more stores for groceries and house stuff. That means they will need stores to supply people with their wants and needs.

Score: 3

Scorer Explanation: The student clearly provides a response to the two tasks in the question using evidence in the image to support his first response. The answer to the second question was unsupported by evidence from the text; the student didn't identify the effects of Main Street in the year 2000. The student shows a thorough understanding of economic concepts by extending his response to include an increase in demand based on an increase in population.

LESSON 110

ANSWERS

0:20

ACE

1. Identify one type of transportation used by the people of the Asian community shown in this picture. Explain the importance of the river to the people of this Asian community.

Possible Answer(s):
by ship
by boat
by canoe
by water

Possible Cite(s):
In the picture there are:
*   many different types of boats.
*   people traveling on canoes.
*   people loading cargo on ships.

Possible Extension(s):
Refer to history of travel in the United States: canals, railroad, ships.
Show a connection to the colonies on the East Coast.
Show a connection to personal travel by boat.
Show a connection to transporting goods and services by water.
Show a connection to Asian community then and now.

LESSON 114　　　　ANSWERS

0:05

Use evidence from the poem and your knowledge to answer the following question.

Mrs. Bertges read the following poem to her class. After reading the poem, Eliana observed, "This poem doesn't begin in the month of December." Levi did not support Eliana's statement and thinks that the poem only talks about the month of December.

ACE

1. Evaluate both points of view and determine whose view you agree with. Use evidence from the text to support your answer.

Possible Answer(s):
The author begins the poem in the fall months.
The poem begins in the month of October or November.
I agree with Eliana's observation.
Levi should agree with Eliana's observation.
Eliana's observation is correct; the poem doesn't begin in the month of December.

Possible Cite(s):
The author starts the poem with...
The author states...
When the author states...
- warm fall colors on the leaves, it means it is fall and the leaves are changing.
- the chill of winter air comes rushing in, it could mean that winter hasn't started.
- there are still leaves on the trees, it could mean it is still fall.

Possible Explanation(s):
Winter doesn't officially begin until December 21.
Text-to-self: anticipate winter beginning, enjoy snow, like when the leaves change, personal appreciation for a white winter, personal connection to not being able to see seasons, special holiday food.
Text-to-world: not all areas get to see changing leaves, some families don't celebrate Christmas, special food for holidays, knowledge of holiday celebrations in other countries.

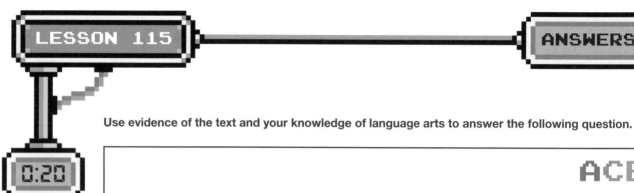

LESSON 115   ANSWERS   0:20

Use evidence of the text and your knowledge of language arts to answer the following question.

ACE

1. Identify the author's purpose of the passage. Evaluate the response and draw a conclusion on the author's feelings about visiting New York City.

The author's purpose was to persuade the reader to visit New York City. "New York is an outstanding place to live." The author wants to live there. I don't want to live in New York City because it is too crowded and I might get lost and scared. The author may not have went to New York City and doesn't know what it would be like to live there. That is why I know that the author is trying to persuade.

Score: 1

Scorer Comments: The student clearly identified the author's purpose but didn't answer the task of evaluating the author's feelings about New York City. Also, the student quoted directly from the text and didn't use the evidence provided to support the response. The student should have summarized the text to support the response that the sentence is evidence of a persuasive essay. The student's personal reflection doesn't support the answer or evidence from the text. When the student "explains his brain," he should evaluate his personal opinion or feelings on the passage's ability to persuade or not persuade him. A better explanation could be:

The author didn't persuade me to visit New York, because I think that New York is too crowded and that would scare me.

LESSON 116

ANSWERS

0:05

Use evidence from the news article and your knowledge to answer the following question.

ACE

1. Trace through the events that caused the popcorn explosion. Explain at least one effect the explosion had on Kettle Township and decide if it was a negative consequence or a positive consequence.

Possible Answer(s):
A consequence of the popcorn explosion was…
- two tons of popcorn spilled.
- no one was hurt.
- no real damage to the factory.
- people helped with the clean up.
- the town had to figure out how to clean up the popcorn.
- free popcorn for the entire week.

Possible Cite(s):
The entire community was working together.
Mr. and Mrs. Poplar's arguing caused the explosion.
The manager of the local grocery store helped with the clean up.
The Poplars will continue popcorn production when clean up is complete.

Possible Explanation(s):
Connections can be made with text-to-text, text-to-self, or text-to-world.
Learning that arguing never ends well.
Bringing the community together is a positive.
Compare to a similar story that had consequences due to an argument.

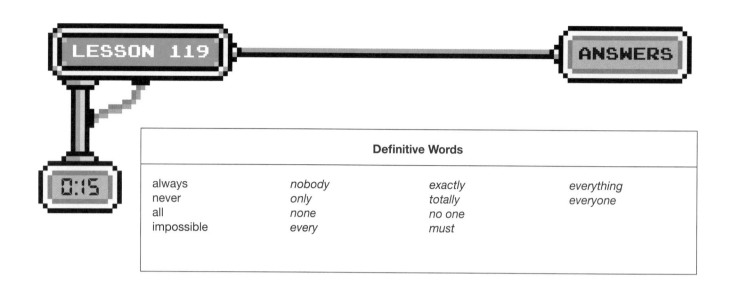

LESSON 119

ANSWERS

0:15

Definitive Words

always	*nobody*	*exactly*	*everything*
never	*only*	*totally*	*everyone*
all	*none*	*no one*	
impossible	*every*	*must*	

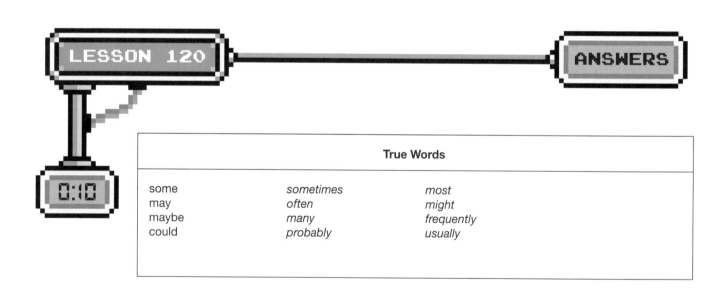

LESSON 120

ANSWERS

0:10

True Words

some	*sometimes*	*most*
may	*often*	*might*
maybe	*many*	*frequently*
could	*probably*	*usually*

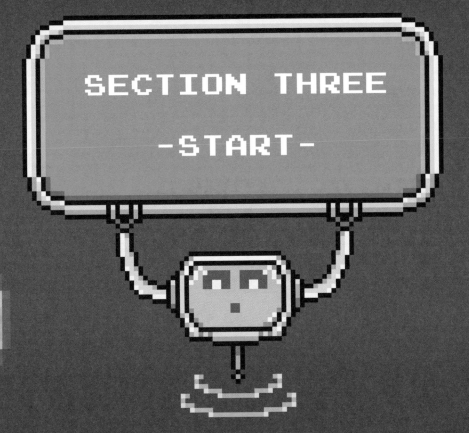

SECTION THREE

-START-

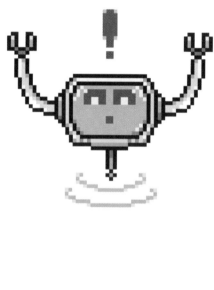

SECTION 1: MULTIPLE CHOICE QUESTIONS

There are 28 questions in Section 1. In the section, you will do some reading. Then you will answer questions about what you have read. Each question is followed by three or four choices. Read each question and decide which choice is the best answer. Mark your answer by completely filling in the bubble next to the answer choice. Use a No. 2 pencil to mark the answer sheet.

Read this passage. Then answer questions 1 through 4.

Latasha and Ella
by Michael Scotto

I named Ella for my favorite singer, Ella Fitzgerald. You might not have heard of her, but she was famous a long time ago. My puppy's full name is Ella Fitzgerald Gandy, because she is a real part of my family, the Gandys. I only use her full name when she does something bad, though. I think I picked that up from Momma. She does the same thing with me.

When I leave my books all over the living room floor, or if I flush the toilet while Momma is in the shower, her voice gets deep and serious and she calls out, "Latasha Esther Gandy!"

I've really been trying to be good, though. Honest, I have. And not just because I hate hearing my middle name—which I do! I'm trying to be good because I'm not just some little kid anymore. I'm eight years old. That's halfway to being a grown-up.

You know, there's a more grown-up way to say "grown-up." It is called being mature. I learned it from my pocket dictionary.

That's what I want to be—mature. I want to be mature for Momma, because she is looking for a new job and she needs my help. And I want to be mature for Ella. If I set a good example for her, maybe that dog switch will turn on and she'll finally settle down.

Question 1:

This passage is **mostly** about a girl who _____.

- ○ loves her dog
- ○ uses a dictionary
- ○ who wants to be thought of as an adult
- ○ learned from her mother

Question 2:

Latasha uses her dog Ella's full name when _____.

- ○ Ella is misbehaving
- ○ her mother is around
- ○ she needs to sound like an adult
- ○ Ella leaves her books on the living room floor

Question 3:

Which sentence from the passage **best** shows that Latasha thinks she is mature?

- ○ "I learned it from my pocket dictionary."
- ○ "I named Ella for my favorite singer, Ella Fitzgerald."
- ○ "I think I picked that up from Momma."
- ○ "I'm trying to be good because I'm not just some little kid anymore."

Question 4:

The author **most likely** wrote this story _____.

- ○ to entertain the reader
- ○ to inform the reader
- ○ to persuade the reader
- ○ to convince the reader that Latasha is mature

Read this passage. Then answer questions 5 through 10.

Chapter II: Danny Meadow Mouse and His Short Tail
by Thornton W. Burgess

All Danny Meadow Mouse could think about was his short tail. He was so ashamed of it that whenever anyone passed, he crawled out of sight so that they should not see how short his tail was. Instead of playing in the sunshine as he used to do, he sat and sulked. Pretty soon his friends began to pass without stopping. Finally one day old Mr. Toad sat down in front of Danny and began to ask questions.

"What's the matter?" asked old Mr. Toad.

"Nothing," replied Danny Meadow Mouse.

"I don't suppose there really is anything the matter, but what do you think is the matter?" said old Mr. Toad.

Danny fidgeted, and old Mr. Toad looked up at jolly, round, red Mr. Sun and winked. "Sun is just as bright as ever, isn't it?" he inquired.

"Yes," said Danny.

"Got plenty to eat and drink, haven't you?" continued Mr. Toad.

"Yes," said Danny.

"Seems to me that that is a pretty good-looking suit of clothes you're wearing," said Mr. Toad, eyeing Danny critically. "Sunny weather, plenty to eat and drink, and good clothes—must be you don't know when you're well off, Danny Meadow Mouse."

Danny hung his head. Finally he looked up and caught a kindly twinkle in old Mr. Toad's eyes. "Mr. Toad, how can I get a long tail like my cousin Whitefoot of the Green Forest?" he asked.

"So that's what's the matter! Ha! ha! ha! Danny Meadow Mouse, I'm ashamed of you! I certainly am ashamed of you!" said Mr. Toad. "What good would a long tail do you? Tell me that."

For a minute Danny didn't know just what to say. "I—I—I'd look so much better if I had a long tail," he ventured.

Old Mr. Toad just laughed. "You never saw a Meadow Mouse with a long tail, did you? Of course not. What a sight it would be! Why, everybody on the Green Meadows would laugh themselves sick at the sight! You see you need to be slim and trim and

handsome to carry a long tail well. And then what a nuisance it would be! You would always have to be thinking of your tail and taking care to keep it out of harm's way. Look at me. I'm homely. Some folks call me ugly to look at. But no one tries to catch me as Farmer Brown's boy does Billy Mink because of his fine coat; and no one wants to put me in a cage because of a fine voice. I am satisfied to be just as I am, and if you'll take my advice, Danny Meadow Mouse, you'll be satisfied to be just as you are."

Mr. Toad gave Danny some good advice.

"Perhaps you are right," said Danny Meadow Mouse after a little. "I'll try."

Question 5:

This passage is **mostly** about _____.

- ○ how a mouse can live in a meadow
- ○ how a toad helps a mouse like his appearance
- ○ how a toad has more friends than a mouse
- ○ how a mouse wants to move away from a meadow

Question 6:

What did Mr. Toad point out to Danny Meadow Mouse at the beginning of the passage?

- ○ the positive things in Danny Meadow Mouse's life
- ○ that Danny Meadow Mouse's tie was crooked
- ○ that Danny Meadow Mouse didn't have a long tail
- ○ Danny Meadow Mouse didn't have a lot of friends

Question 7:

Why does Mr. Toad laugh when he hears Danny Meadow Mouse's feelings about his tail?

- ○ He thinks that Danny Meadow Mouse's tail is funny.
- ○ He thinks that Danny Meadow Mouse doesn't appreciate all the good things in his life.
- ○ He plans to help Danny Meadow Mouse make friends.
- ○ He thinks that he has more friends than Danny Meadow Mouse.

Question 8:

Which of these details is **most** important to what happens in the passage?

- ○ how a mouse learns to be nicer to his friends
- ○ how a toad learns to be thankful for the sun
- ○ how a toad helps a mouse appreciate his tail
- ○ how a mouse is thankful for having enough food to eat

Question 9:

This passage is **most** like a _____.

- ○ folktale
- ○ real-life story
- ○ news story
- ○ textbook article

Question 10:

In the passage, the **most** important lesson Danny Meadow Mouse learns is _____.

- ○ he has to be satisfied with the way he looks
- ○ his friends will laugh at his long tail
- ○ the bright sun should cheer him up
- ○ you should be nice to all your friends

L ARTS

Read this passage. Then answer questions 11 through 17.

Amazing National Parks: Volcanoes and Mountains
by Jill Fisher

There are nearly sixty national parks in the United States. The US government cares for these areas. The government has written many special laws to help. These laws keep the land safe. They guard the animals that live there. The national parks are known for many reasons. They have incredible wildlife and pretty landscapes. They offer a range of outdoor activities. Millions of tourists visit them each year. They come from all parts of the world. Two of the most popular parks to see are Hawaii Volcanoes and Rocky Mountain National Parks. This splendid pair has many similarities and differences.

Hawaii Volcanoes and Rocky Mountain National Parks are similar in many ways. Both are open every day of the year. They became national parks in the early 1900s. Each has a gorgeous view. They offer a variety of fun activities, like hiking and horseback riding. Each place is perfect to relax. They are also both known for their unpredictable weather. Either place can be cold and rainy on any given day. It is best to wear layers of clothing. This way you are ready for all weather. Both of these parks are partly created with igneous rock. Igneous rock forms when hot lava cools.

These two parks also have key differences. One is a group of volcanoes. The other is a mountain range. They are found in very different locations. Hawaii Volcanoes stands on the southern part of Hawaii, also known as the Big Island. There you will find two of the world's most active volcanoes. Rocky Mountain National Park is in northern Colorado. It is one of the longest mountain ranges in the world. The parks were shaped in different ways. Over millions of years the lava from the volcanoes formed the shape of the Hawaiian island. The Rocky Mountains were slowly shaped by glaciers and rivers.

Hawaii Volcanoes has less extreme weather than Rocky Mountain National Park. In Hawaii Volcanoes, the temperature stays between fifty and seventy degrees for most of the year. At Rocky Mountain, it can range from below zero to the upper eighties. The animals found at each park are quite different. Hawaii is home to many rare birds. You may also see an endangered sea turtle. In the Rocky Mountains, many animals have thick fur. They need it to keep warm in the cold weather. Some examples are elks, moose, bears, and bighorn sheep.

Hawaii Volcanoes and Rocky Mountain National Parks have many similarities. They also have many differences. Yet each is a treasure in its own way. It is important to care for the national parks. In doing so, the natural beauty of the land will be saved. The animals will be protected. Plants, animals, and rock forms will remain for future generations to enjoy them. Whether you'd like to view an active volcano or climb a mountain, everyone can agree that the sights at both of these parks are out of this world.

Question 11:

What is this article **mostly** about?

- ○ the number of visitors to national parks in the United States
- ○ how national parks are home to many rare birds
- ○ a comparison of Hawaii Volcanoes and Rocky Mountain National Parks
- ○ the way that volcanoes and mountains are formed

Question 12:

Which fact would be **best** to include in a report about volcanoes?

- ○ Igneous rock forms when hot lava from volcanoes cools.
- ○ Some parks are home to many rare birds.
- ○ The US government cares for national parks.
- ○ Saving the natural beauty of parks is important.

Question 13:

Which fact from the article **best** supports the idea that Hawaii Volcanoes and Rocky Mountain National Parks should be protected?

○ Either place can be cold and rainy on any given day.

○ Each is a perfect place to relax.

○ Each was designated a national park in 1900.

○ Each was partly created with igneous rock.

Question 14:

Here is a web about the article.

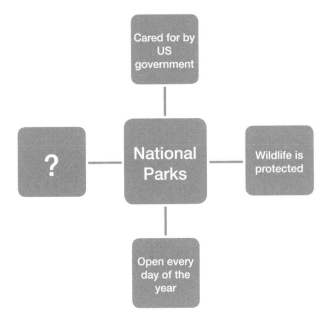

Which fact could be added to this web?

○ endangered sea turtles

○ active volcanoes

○ longest mountain range

○ sixty national parks

Question 15:

According to this article, which statement about Rocky Mountain National Park is **true**?

○ The park was formed by a group of volcanoes.

○ It is home to many rare birds.

○ The animals in the park have thick fur.

○ It has less extreme weather than Hawaii Volcanoes.

Question 16:

After reading the article, the reader could conclude that _____.

○ all national parks are partially formed by igneous rocks

○ there are no birds in Rocky Mountain National Park

○ visiting a national park is a great way to spend a day

○ people should always wear protective clothing in national parks

Question 17:

The author **most likely** wrote this article to _____.

- ○ give information about national parks in the United States
- ○ explain how animals survive in national parks
- ○ entertain with a story about fun activities in national parks
- ○ convince people to stay away from national parks

Read this story about a director and his experiment to control his temper. Then answer questions 18 through 23.

Keeping Your Cool
by Michael Scotto

Broadway owned the Portal Theater in Midlandia. At his theater, Broadway wrote and directed plays for everyone to enjoy.

Broadway kept a close eye on every detail of his plays. He had to be sure that everything turned out just how he wanted. "I loved the way you said that line, Beaker," he said. "However, try it again, just a touch more quietly. That will be much more dramatic."

Everyone tried to do exactly as Broadway said, because if they did not…

"No, no, no!" Broadway hollered. "That was too slow! I said a little slower, not slow like a turtle! I can't believe this!"

Broadway had an awful temper. "Nobody ever listens!" he cried, stomping his feet. "It's a tragedy! It could make a Midlandian weep. In fact, that's just what I'll do!"

After Broadway had calmed down, he noticed that his tummy was grumbling. "Boy, all that jumping around made me hungry!" he thought.

Broadway decided to stop for his favorite snack: a blueberry muffin at his friend Bun's bakery.

Broadway reached the counter. "One blueberry muffin, please!" he said.

Bun gulped nervously. "I'm sorry, Broadway," he stammered. "I just sold my last one."

Broadway could not believe his ears! "You're out of blueberry muffins?" he asked.

Bun nodded nervously. He knew that when Broadway lost his temper, he could be very tough to handle. "If you like…I do have some banana muffins," Bun suggested. "Perhaps you might enjoy something new."

That really got Broadway steamed. He felt his face getting hot. "But I didn't come for something new!" he yelled.

Meanwhile, Harmony watched from her table. She was a musician, and Broadway let her play shows at his theater.

"Uh-oh…" Harmony whispered. She knew what was coming next.

In the blink of an eye, Broadway climbed onto the counter and started toppling things over like an angry whirlwind. "I just want my blueberry muffin!" he howled. "This is a tragedy!"

As Broadway stamped his feet, he felt a hand touch his ankle. It was Harmony! "Can we go somewhere and talk?" she asked.

Harmony and Broadway sat together in the park. Broadway was no longer mad—he was worried.

"Oh, gracious, I was really rude to Bun," he said. "I am so embarrassed."

"Why do you think you got so upset?" asked Harmony.

"I just get so frustrated when things don't go my way," Broadway said. "I try not to get upset, but I feel like I can never hold my temper in!"

"Everybody feels upset, or disappointed, or even angry sometimes. But losing your temper is never a good idea. It can be scary, and it is hurtful to others," Harmony said. "Would you like to know how I keep my cool?"

"I would love to know," Broadway replied.

"When I think I might lose my temper," Harmony said, "I like to count to ten. It gives me time to calm down."

"I don't know, Harmony," Broadway said. "With my temper I might need to count to a million. Do you have any other ideas?"

"How about this?" Harmony said. "When I'm upset, sometimes it helps me to think of things that make me laugh or smile. What makes you smile?"

"I always smile when I think about my theater," Broadway said. "After each show, I get to come out and take a bow. Everybody claps for me!"

"If you thought about that, there's no way you could stay angry!" Harmony said.

"Maybe you're right," Broadway replied doubtfully.

"I also have one more solution you can try!" Harmony said. "Instead of trying to hold your temper in, you could use it to do something creative!"

"I've heard of losing your temper, but I've never heard of using your temper," Broadway said. "How can I do that?"

"Sometimes," Harmony said, "I dance to some music! Or, I'll take out my banjo and make up a song."

"I'm not very good at dancing or singing," Broadway said. "Could I write a story or a play instead?"

"Good thinking!" Harmony exclaimed. "You could write your feelings down, or you could draw a picture about them."

"Maybe I'll write my next big hit!" Broadway said. "Thanks for helping me, Harmony. I should go apologize to Bun."

As Broadway waited in line to apologize, he began to feel frustrated. "One, two, three, four…" he whispered to himself. As he counted, the line moved along. Soon, it was his turn to talk with Bun.

"I'm so sorry for losing my temper with you," Broadway told Bun. "It was not fair to treat you that way. From now on, I'll try to be a little more patient and kind. Can we still be friends?"

"Friends," Bun replied, and he shook Broadway's hand.

"Good!" Broadway said. "Because the next time I have a new play opening, there will be a front row ticket waiting for you!"

From that day on, Broadway always tried to control his temper. He counted, he hummed songs, he thought of funny things… he even wrote a new play.

Keeping his cool was very hard work. But as you can see, it gave Broadway plenty to smile about.

Question 18:

How does Broadway get the idea to keep his cool?

- ○ He thinks of it himself.
- ○ His friend suggests it.
- ○ He visits a bakery.
- ○ He needs more friends.

Question 19:

Broadway first tries his experiment at the _____.

- ○ bakery
- ○ park
- ○ theater
- ○ play

Question 20:

According to Harmony, what is the consequence of losing your temper?

- ○ You can't write a play.
- ○ It will scare people.
- ○ You can't buy blueberry muffins.
- ○ You will not laugh.

Question 21:

Read this sentence from the story.

That really got Broadway steamed.

According to this sentence, Broadway appears to be _____.

- ○ feeling sick
- ○ ready to write a great play
- ○ losing his temper
- ○ directing a play

Question 22:

Broadway's experiment to control his temper is successful because he _____.

- ○ made new friends
- ○ wrote a new play
- ○ only ate blueberry muffins
- ○ learned to sing

Question 23:

According to Harmony, which strategy may be the **least likely** to use when trying to control her temper?

- ○ write a story
- ○ dance
- ○ sing
- ○ eat

Emma wrote this letter to her new pen pal, Dae. There are several mistakes in her letter. Read the letter. Then answer questions 24 through 28.

Letter to a Pen Pal
by Jill Fisher

923 Logan Street, Apt. 4
Columbus, Ohio 43001
October 15, 2010

Dear Dae,

(1)   How are you? I really enjoyed the letter you sent me. I am so happy to have a new pen pal. I've never gotten a letter from another country before. I found Korea on a map. You are really far from Ohio! Sorry it has taken me two weeks to write back to you. I have been very busy with schoolwork. My favorite subject is math. We are learning about money. In the United States, we call our money dollars and cents. What do you call money in you're country?

(2)   Thank you for the photo you sent with your last letter. The house in the picture is beautiful. I did not know that Korean buildings are known for their curved roofs. The roof on the house reminds me of a big smile. Is that your house? I live in an apartment building with my mom, dad, little sister, and pets. Who lives with you?

(3)   We have two pets. Oscar is our dog. He is very small and brown. He was my birthday present when I turned five. He sleeps with me every night. We also have a cat. He is a boy, too. His name is Tiger. My sister named him that because he has stripes on his belly. He is really cute and fluffy. Do you have any pets?

(4)   I like animals so much that I would like to be a veterinarian when I grow up. I think it would be awesome to work on a farm and take care of horses. My mom told me to work very hard in school so that I can become a vet. What would you like to be when you grow up?

(5)   I am excited for tomorrow. I am going to my first wedding. It is my cousin's. My parents think I am finally old enough to sit with the adults. My sister is still too young to go to a wedding. She will stay with a babysitter. It should be a lot of fun. There will be a fancy dinner after the wedding. Then everyone will eat wedding cake. After that, we will dance. My mom bought me a pretty dress to wear. It is pink with long sleeves and a bow on the skirt. What do you wear to special occasions?

(6)   Did I tell you that I went camping? It was so cool! I got to sleep in a tent for three nights. My whole family went, including grandparents, aunts, uncles, and cousins. We couldn't play video games, watch television, or get on the computer, but we had a lot of fun. During the day we went for hikes. After lunch we went swimming in the lake.

(7)   My dad made a fire every night. The whole family sang campfire songs. Then we made s'mores. S'mores are delicious treats. They are made with roasted marshmallows, pieces of chocolate, and graham crackers. It was a great vacation. What do you like to do for fun?

(8)   It's fall in Ohio. The weather is cool. The leaves on the trees are changing colors. They were green and are now changes to red, orange, and yellow. They look very pretty. Soon all of the leaves will fall to the ground. Then we will rake them up. My sister and I will have fun jumping into the big piles of leaves.

(9)   Another one of my favorite fall activities is going to a pumpkin patch. My family is going later this month. Last year I carved a pumpkin. My dad helped me carve a silly face. Then my sister and I took a hayride. The best part about the pumpkin patch were bobbing for apples. Let me tell you about bobbing for apples. Everyone takes a turn trying to grab an apple from a big bucket of water using only his or her teeth. Sometimes it gets messy. We always have so much fun. I'll ask my mom to take some pictures when we go this year. I will send you some soon. Do you do anything special in the fall?

(10)   Well, it is getting late. I'd better end this letter. It is almost my bedtime. I have to wake up very early tomorrow to get ready for the wedding. I'll tell you all about it in the next letter I write. I'm so glad we are becoming friends. I am excited to hear more about Korea. Have a great day.

Your friend,
Emma

P.S. I can't wait to hear from you!

Question 24:

Which of these **best** states the writer's purpose?

- ○ To tell her friend about her life in Ohio
- ○ To persuade her friend to come for a visit
- ○ To inform her friend about the weather in Ohio
- ○ To describe to her friend how to make s'mores

Question 25:

Read this sentence from Paragraph 9 of Emma's letter.

The best part about the pumpkin patch <u>were</u> bobbing for apples.

Which form of the underlined verb agrees with its subject?

- ○ is
- ○ was
- ○ has been
- ○ no change

Question 26:

Read this sentence from Paragraph 8 of Emma's letter.

They were green and are now changes to red, orange, and yellow.

Which of these is the **best** way to write the sentence to show correct parallelism?

- ○ They were green and are now changed to red, orange, and yellow.
- ○ They were green and are now change to red, orange, and yellow.
- ○ They were green and are now changing to red, orange, and yellow.
- ○ no change

Question 27:

Read these sentences from Paragraph 3 of Emma's letter.

We also have a cat. He is a boy, too. His name is Tiger.

Which of these is the **most** effective way of combining these three sentences?

- ○ Also we have a cat that is a boy named, Tiger.
- ○ We also have a cat, he is a boy, too, his name is Tiger.
- ○ Tiger is also our cat; he is a boy, too.
- ○ We also have a boy cat named Tiger.

Question 28:

Read this sentence from Paragraph 1 of Emma's letter.

What do you call money in <u>you're</u> country?

What should the underlined word be?

- ○ you
- ○ your
- ○ one's
- ○ no change

SECTION 2: LISTENING AND WRITING

GUIDE NOTES: The story for the *Listening and Writing* activity appears below the Section 4 Answer Key for Language Arts.

In this section of the test, you will listen to a story called "The Porcupine and the Firefly." Then, you will answer some questions about the story. You will listen to the story twice. The first time you hear the story, listen carefully but do not take notes. As you listen to the story the second time, you may want to take notes. Use the space below for your notes. You may use these notes to answer the questions that follow. Your notes on these pages will NOT count toward your final score.

Please ask your Guide to begin reading once you have turned to the Notes Page of this exam and reviewed the vocabulary words from the story.

Notes

Here are words you will need to know as you listen to the story:

reckless: unconcerned about danger; foolhardy
dreadful: causing fear or terror
rustling: soft sounds; light noise
flitted: to flutter

L ARTS

Question 29:

The chart below shows what happens in the story. Complete the chart with details from the story.

The Porcupine and the Firefly

Penelope likes to be alone in the forest.

↓

↓

↓

Penelope and Lightning became inseparable.

Question 30:

At the end of the story, why did Lightning and Penelope become friends? Use details from the story to support your answer.

Planning Page

You may PLAN your writing for question 31 here if you wish, but do NOT write your final answer on this page. Your writing on this Planning Page will NOT count toward your final score.

Question 31:

How does Penelope Porcupine act at the beginning of the story? How does her behavior change by the end of the story? What causes this change? Use details from the story to support your answer.

In your answer, be sure to include:
- how Penelope Porcupine feels and acts at the beginning of the story.
- how Penelope Porcupine's behavior changes as the story goes along.
- how Penelope Porcupine acts by the end of the story.
- what causes Penelope's behavior to change.
- details from the story to support your answer.

Check your writing for correct spelling, grammar, capitalization, and punctuation.

SECTION 1: MULTIPLE CHOICE QUESTIONS

There are 30 questions in Section 1. Each question is followed by three or four choices. Read each question and decide which choice is the best answer. Mark your answer by completely filling in the bubble next to the answer choice. Use a No. 2 pencil to mark the answer sheet.

Test Taking Tips

You may use the following strategies to help you do your best:
- Read all the directions before each section of the test.
- Use all the allowed tools to help you solve problems on the test.
- The tools you are allowed to use are:

Ruler   **Pattern blocks**   **Counters**

- Read each question carefully and check your work before choosing your response.

Question 1:

Which number is the same as five thousand ninety-six?

- ○ 596
- ○ 5,906
- ○ 5,096
- ○ 5,960

MATH

Question 2:

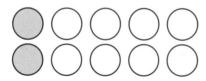 Use your ruler to help you solve this problem.

Angela drew the picture of a frog below.

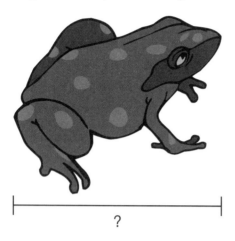

?

How many inches long is the frog?

- ○ 2
- ○ $2\frac{1}{4}$
- ○ $2\frac{1}{2}$
- ○ $3\frac{3}{4}$

Question 3:

Brianne, Ryan, and Marcy together earned $27.00 at their lemonade stand. They decide to share the money equally. Which number sentence could they use to find out how much money they will each earn?

- ○ $27.00 + 3 = □
- ○ $27.00 − 3 = □
- ○ $27.00 x 3 = □
- ○ $27.00 ÷ 3 = □

Question 4:

What is 794 rounded to the nearest ten?

- ○ 700
- ○ 790
- ○ 800
- ○ 810

Question 5:

Lenny shaded $\frac{2}{10}$ of the circles below.

Which fraction is equivalent to $\frac{2}{10}$?

- ○ $\frac{1}{10}$
- ○ $\frac{1}{5}$
- ○ $\frac{2}{5}$
- ○ $\frac{1}{2}$

Question 6:

Last week, Brian's mother spent $36.00 on groceries. This week, she spent $27.89 on groceries. How much **less** did Brian's mother spend on groceries this week than last week?

- ○ $11.89
- ○ $ 8.11
- ○ $ 7.81
- ○ $ 8.09

Question 7:

$$\begin{array}{r} 47 \\ \times\ 6 \\ \hline \end{array}$$

- ○ 53
- ○ 244
- ○ 186
- ○ 282

Question 8:

Which expression has the smallest value?

56 x 1   89 x 0   56 ÷ 7   81 ÷ 9

- ○ 56 x 1
- ○ 89 x 0
- ○ 56 ÷ 7
- ○ 81 ÷ 9

Question 9:

Mr. Dixon bought cartons of eggs at the grocery store. Each carton contains a dozen eggs. Which could be the total number of eggs that Mr. Dixon bought?

- ○ 44
- ○ 56
- ○ 76
- ○ 60

Question 10:

Mrs. Lyons writes the following number sentence on the board.

$$\square\ >\ \frac{1}{4}$$

- ○ $\frac{1}{8}$
- ○ $\frac{1}{6}$
- ○ $\frac{1}{5}$
- ○ $\frac{1}{2}$

Question 11:

Alexis and her friends wash cars each weekend. The bar graph below shows the number of cars they washed in the past four weeks.

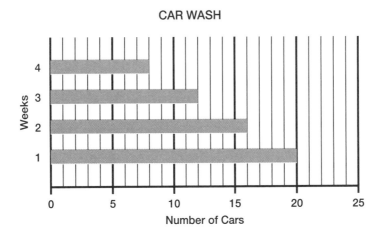

CAR WASH

Based on the data in the bar graph, how many cars will Alexis and her friends **most likely** wash in Week 5?

- ○ 0
- ○ 2
- ○ 4
- ○ 6

MATH

Question 12:

Rick, Amber, Megan, Aubrey, and Robert are in a math group today. Robert wrote the following number pattern rule for his math group:

subtract 1, add 3, subtract 1, add 3

Robert asked his math group to follow the rule starting with the number 20. Which pattern was made using Robert's rule?

- ○ 20, 19, 16, 13, 10
- ○ 20, 23, 22, 25, 24
- ○ 20, 19, 22, 21, 24
- ○ 20, 18, 16, 14, 12

Question 13:

Kelly, Caleb, and Diego checked out books from the library. Kelly has an even number of library books. Caleb has 3 more library books than Kelly. Diego has 2 more library books than Caleb. Which statement is true about the number of library books Caleb and Diego have?

- ○ Caleb's number is odd, and Diego's number is odd.
- ○ Caleb's number is odd, and Diego's number is even.
- ○ Caleb's number is even, and Diego's number is odd.
- ○ Caleb's number is even, and Diego's number is even.

Question 14:

Crystal quickly estimated the product of 898 x 18 this way:

- • She rounded each number to the nearest ten.
- • She multiplied these new numbers together.

What was Crystal's estimate?

- ○ 17,800
- ○ 18,000
- ○ 20,000
- ○ 19,100

Question 15:

What fraction on the number line below is in the wrong place?

- ○ $\frac{1}{2}$
- ○ $\frac{1}{4}$
- ○ $\frac{3}{4}$
- ○ $\frac{1}{8}$

Question 16:

 Use your ruler to help you solve this problem.

How many inches tall is the toy panda shown below?

- ○ $1\frac{1}{4}$
- ○ $2\frac{1}{4}$
- ○ $1\frac{1}{2}$
- ○ 2

Question 26:

What is the name of the shape below?

- ○ pentagon
- ○ trapezoid
- ○ hexagon
- ○ parallelogram

Question 27:

Which number sentence always results in an answer that is an odd number?

- ○ even number x even number = □
- ○ even number x odd number = □
- ○ odd number x even number = □
- ○ odd number x odd number = □

Question 28:

Which measurement is **most likely** to be the length of a motorcycle?

- ○ 2 millimeters
- ○ 2 centimeters
- ○ 2 meters
- ○ 2 kilometers

Question 29:

Paula made a drawing that has exactly 3 triangles and 1 rectangle. Which drawing below could be the one Paula made?

 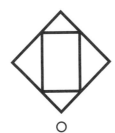  

○   ○   ○   ○

Question 30:

Nathan wrote the following number sentence.

378 ÷ 18 = 21

Which expression can be used to find out if Nathan's number sentence is correct?

- ○ 21 + 18
- ○ 21 ÷ 18
- ○ 21 − 18
- ○ 21 x 18

SECTION 2: SHOW YOUR WORK

There are 5 questions in Section 2. Read each question carefully and think about your answer before beginning your work. Be sure to show all your work. You may receive partial credit if you have shown your work. Use a No. 2 pencil to mark the answer sheet.

 There are some questions that will require you to use your ruler.

MATH

Question 31:

Mr. Billingsly is going on a group hike at the Grand Canyon. They will camp out for the night on the other side of the trail. The group's guide tells them the trail is 9,981 feet. After walking 5,276 feet, the group decides to stop and rest. How many more feet must the hiking group walk to get to the other end of the trail?

Show your work.

Answer: _____ feet

Question 32:

Melvin has collected 90 baseball cards. He places 9 cards on each page of his baseball card album. There are 8 pages in his album. How many baseball cards does Melvin have left over?

Show your work.

Answer: _____ baseball cards

Question 33:

Allison makes friendship bracelets using beads. She has 47 beads for each friendship bracelet. How many beads does Allison need to make 6 bracelets?

Show your work.

Answer: _____beads

Question 34:

Skates and Fun Company is building a new skateboarding arena in a park. The diagram of the new skateboarding arena is shown on the grid below.

Skates and Fun Company Skateboarding Arena

KEY

[   ] = 1 Unit

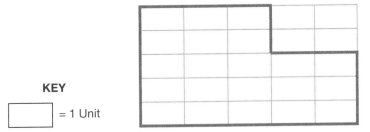

What is the perimeter, in units, of the playground?

Show your work.

Answer: _____units

Question 35:

Mickey bought a burger for $2.75 and a soft drink for $1.50. He gave the cashier $10.00. How much money did Mickey receive in change?

Show your work.

Answer: $_____

SECTION 3: EXTENDED RESPONSE QUESTIONS

There are 6 questions in Section 3. Reach each question carefully and think about your answer before beginning your work. Be sure to answer all parts of a question. You may receive partial credit if you have shown your work. Your answers to the extended-response questions should be written only in the space provided for each question. Use a No. 2 pencil to mark the answer sheet.

There are some questions that will require you to use your ruler.

Question 36:

Albert is using toothpicks to make a pattern of squares.

Part A

He made the table below to show the number of toothpicks needed to make the squares. Write the missing numbers in the table.

Number of Squares	1	2	3	4	5
Number of Toothpicks	4	7	10		

Part B

If the pattern continues, how many toothpicks will it take to make 8 squares?

Answer: _____

Part C

On the lines below , describe the pattern.

_____

_____

_____

Question 37:

Debbie writes the number pattern below.

52, 48, 44, 40, 36, <u>?</u>

Part A

What is the next number in the pattern?

Answer: _____

Part B

On the lines below, complete the number pattern using the same rule as Debbie's pattern.

Pattern: _____, 22, _____, _____, _____

Part C

On the lines below, write the rule for Debbie's pattern. Explain how you determined the pattern.

_____

_____

_____

_____

_____

Question 38:

Tonya puts these blocks into a bag:

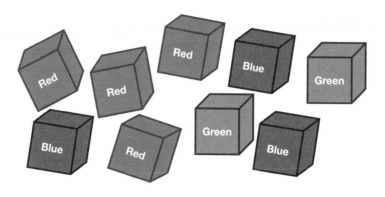

Part A

Tonya shakes the bag. Then, without looking, she chooses one block from the bag. Which color block is she **least** likely to choose?

Answer: _____

Part B

What is the probability that Tonya will choose a red block?

Answer: _____

Part C

Use your knowledge of probability and the cubes provided to support your answer. If Tonya chooses a green cube, leaves it out of the bag, and then selects another cube, does the probability of choosing another green cube change? Explain your answer using evidence from the diagram.

_____

_____

_____

_____

_____

Question 39:

Mrs. Nelson is giving a quiz worth 100 points to her fourth grade class. Some questions on the quiz are worth 10 points and the rest are worth 5 points. If 7 of the questions are worth 10 points each, how many questions are worth 5 points each?

Part A

Show your work.

Answer: _____

Part B

If all questions were worth 2 points each, how many questions would be on the quiz?

Show your work.

Answer: _____

Part C

Mrs. Nelson wants to give a 100-point quiz with 15 questions worth 6 points each. Evaluate Mrs. Nelson's plan for a 100-point quiz. Explain why Mrs. Nelson's plan for a quiz might not be possible.

_____

_____

_____

_____

Question 40:

Mr. Feldman is making model airplanes. The table below shows the total number of model airplanes he has built by the end of Weeks 2 through 5.

Mr. Feldman's Model Airplanes	
Week	Total Number of Airplanes
2	11
3	18
4	25
5	32

Part A

If the pattern in the table continues, how many model airplanes will Mr. Feldman build by the end of Week 6?

Answer: _____ model airplanes

Part B

On the lines below, explain how you found your answer.

_____

_____

_____

_____

_____

Part C

If the pattern in the table continues, by the end of which week will Mr. Feldman have built the 60th model airplane?

Answer: week _____

Question 41:

Part A

Each expression in the first column below is equivalent to one of the expressions in the second column. Draw a line between the pairs of expressions that are equivalent.

6 x (4 x 8)   9 + 8

(3 + 6) + 8   3 + 12

(4 x 2) x 5   (6 x 4) x 8

3 + (4 + 8)   4 x (2 x 5)

MATH

Part B

Dana wrote the number sentence below. Solve for the answer.

$$(2 \times 3) \times 4 = \square$$

Part C

Olivia rewrote Dana's number sentence and grouped the numbers differently. Complete Olivia's number sentence below to show the new grouping. Use all the numbers and symbols from Dana's number sentence. Explain the law of arithmetic used to write the number sentence.

Olivia's Number Sentence:

_____

_____

_____

_____

PRACTICE

SCIENCE EXAM

SECTION 1: MULTIPLE CHOICE QUESTIONS

There are 19 questions in Section 1. Each question is followed by three or four choices. Read each question and decide which choice is the best answer. Mark your answer by completely filling in the bubble next to the answer choice. Use a No. 2 pencil to mark the answer sheet.

Use the food chain diagram below to answer questions 1 – 3:

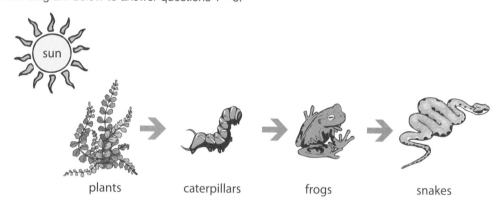

Question 1:

Which organisms in this food chain are needed for all the other organisms to survive?

- ○ caterpillars
- ○ frogs
- ○ plants
- ○ snakes

Question 2:

Which organisms in this food chain are predators?

- ○ plants and caterpillars
- ○ caterpillars and frogs
- ○ frogs and snakes
- ○ snakes and plants

Question 3:

If the population of plants increased, the population of caterpillars would most likely _____.

- ○ decrease
- ○ increase
- ○ remain the same

Question 4:

Which substance is usually found in nature as a liquid, solid, and gas?

- ○ water
- ○ rock
- ○ metal
- ○ glass

Question 5:

A duck's feathers are covered with natural oil that keeps the duck dry. This is a special feature ducks have that helps them _____.

○ feed their young

○ adapt to their environment

○ attract a mate

○ search for food

Question 6:

Which food is a fruit?

○ a potato

○ an onion

○ a carrot

○ a pumpkin

Question 7:

The sunrise and sunset times for three days in February are recorded in the chart below.

Date	Sunrise	Sunset
February 8	7:31 am	5:50 pm
February 15	7:22 am	5:58 pm
February 22	7:12 am	6:07 pm

Which statement is an accurate conclusion based on this information?

○ There are more hours of daylight as the month goes on.

○ There are fewer hours of daylight as the month goes on.

○ The sun rises later as the month goes on.

○ The sun sets earlier as the month goes on.

Question 8:

Temperatures below freezing are expected overnight. What might be done to protect plants growing outside?

○ trim the leaves

○ weed them

○ cover them

○ give them plant food

SCIENCE

Question 9:

Which is the **best** example of evaporation?

○ raindrops freezing

○ an ice cube melting

○ a puddle drying in the sun

○ a sponge soaking up water

Question 10:

The energy that all organisms need to survive comes from _____.

○ the air

○ the sun

○ water

○ grass

Question 11:

In the diagram below, letters A, B, C, and D show processes in the water cycle.

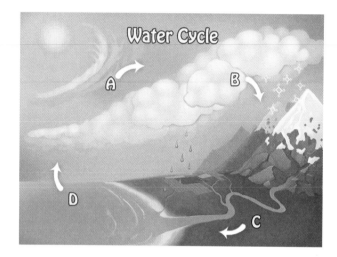

Which letter shows runoff?

- ○ A
- ○ B
- ○ C
- ○ D

Question 12:

The diagram below shows four parts of a plant.

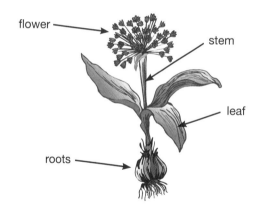

Complete the chart below by matching each plant part with its function.

Plant Function	Plant Part
uses sunlight to make food	
takes in water and nutrients	
produces seeds	

Question 13:

Place a number (2, 3, or 4) on the line below each image to show the order of the four stages in the life cycle of a butterfly. Stage 1 is already numbered.

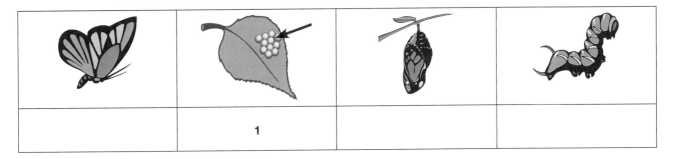

	1		

Base your answers to questions 14 – 17 on the information below and on your knowledge of science.

A group of fourth grade students recorded their eye colors. The tallies in the data table below show their results. Each / equals one fourth grade student. The symbol /// equals 5 fourth grade students.

Data Table

Eye Color	Number of Fourth Grade Students
blue	/// /// ///
brown	/// /// /// /// /// ///
green	/// ///

Question 14:

Which eye color was most common in this group of students? _____

Question 15:

Use the results in the data table to complete the bar graph below.

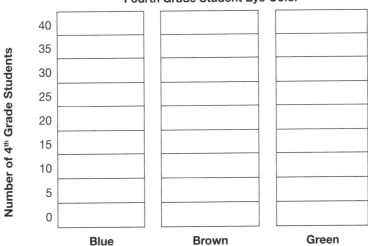

Fourth Grade Student Eye Color

SCIENCE

Question 16:

Identify one trait, other than eye color, that children can inherit from their parents.

_____

Question 17:

Identify one characteristic that children learn and do not inherit from their parents.

_____

Question 18:

The chart below shows three properties of five objects.

Object	Properties		
	Color	**Texture**	**Shape**
1	red	smooth	round
2	yellow	rough	oval
3	green	rough	round
4	red	smooth	oval
5	blue	rough	rectangle

What color is the round object that has a rough surface?

○ blue

○ green

○ red

○ yellow

Question 19:

Base your answer to the question below on the bar graph, which shows the average life span of four animals.

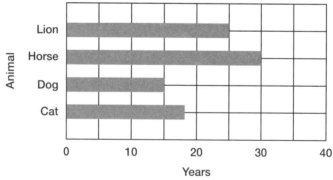

Which statement is supported by the data in the bar graph?

○ The life span of a dog is longer than the life span of a cat.

○ The life span of a lion is longer than the life span of a horse.

○ The life span of a cat is longer than the life span of a lion.

○ The life span of a horse is longer than the life span of a dog.

SECTION 2: BRIEF CONSTRUCTED RESPONSE AND EXTENDED RESPONSE QUESTIONS

There are 10 questions in Section 2. Read each question carefully and construct your responses in the space provided. Use a No. 2 pencil to completely answer each question.

Question 20:

A fourth grade class visited a pond. They saw a green frog, a beaver, and a smooth, brown snake. The teacher thought the frog was pretty. The students used nets to catch pond insects. The students looked at several insects. They counted six legs on each insect. Some students thought the insects looked scary.

A.   Identify one opinion that is stated in the paragraph.

_____

_____

B.   Identify two observations that are stated in the paragraph.

1. _____

2. _____

Question 21:

After walking in a field, a student finds seeds stuck to his clothing. He knows this is one way seeds can be dispersed. Explain one other way that seeds can be dispersed.

_____

_____

_____

_____

_____

SCIENCE

Base your answers to the questions 22 and 23 on the diagrams below and on your knowledge of science. The diagrams show the same piece of land in the summer of 2005 and the summer of 2010 after the trees were cut down.

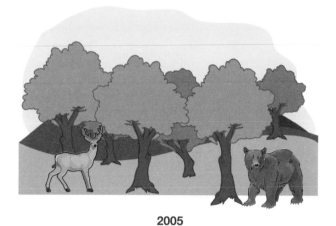

2005

2010

Question 22:

Describe one positive thing that might result from cutting down the trees.

_____

_____

Question 23:

Describe one negative thing that might result from cutting down the trees.

_____

_____

Question 24:

Monarch butterflies migrate from the state of New York at a certain time of the year. Explain how migration helps butterflies survive.

_____

_____

Base your answers to questions 25 and 26 on the Venn diagram below. The diagram compares some physical structures of cats and birds.

Question 25:

Identify two physical structures that birds and cats have in common.

1. _____

2. _____

Question 26:

Identify two physical structures that cats have but birds do **not** have.

1. _____

2. _____

Question 27:

A scientist studies a population of black bears in an area. Two years later, half of the black bear population had moved to another area. Identify two factors that might have caused the black bears to move.

1. _____

2. _____

Question 28:

Use your knowledge of adaptations to answer the following question.

Identify the changes in the environment that cause some animals to hibernate during the winter.

1. _____

2. _____

3. _____

4. _____

5. _____

Question 29:

The diagram below shows an Arctic bird in summer and the same bird in winter.

Summer   **Winter**

Identify two different characteristics of the Arctic bird that changed from summer to winter.

1. _____

2. _____

PRACTICE

SOCIAL STUDIES EXAM

SECTION 1: MULTIPLE CHOICE QUESTIONS

There are 30 questions in Section 1. Each question is followed by three or four choices. Read each question and decide which choice is the best answer. Mark your answer by completely filling in the bubble next to the answer choice. Use a No. 2 pencil to mark the answer sheet.

Question 1:

Which part of the federal government decides if a law follows the United States Constitution?

- ○ the Senate
- ○ the president
- ○ the Supreme Court
- ○ the House of Representatives

Question 2:

Which action best identifies a person using a money system?

- ○ Chace receives a birthday card from Adam.
- ○ Elizabeth gives her extra bag of chips to Allison.
- ○ Arnold trades a basketball card for Emmanuel's baseball card.
- ○ Cailyn pays twenty dollars for a new soccer ball.

Base your answers to questions 3 and 4 on the map below, which shows time zones of the United States.

Time Zones of the United States

Question 3:

If it is 1:30 p.m. in Washington, DC, what time is it in Phoenix, AZ?

- ○ 12:30 a.m.
- ○ 10:30 a.m.
- ○ 11:30 a.m.
- ○ 9:30 a.m.

Question 4:

Which time zone is Minnesota in?

- ○ Pacific
- ○ Mountain
- ○ Eastern
- ○ Central

Question 5:

The three houses shown are found in different regions of the world. The builders probably chose to construct these houses differently because the builders had _____.

- ○ different amounts of money to spend
- ○ different natural resources available to them
- ○ different ideas of what was beautiful
- ○ different amounts of space they had to provide in their homes

Question 6:

Which sentence explains one reason the United States Constitution was written?

- ○ There were too many forms of currency.
- ○ The government had no judicial branch.
- ○ Farmers owed too many taxes.
- ○ The country was divided over slavery.

Question 7:

Which Native American group lived in the present-day Northeastern Woodlands region?

- ○ Hopi
- ○ Seminole
- ○ Sioux
- ○ Iroquois

Question 8:

The first factories in the Northeast region were built near rivers and streams because _____.

○ factories used water to power machines

○ all factories depended on railroads for transportation of goods and services

○ most farmland was located nearby

○ all of the raw materials the factories needed were located nearby

Question 9:

If a tire company experienced a drop in its supply of rubber, the company can raise the price of tires to _____.

○ build more tires

○ lower the cost of truck tires

○ hire more workers to make tires

○ lower the demand for tires

Question 10:

The capital city of a state is important because it _____.

○ is located in a city with many buildings

○ is the center of state government

○ is a good place to raise a family

○ has many museums

Question 11:

Which geographic feature provides all the needs listed below?

| Transportation |
| Boundaries |
| Sources of food and water |

○ deserts

○ mountains

○ rivers

○ grasslands

Question 12:

Which statement about the Hopi is an opinion?

○ The Hopi lived in villages called pueblos.

○ The Hopi raised corn, beans, squash, melons, pumpkins, and fruit.

○ The men planted and harvested.

○ The Hopi had the best ceremonies in the Southwest region.

Question 13:

In the United States, Memorial Day is celebrated as a national holiday to honor_____.

○ the men and women who died while serving in the United States Armed Services

○ the people who signed the Declaration of Independence

○ all the people that work

○ former vice presidents

S STUDIES

Base your answers to questions 14 and 15 on the map below.

United States Resourses

Question 14:

Most states along the Northeast and Southeast regions produce the following resource.

- ○ fish
- ○ oil
- ○ apples
- ○ livestock

Question 15:

Texas and Louisiana are along the Gulf of Mexico. Which statement describes the resources of Texas and Louisiana?

- ○ Texas and Louisiana both produce oil as a resource.
- ○ Texas does not have fish as a natural resource and Louisiana raises corn.
- ○ Both Texas and Louisiana produce corn.
- ○ Louisiana produces fish and cotton.

Question 16:

Prior to the American Revolution, colonists were forced to provide British soldiers with _____.

- ○ housing
- ○ clothing
- ○ food
- ○ weapons

Question 17:

In the 1500s, which European group settled in Florida?

- ○ Dutch
- ○ Spanish
- ○ German
- ○ French

Question 18:

Which imaginary line circles Earth at 0° longitude?

○ equator

○ Tropic of Capricorn

○ prime meridian

○ Tropic of Cancer

Question 19:

The main purpose of a physical map is to show _____.

○ political boundaries

○ landforms

○ streets and highways

○ resources

Use the timeline and your own knowledge to complete questions 20 and 21.

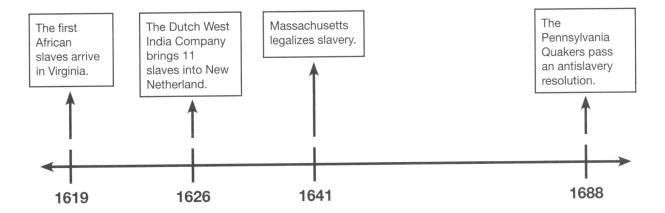

| The first African slaves arrive in Virginia. | The Dutch West India Company brings 11 slaves into New Netherland. | Massachusetts legalizes slavery. | | The Pennsylvania Quakers pass an antislavery resolution. |

1619   **1626**   **1641**   **1688**

Question 20:

According to the timeline, when did the slave trade begin in the regions around New York?

○ 1619

○ 1626

○ 1641

○ 1688

Question 21:

From 1619 to 1688, what does the timeline say about slavery in the colonies?

○ There was slavery throughout the colonies.

○ Slaves were used only in the south.

○ All people in the colonies approved of slavery.

○ All slave owners lived in Virginia.

Question 22:

Dr. O'Brien opened a letter that notified him to report to the court house for jury duty. Jury duty is his responsibility as a _____.

○ physician

○ customer

○ man

○ citizen

Question 23:

Which statement **best** describes one of the responsibilities of the United States Congress?

○ decides if the laws follow the Constitution

○ approves justices for the Supreme Court

○ vetoes bills from a becoming law

○ reports on the State of the Union in front of all of Congress

S STUDIES

Question 24:

Which was one result of the Lewis and Clark expedition?

- ○ Maps of the Mississippi River were completed for all traders.
- ○ Mexico signed a peace treaty with the United States.
- ○ Florida became a territory of the United States.
- ○ Citizens learned about western Native Americans.

Question 25:

Which right does the First Amendment grant to citizens of the United States?

- ○ a trial by jury
- ○ freedom of speech
- ○ protection against search and seizure
- ○ the right to bear arms

Question 26:

How is the Mayflower Compact a symbol of the first United States government?

- ○ It gave a good example of self-rule.
- ○ It committed colonists to follow the laws of England.
- ○ It started a trade economy.
- ○ It outlined a system of fair taxation.

Question 27:

The goal of an abolitionist was to _____.

- ○ allow each state to make its own decision about slavery
- ○ persuade the government to end slavery
- ○ force plantation owners to give half their land to slaves
- ○ return escaped slaves to plantation owners

Question 28:

Which list shows the correct order in which these three important documents were written, from earliest to the most recent?

- ○ Declaration of Independence → United States Constitution → Mayflower Compact
- ○ United States Constitution → Mayflower Compact → Declaration of Independence
- ○ Declaration of Independence → Mayflower Compact → United States Constitution
- ○ Mayflower Compact → Declaration of Independence → United States Constitution

Question 29:

Which of these is an example of using a barter system?

- ○ Felix gives Mandy money for her baseball glove.
- ○ Maura gives his credit card to an auto repair shop to pay for his car repairs.
- ○ Lon gets a weekly allowance from his mother for completing all his chores.
- ○ Polly gives Abe a basketball in exchange for a football.

Question 30:

Which physical landmark in the United States was **most likely** created by erosion?

- ○ the Great Lakes
- ○ the Mississippi River
- ○ the Grand Canyon
- ○ the Rocky Mountains

SECTION 2: BRIEF CONSTRUCTED RESPONSE QUESTIONS

There are 5 short answer questions in Section 2. Read each question carefully and construct your responses in the space provided. Use a No. 2 pencil to completely answer each question.

Base your answers to questions 31 and 32 on the graphic and passage below.

The Transcontinental Railroad connected California to the East.

Excerpt from:
pbs.org
(http://www.pbs.org/wgbh/americanexperience/films/tcrr/)
Transcontinental Railroad
PBS Home Video

"As white explorers and settlers entered Western territory, they disrupted a centuries-old culture -- that of the Plains Indians. The arrival of the railroad and, with it, more permanent and numerous white settlements, spelled growing conflict between whites and natives. The troubles would erupt into an all-out war."

Question 31:

Identify one explanation for the increase in population in the West that was the result of building the Transcontinental Railroad.

Question 32:

State **two** reasons the Native Americans may have been concerned for the buffalo population in the Plains region.

S STUDIES

Base your answers to questions 33 – 35 on the passage below.

Homowo Festival in Ghana

Excerpt from:
http://www.everythingesl.net/lessons/harvest_festivals_around_world_79423.php

African people have always had festivals at the time of the harvest. In Ghana, the Yam Festival (Homowo) lasts three days. Yams are an important crop in Ghana. During Homowo, they are taken from the ground and are carried to the village. Then they are blessed by the chief. Special foods made from yams are served. Mashed yams with hard boiled eggs are an important part of the festival. People also eat Kpekpele which is made from cornmeal and palm oil. During Homowo, people wear a kind of toga made from kente cloth which is brightly colored. The festival ends with a big feast. People dance and sing to the sounds of drums.

There are similarities and differences between Thanksgiving in the United States and Ghana's Homowo celebration. Compare Thanksgiving in the United States to Homowo by filling in the boxes below.

Compare	Homowo	Thanksgiving in the United States
Purpose of Celebration	Give thanks for the Yam Harvest.	**Question 33:**
Traditional Food	**Question 34:**	Turkey
How People Celebrate	People wear a special toga. People have a big feast. People dance and sing.	**Question 35:**

S STUDIES

SECTION 3: EXTENDED RESPONSE QUESTIONS

There are 2 parts in Section 3. Part A is based on sets of artifacts. Each set of artifacts is followed by one or more questions. Write your answer to each question in the space provided. Part B contains one essay question based on the artifacts. Write your answer to this question on the pages provided. Read each question carefully and construct your responses in the space provided. Use a No. 2 pencil to completely answer each question.

Part A: Artifact Evaluation

Directions: The task below is based on artifacts 1 through 6. This task is designed to test your ability to work with artifacts and other historical documents. Look at each set of artifacts and answer the question or questions after each. Use your answers to the questions to help you write your essay.

Northeastern Woodland Region Native Americans

The Native Americans of the Northeast include: Wampanoag, Iroquois, Creek, Massachusett, Narrangansett, and Nauset. The Native Americans of this region always used nature and natural resources to meet their needs and wants.

Artifact 1

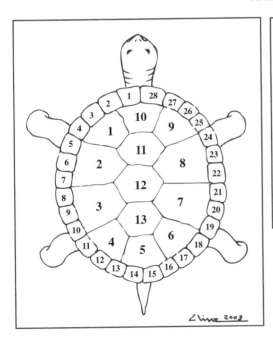

Native Americans have always depended on nature and natural resources for their survival. Many Native Americans believe that the turtle's back represents the thirteen new moons of a lunar year. The twenty-eight segments on a turtle's back represent the number of days between each new moon.

Native Americans have used those thirteen moons to keep track of the changing seasons and the effects those changes had on the natural world around them.

1. Interpret the importance of how Native Americans have used the turtle to explain changes in their natural world.

_____

_____

_____

_____

Artifacts 2

Figure 1: deerskin leggings with porcupine quills

Figure 2: Rattles made of deer hooves are worn strapped to the knee of a Native American dancer.

Figure 3: Iroquois woman in a buckskin dress

Figure 4: wooden headdress with eagles feathers (Negative 963 B, National Anthropological Archives, Smithsonian Institution)

Figure 5: moccasin with dyed porcupine quills

Figure 6: Iroquois men in buckskin garments

Based on Artifacts 2, complete the lists below by giving three examples of a Northeastern region Iroquois native using different parts of animals to make clothing. In Column A, list the animal and parts used to make clothing. In Column B, name the clothing made from the animal part listed in Column A.

Column A	Column B
Animal Part Used	**Clothing Made**
(1)	(1)
(2)	(2)
(3)	(3)

Artifacts 3

Figure 7: Native American holding a feathered fan used in ceremonial dances

Figure 8: horn rattle used in ceremonial dances

Figure 9: Native Americans believe that ceremonial dance masks (this one made from cornhusks) were representative of hunting and farming.

Figure 10: turtle shell rattles used in ceremonial dances

Figure 11: water-filled drum used in ceremonial dances

Based on the artifacts above, identify **two** examples of how Northeastern Native Americans have used plants or animals to make objects for their ceremonial dances.

1. _____

2. _____

S STUDIES

Artifacts 4

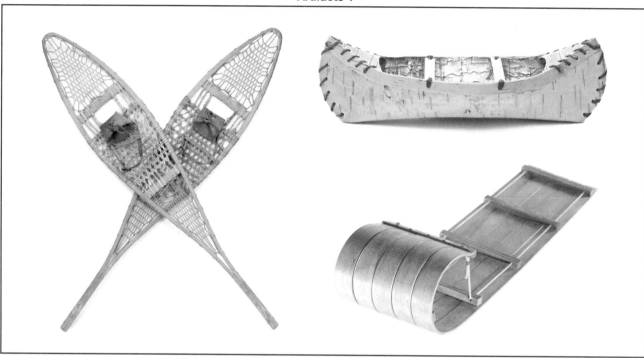

Based on the artifacts, explain the **three** ways that Northeastern region Native Americans used trees to meet their transportation needs.

1. _____

_____

2. _____

_____

3. _____

_____

S STUDIES

Artifacts 5

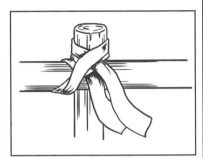

Longhouse of the Iroquois

Poles and bark were the basic components of longhouse structure. The frame of the longhouse started with rows of posts dug into the ground. Other poles were lashed to the posts, both across and along the length of the longhouse to strengthen the structure. The roof was supported by poles that were attached at the tops of the posts and were bent into an arch. The parts of the frame were tied together with strips of bark. The Iroquois tied or lashed their buildings together with long strips of bark, or with ropes made by braiding strips of bark. When the bark is fresh and wet, it is flexible and can be wound around poles and posts to tie them together. When it dries, it shrinks a little and becomes stiff, thereby tightening the poles together.

Using the picture above, in Column A identify **two** different natural resources or parts of a natural resource that the Northeastern region Native Americans used to meet their need for shelter. Then, in column B, tell **how** each resource has been used. In Column B, name specific parts of the longhouse made from the natural resource listed in Column A.

Column A	Column B
Natural Resource	**How Resource Was Used**
(1)	(1)
(2)	(2)

Part B: Essay

Write a well-organized essay using your knowledge of social studies and the artifacts in Part A as evidence. Be sure to use proper capitalization and punctuation.

The Northeastern Region Native Americans used nature and natural resources to meet their needs and wants. Using information from the artifacts and your knowledge of social studies, write an essay evaluating how the Northeastern Native Americans used nature and natural resources around them to meet their needs and wants.

S STUDIES

In your essay, remember to:
- include an introduction.
- include in the body of your essay:
  - an explanation of how the Northeastern region Native Americans used nature and natural resources to meet their needs and wants.
  - information from the artifacts.
  - an interpretation of the reasons why Native Americans used the natural resources to meet their wants and needs.
- include a conclusion paragraph.

ESSAY

SECTION FOUR

-START-

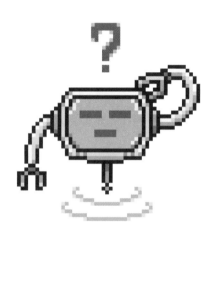

LANGUAGE ARTS EXAM

ANSWERS

Question	Skills and Categories
1. who wants to be thought of as an adult	Main Idea, Reading Comprehension, Thinking Skills, Use of Literary Information
2. Ella is misbehaving	Evidence from the Text, Reading Comprehension, Use of Literary Information
3. "I'm trying to be good because I'm not just some little kid anymore."	Reading Comprehension, Thinking Skills, Use of Literary Information
4. to entertain the reader	Author's Purpose, Analysis of Fiction and Nonfiction Text
5. how a toad helps a mouse like his appearance	Main Idea, Reading Comprehension
6. the positive things in Danny Meadow Mouse's life	Inference, Reading Comprehension, Thinking Skills
7. He thinks that Danny Meadow Mouse doesn't appreciate all the good things in his life.	Reading Comprehension, Inference, Evidence from the Text
8. how a toad helps a mouse appreciate his tail	Main Idea, Reading Comprehension, Thinking Skills, Use of Literary Information
9. folktale	Analysis of Fiction and Nonfiction Text
10. he has to be satisfied with the way he looks	Drawing Conclusions, Inference, Reading Comprehension, Thinking Skills, Use of Literary Information
11. a comparison of Hawaii Volcanoes and Rocky Mountain National Parks	Main Idea, Reading Comprehension, Thinking Skills, Use of Literary Information
12. Igneous rock forms when hot lava from volcanoes cools.	Analysis of Fiction and Nonfiction Text, Thinking Skills
13. Each was designated a national park in 1900.	Evidence from the Text, Use of Literary Information, Thinking Skills
14. sixty national parks	Evidence from the Text, Reading Comprehension, Thinking Skills, Use of Literary Information
15. The animals in the park have thick fur.	Evidence from the Text, Reading Comprehension
16. visiting a national park is a great way to spend a day	Inference, Analysis of Fiction and Nonfiction Text, Reading Comprehension, Thinking Skills
17. give information about national parks in the United States	Author's Purpose, Analysis of Fiction and Nonfiction Text, Thinking Skills
18. His friend suggests it.	Evidence from the Text, Reading Comprehension, Use of Literary Information
19. bakery	Evidence from the Text, Reading Comprehension, Use of Literary Information
20. It will scare people.	Evidence from the Text, Inference, Reading Comprehension, Use of Literary Information
21. losing his temper	Inference, Thinking Skills, Reading Comprehension

22.	wrote a play	Inference, Thinking Skills, Reading Comprehension, Use of Literary Information
23.	eat	Evidence from the Text, Reading Comprehension, Use of Literary Information
24.	To tell her friend about her life in Ohio.	Author's Purpose, Analysis of Fiction and Nonfiction Text
25.	was	Word Usage, Grammar, Conventions of Writing, Thinking Skills
26.	They were green and are now changing to red, orange, and yellow.	Grammar, Conventions of Writing, Thinking Skills
27.	We also have a boy cat named Tiger.	Grammar, Conventions of Writing, Thinking Skills
28.	your	Word Usage, Grammar, Conventions of Writing, Thinking Skills
29.	**Penelope likes to be alone in the forest.** Box 2: Student should reference the skunk and opossum (Example: Penelope tries to make friends with a skunk and an opossum.) Box 3: Student should reference the encounter with the firefly, Lightning. (Example: A firefly accidentally flies into Penelope's nose.) **Penelope and Lightning became inseparable.**	Main Idea, Summarization, Main Idea, Reading Comprehension, Use of Literary Information, Analysis of Fiction and Nonfiction Text
30.	ACE Strategy Possible Answer(s): Lightning did not run away. Lightning wasn't afraid of Penelope. Penelope did not tease Lightning. Possible Cite(s): Penelope states that she doesn't see anything wrong with Lightning's light. Lightning is not afraid of Penelope's quills. Penelope and Lightening became inseparable. Penelope and Lightning laughed and played. Lightning helped Penelope find food. Possible Explanation(s): Connection to another fable. Connection to lessons learned. Understanding of purpose of fable. Connection to an event in student's life.	Reading Comprehension, Analysis of Fiction and Nonfiction Text, Thinking Skills, Use of Literary Information
31.	ACE Strategy Possible Answer(s): Answer should include: how Penelope Porcupine feels and acts at the beginning of the story. how Penelope Porcupine's behavior changes as the story goes along. how Penelope Porcupine acts by the end of the story. what causes Penelope's behavior to change. Possible Cite(s): Each bullet point should include a specific detail to support the answer. Possible Explanation(s): Connection to another fable with similar events. Understanding of purpose of fable. Connection to an event in student's life.	Conventions of Writing, Summarizing, Sequencing, Reading Comprehension, Thinking Skills, Use of Literary Information, Analysis of Fiction and Nonfiction Text

The Porcupine and the Firefly
by Nicole Costlow

Penelope was a loner. It wasn't because of her personality; she was as friendly as any porcupine could be. It just seemed to Penelope that no one would give her a chance. Every time she would get brave enough to try to make a friend, whomever it was Penelope said hello to would take one look at her sharp, pointy quills and run in the other direction.

The nighttime crowd in the forest where Penelope lived presented its own challenges. The badgers didn't want to be bothered and weren't very nice. The raccoons were just plain reckless in their search for food. When the fox said he wanted to "have her over for dinner," Penelope was thankful for her quills.

One evening while she was out, Penelope encountered a black-and-white animal just about her size. Feeling braver than usual, she waddled over to the skunk to introduce herself.

"Hello," she said, "my name is Penelope! How are you tonight? What are you having for dinner?" She pointed to the tasty-looking, colorful plant that the skunk was eating.

"Whoa, you scared me! You shouldn't sneak up on me like that!" the nervous animal said, quivering. "You aren't going to hurt me with those sp…sp…spikes, are you?"

"No, I just thought you might like some company," Penelope replied, moving a bit closer.

"Wh-wha-what are you doing? Don't come any closer! I'm warning you…"

"Please don't be afraid," Penelope interrupted. "I promise I won't hurt you. I was just hoping we could be friends. What is your name?" She reached her paw out toward the animal, for a handshake.

"I warned you! They don't call me Squirt for nothing!"

Before she even knew what was happening, Squirt the skunk had already turned around, pointed his tail straight up, and filled the air with an awful odor. Sniffing, Penelope felt her stomach turn from the dreadful scent that Squirt had released.

"Cough! Cough! What did you do?" Penelope asked through her coughs.

"I tried to warn you," Squirt replied. "Now leave me alone. I can't trust anyone who looks as prickly as you!"

"I just thought you might like some company," Penelope said. She could feel her eyes starting to well up with tears, but she wasn't sure if it was from the smell or Squirt's reaction to her appearance. "I guess I'll leave you alone then."

"Good riddance!" Squirt shouted, as Penelope walked away sadly.

The next night didn't prove to be much better for Penelope. While nibbling on some tasty tree bark, she noticed a short, plump gray animal heading in her direction, its bright pink nose to the ground as it scavenged for a snack.

"Hi there," Penelope shouted to the opossum.

The animal stopped in its tracks, took one look at her, froze, and fell over. Penelope ran to it as fast as her little legs could carry her to try to help.

"Hey, are you okay? I didn't mean to frighten you! Hello? Heeellllloooo!" But the animal lay very still and did not move a muscle.

"Hello? Mister, are you all right?"

Still nothing.

Penelope felt horrible. What had she done? She paced back and forth near the animal for a few minutes, deciding what to do to help him. Finally, she thought it would be best to leave him alone and head toward home. She was terrified that she might make the situation worse. Was she really so frightening that she had made the animal faint? As she began to walk away, she heard a rustling in the brush behind her. When she turned back, she saw the animal's long, skinny tail disappear into the forest.

Penelope headed home that night feeling defeated. No matter what she did or how hard she tried, no one wanted to be her friend. She just couldn't understand it. As she walked, she began to think about all the ways she could try to improve her approach to meeting other forest creatures.

"If these quills just didn't look so scary," she thought. "Maybe if I covered them in mud, no one would notice them. Or maybe if I—"

Smack!

Penelope jumped when she felt something small crash into her forehead. She looked up to find a tiny glowing light in front of her.

"Ouch! Are you okay? I'm really sorry for flying into you. I should watch where I'm going, but I'm just so upset. I hope I didn't hurt you."

"Yes, I'm ok," Penelope said, trying not to laugh at the idea of the tiny insect hurting her. "What's wrong?"

"I'm so tired of it. I just had to get away!"

"Get away from what?"

"My so-called friends," the bug said.

"Why would you want to get away from your friends?" Penelope thought, but was surprised to hear herself speaking the words aloud.

"Well, you see, my parents named me Lightning because they just knew that I was going to have the strongest, brightest flashing light in the forest, just like the lightning when it rains. It turns out that my light is just a faint, dim glow. Now all the other fireflies laugh at it and tease me."

"Well, I don't see anything wrong with your light at all. Look how it shines so brightly on this path," Penelope said as she looked around.

"I guess," Lightning sighed. "Hey, what's your name?"

"What?" she asked, surprised. "You're not going to run away?"

"Well, I've already run into you, so why would I run away?"

"But aren't you afraid of my quills?" she asked nervously.

Lightning flitted around to Penelope's backside and lit up the night to take a peek at her prickly prongs.

"You mean these crazy-looking things? I actually think they go quite nicely with your spiky hairdo."

"My name is Penelope," the porcupine chuckled.

"It's a pleasure to meet you, Penelope, quills and all."

From that night on, Penelope and Lightning became inseparable. They spent their time together in the forest, laughing, playing, and enjoying each other's company. Soon they were the best of friends. Lightning helped Penelope find the most delicious plants to eat on the darkest of nights, while Penelope scared off any creatures looking for a firefly feast. By looking just a little bit deeper, Penelope and Lightning were able to find the true friendship they had both been missing for so long.

MATH EXAM

ANSWERS

Question	Skills and Categories
1. 5,096	Number, Number Sense, and Operations
2. $2\frac{1}{4}$ inches	Measurement
3. $27.00 ÷ 3 = □	Number, Number Sense, and Operations; Patterns, Functions, and Algebra
4. 790	Number, Number Sense, and Operations
5. $\frac{1}{5}$	Number, Number Sense, and Operations
6. $8.11	Number, Number Sense, and Operations; Patterns, Functions, and Algebra
7. 282	Number, Number Sense, and Operations
8. 89 x 0	Number, Number Sense, and Operations
9. 60	Number, Number Sense, and Operations; Patterns, Functions, and Algebra
10. $\frac{1}{2}$	Number, Number Sense, and Operations; Patterns, Functions, and Algebra
11. 4	Data Analysis and Probability
12. 20, 19, 22, 21, 24	Patterns, Functions, and Algebra
13. Caleb's number is odd, and Diego's number is odd.	Patterns, Functions, and Algebra
14. 18,000	Patterns, Functions, and Algebra
15. $\frac{1}{8}$	Number, Number Sense, and Operations; Patterns, Functions, and Algebra; Data Analysis and Probability
16. $1\frac{1}{4}$ inches	Measurement
17. 1,372	Number, Number Sense, and Operations; Patterns, Functions, and Algebra
18. 10	Data Analysis and Probability
19. cream cheese > bagels + jam	Patterns, Functions, and Algebra
20. They can all be divided evenly by 3.	Number, Number Sense, and Operations; Patterns, Functions, and Algebra
21. 162 yards	Measurement; Data Analysis and Probability; Patterns, Functions, and Algebra
22. 42 x (18 x 27)	Number, Number Sense, and Operations; Patterns, Functions, and Algebra
23. 1 hour and 30 minutes	Measurement
24. gram	Measurement

25.	80%	Number, Number Sense, and Operations; Patterns, Functions, and Algebra
26.	pentagon	Geometry and Spatial Sense
27.	odd number x odd number =	Number, Number Sense, and Operations; Patterns, Functions, and Algebra
28.	2 meters	Measurement
29.		Geometry and Spatial Sense
30.	21 x 18	Number, Number Sense, and Operations; Patterns, Functions, and Algebra
31.	4,705 feet	Measurement; Number, Number Sense, and Operations; Patterns, Functions, and Algebra
32.	18 baseball cards	Number, Number Sense, and Operations; Patterns, Functions, and Algebra
33.	282 beads needed	Number, Number Sense, and Operations; Patterns, Functions, and Algebra
34.	21 units	Measurement; Data Analysis and Probability
35.	$5.75	Number, Number Sense, and Operations; Patterns, Functions, and Algebra; Data Analysis and Probability
36A.	13, 16	Number, Number Sense, and Operations; Patterns, Functions, and Algebra; Data Analysis and Probability
36B.	25	Number, Number Sense, and Operations; Patterns, Functions, and Algebra; Data Analysis and Probability
36C.	Possible Answer(s): Every time you add a square you have to add an additional 3 toothpicks. Possible Cite(s): Each pattern increases by one square. Possible Explanation(s): A square has four sides and adding a square will only need to add three sides. The squares share one side when side by side.	Number, Number Sense, and Operations; Patterns, Functions, and Algebra; Data Analysis and Probability
37A.	32	Number, Number Sense, and Operations; Patterns, Functions, and Algebra
37B.	26, **22**, 18, 14, 10	Number, Number Sense, and Operations; Patterns, Functions, and Algebra

37C.	Possible Answer(s): Debbie's pattern is subtracting 4 from the previous number. Possible Cite(s): Start at the 36 and work up to 40. Subtract 52 from 48 and 48 from 44 to see if you can match. Possible Explanation(s): Describe that addition is easier. Find the first pattern and see if it can be applied to all numbers.	Number, Number Sense, and Operations; Patterns, Functions, and Algebra; Data Analysis and Probability
38A.	green	Data Analysis and Probability
38B.	4 out of 9 or 4:9 or $\frac{4}{9}$	Data Analysis and Probability
38C.	Possible Answer(s): The probability changes if you leave a cube out of the bag. Possible Cite(s): You will be left with 8 cubes instead of 9. You only have one chance to get a green. You will no longer have two chances to pull a green. Possible Explanation(s): The probability goes from 2 out of 9 to 1 out of 8. The other colors have the same number of cubes but green has only one.	Data Analysis and Probability
39A.	6 questions	Number, Number Sense, and Operations; Patterns, Functions, and Algebra
39B.	50 questions	Number, Number Sense, and Operations; Patterns, Functions, and Algebra
39C.	Possible Answer(s): Mrs. Nelson's plan is not possible. Possible Cite(s): (Calculate) 15 x 6 = 90; does not = 100 Possible Explanation(s): Increasing points to 7 does not work: 15 x 7 = 105. Some questions will have to be worth more. Mrs. Nelson can make harder questions worth more. Her original plan of making some questions worth 10 and other questions 5 is better.	Number, Number Sense, and Operations; Patterns, Functions, and Algebra
40A.	39 model airplanes	Patterns, Functions, and Algebra
40B.	Possible Answer(s): I found my answer by solving for the pattern. Possible Cite(s): Subtracted 18 from 11 to get 7. Checked to see if the pattern matched other numbers. Add 7 to each number to get next number. Possible Explanation(s): I recognized that this was a pattern. The pattern has to be the same for all numbers. Mr. Feldman builds 7 airplanes a week.	Patterns, Functions, and Algebra; Number, Number Sense, and Operations
40C.	Week 9	Patterns, Functions, and Algebra

41A. 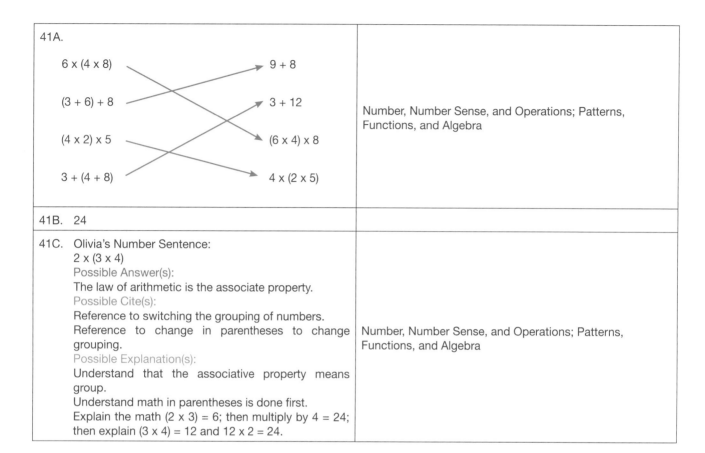	Number, Number Sense, and Operations; Patterns, Functions, and Algebra
41B. 24	
41C. Olivia's Number Sentence: 2 x (3 x 4) Possible Answer(s): The law of arithmetic is the associate property. Possible Cite(s): Reference to switching the grouping of numbers. Reference to change in parentheses to change grouping. Possible Explanation(s): Understand that the associative property means group. Understand math in parentheses is done first. Explain the math (2 x 3) = 6; then multiply by 4 = 24; then explain (3 x 4) = 12 and 12 x 2 = 24.	Number, Number Sense, and Operations; Patterns, Functions, and Algebra

For 41A, the matching:

- 6 x (4 x 8) → (6 x 4) x 8
- (3 + 6) + 8 → 3 + 12
- (4 x 2) x 5 → 4 x (2 x 5)
- 3 + (4 + 8) → 9 + 8

SCIENCE EXAM

ANSWERS

Question	Skills and Categories
1. plants	Food Chain, Biological Science/Life Science
2. frogs and snakes	Interactions of Living Things, Biological Science/Life Science
3. increase	Environment, Biological Science/Life Science
4. water	Water Cycle; Solid, Liquid, Gas; Physical Science
5. adapt to their environment	Adaptations, Biological Science/Life Science
6. a pumpkin	Botany, Biological Science/Life Science
7. There are more hours of daylight as the month goes on.	Earth's Systems, Earth and Space Science
8. cover them	Temperature, Meteorology, Earth and Space Science
9. a puddle drying in the sun	Water Cycle, Physical Science
10. the sun	Processes of Life, Biological Science/Life Science
11. C	Water Cycle, Physical Science, Scientific Investigation and the Nature of Science
12A. leaves	Characteristics of Living Things, Botany, Biological Science/Life Science
12B. roots	Characteristics of Living Things, Botany, Biological Science/Life Science
12C. flower	Characteristics of Living Things, Botany, Biological Science/Life Science
13. butterfly (4), egg (1), chrysalis (3), caterpillar (2)	Characteristics of Living Things, Zoology, Anatomy, Biological Science/Life Science, Scientific Investigation and the Nature of Science
14. brown	Characteristics and Structure of Living Things, Anatomy and Physiology, Scientific Investigation and the Nature of Science
15. 15 blue eyes, 28 brown eyes, 10 green eyes (show on bar graph)	Characteristics and Structure of Living Things, Anatomy and Physiology, Scientific Investigation and the Nature of Science
16. **Answers may include but are not limited to:** hair color, physical features (dimples, freckles, attached earlobes, shape of nose and/or mouth), height, weight, special abilities (athleticism, musical ability, IQ)	Characteristics and Structure of Living Things, Anatomy and Physiology, Scientific Investigation and the Nature of Science
17. **Answers may include but are not limited to:** ability to ride a bike, read, speak a language, and/or play board games; friendliness, personality	Anatomy and Physiology, Scientific Investigation and the Nature of Science
18. green	Evaluate Data, Physical Science, Scientific Investigation and the Nature of Science

19.	The life span of a horse is longer than the life span of a dog.	Evaluate Data, Biological Science/Life Science, Scientific Investigation and the Nature of Science
20A.	The teacher thought the frog was pretty. The insects looked scary.	Observation, Scientific Investigation and the Nature of Science, Biological Science/Life Science
20B.	they counted six legs on each insect; green frog; a beaver; smooth snake or brown snake or smooth brown snake	Observation, Scientific Investigation and the Nature of Science, Biological Science/Life Science
21.	Possible Answer(s): There are many ways that seeds are dispersed: by wind, by water, on animal's fur Possible Cite(s): reference to seed attached to clothing; walking in a field Possible Explanation(s): some seeds blow in the wind; animals in a field will carry seeds	Dispersal, Scientific Investigation and the Nature of Science, Biological Science/Life Science
22.	**Answers may include but are not limited to:** can build houses; can build a park	Environmental Impact, Scientific Investigation and the Nature of Science, Biological Science/Life Science
23.	**Answers may include but are not limited to:** environmental impact, impact on animals, soil erosion (soil will wash away), air quality	Environmental Impact, Scientific Investigation and the Nature of Science, Physical Science, Earth and Space Science
24.	**Answers may include a variation of:** warmer weather for survival	Zoology, Migration, Scientific Investigation and the Nature of Science, Biological Science/Life Science
25.	**Answers should include a variation of:** mouth, lungs, eyes, tail	Data Evaluation, Scientific Investigation and the Nature of Science, Biological Science/Life Science
26.	**Answers should include a variation of:** cats have fur, birds have feathers; cats have teeth, birds have beaks	Data Evaluation, Scientific Investigation and the Nature of Science, Biological Science/Life Science
27.	**Answers may include but are not limited to:** loss of food source, loss of habitat, danger from predators (humans)	Environmental Impact, Biomes, Biological Science/Life Science, Scientific Investigation and the Nature of Science
28.	Possible Answer(s): There are many reasons that animals hibernate in the winter. Student can identify: cold weather, temperature, lack of food source Possible Cite(s): The change in the environment can be identified in answer portion for the citation. cold weather, temperature, lack of food source Possible Explanation(s): connection to animals that hibernate: bears, frogs, moths, snakes, butterflies, mosquitoes, turtles, ladybugs, bees	Weather, Hibernation, Environment, Biological Science/Life Science, Scientific Investigation and the Nature of Science
29.	**Answers may include but are not limited to:** color, feathers, thickness of feathers	Adaptations, Biological Science/Life Science

SOCIAL STUDIES EXAM

ANSWERS

	Question	Skills and Categories
1.	the Supreme Court	Branches of Government; Government: Local, State, and National
2.	Cailyn pays twenty dollars for a new soccer ball.	Money, Monetary System, Meeting Basic Needs and Wants
3.	11:30 a.m.	Time Zones, Maps, Location and Geographic Characteristics
4.	Central	Time Zones, Maps, US States, Location and Geographic Characteristics
5.	different natural resources available to them	Natural, Capital, and Human Resources; Location and Geographic Characteristics; Meeting Basic Needs and Wants
6.	The government had no judicial branch.	United States Constitution; Branches of Government; Government: Local, State, and National
7.	Iroquois	Native Americans, United States Regions, Early Inhabitants and European Encounter, Culture and History of World Communities
8.	factories used water to power machines	Industry, Colonial Life, Meeting Basic Needs and Wants, Location and Geographic Characteristics
9.	lower the demand for tires	Supply and Demand, Economy, Meeting Basic Needs and Wants
10.	is the center of the state government	State; Government: Local, State, and National; Location and Geographic Characteristics
11.	rivers	Geography, Natural Resources, Location and Geographic Characteristics, Meeting Basic Needs and Wants
12.	The Hopi had the best ceremonies in the Southwest region.	Native Americans, Regions, Early Inhabitants and European Encounter, Culture and History of World Communities
13.	the men and women who died while serving in the United States Armed Services	National Holidays; Culture and History of World Communities; Government: Local, State, and National
14.	fish	Natural Resources; US States; Natural, Capital, and Human Resources
15.	Louisiana produces fish and cotton.	Natural, Capital, and Human Resources; Regions; US States; Location and Geographic Characteristics
16.	housing	American Revolution, Colonial Life, Governments
17.	Spanish	Spanish Colony, Early Inhabitants and European Encounter, Location and Geographic Characteristics
18.	prime meridian	Longitude and Latitude, Location and Geographic Characteristics
19.	landforms	Maps, Location and Geographic Characteristics
20.	1626	Early Settlement, Slavery, Northeast Region, Location and Geographic Characteristics, Colonial Life

21.	There was slavery throughout the colonies.	Slavery, Regions, Colonial Life
22.	citizen	Rights and Responsibilities; Citizenship; Government: Local, State, and National
23.	vetoes bills from becoming a law	Branches of Government; United States Congress; Government: Local, State, and National (Special note: Supreme Court Justices are approved by the United States Senate only.)
24.	Citizens learned about western Native Americans.	Exploration, Regions, US States, Culture and History of World Communities, Location and Geographic Characteristics
25.	freedom of speech	Rights and Responsibilities; Bill of Rights; United States Constitution; Government: Local, State, and National
26.	It gave us a good example of self-rule.	Artifacts, History, Culture and History of World Communities, Governments
27.	persuade the government to end slavery	Rights and Responsibilities, Colonial Life
28.	Mayflower Compact -> Declaration of Independence -> United States Constitution	Artifacts; History; Governments; Government: Local, State, and National
29.	Polly gives Abe a basketball in exchange for a football.	Money, Economy, Meeting Basic Needs and Wants
30.	the Grand Canyon	Regions, Landforms, Location and Geographic Characteristics
31.	**Answers may include but are not limited to:** settlers moved west, railroad access, increase in white settlements	Westward Settlement, Pioneers, Railroads, Location and Geographic Characteristics, Meeting Basic Needs and Wants
32.	**Answers should include a variation of:** loss of grazing land, increase in hunting, increase in housing for settlers, hit by trains	Settlers, Pioneers, Westward Settlement, Railroads, Culture and History of World Communities, Location and Geographic Characteristics
33.	**Answers may include but are not limited to:** give thanks for blessings, give thanks to family, celebrate a year of good luck, celebrate family health and happiness	Holiday Celebrations, Customs, Culture and History of World Communities
34.	**Answers may include but are not limited to:** yams, mashed yams, hard-boiled eggs, eggs, Kpekpele, cornmeal, palm oil	Holiday Celebrations, Customs, Culture and History of World Communities
35.	**Answers may include but are not limited to:** give thanks, watch parades, eat a big feast	Holiday Celebrations, Customs, Culture and History of World Communities
Section 3 Part A Artifact 1. Possible Answer(s): used turtle as a calendar, track weather Possible Cite(s): changing seasons, track new moon, types of changes to world around them Possible Explanation(s): know when seasons will change for farming, didn't have clocks to tell time, didn't have calendars like we do today		Artifacts, History, Native Americans, Meeting Basic Needs and Wants, Early Inhabitants and European Encounter, Culture and History of World Communities

Section 3 Artifact 2. **Answers may include but are not limited to:** Column A: (1-3) buckskin, porcupine quills, deerskin, feathers, deer hooves Column B: (1 – 3) dress, moccasin, leggings, headdress, rattles	Artifacts, History, Clothing, Native Americans, Meeting Basic Needs and Wants, Early Inhabitants and European Encounter, Culture and History of World Communities
Section 3 Artifact 3. **Answers for 1 and 2 may include but are not limited to:** cornhusks for masks turtle shells for rattles feathers for fans water for drums wood for drums animal horns for rattles	Artifacts, History, Native Americans, Ceremonies, Meeting Basic Needs and Wants, Early Inhabitants and European Encounter, Culture and History of World Communities
Section 3 Artifact 4. **Answers may include but are not limited to:** 1. Used tree branches to make snowshoes. 2. Used bark or wood to make toboggans. 3. Used branches, bark, and wood to build canoes.	Artifacts, History, Native Americans, Transportation, Meeting Basic Needs and Wants, Early Inhabitants and European Encounter, Culture and History of World Communities
Section 3 Artifact 5. **Answers may include but are not limited to:** Column A: (1 – 2) trees/wood, branches, bark, deerskin, vines Column B: (1 – 2) make longhouse, frame of longhouse, cover roofs, cover sides of longhouse, tie frames together	Artifacts, Regions, Native Americans, Meeting Basic Needs and Wants, Early Inhabitants and European Encounter, Culture and History of World Communities
Section 3 Part B: Essay **4 (Advanced):** • Thoroughly addresses all tasks by relating how Northeast region Native Americans used natural resources to fulfill their needs and wants by including information from the artifacts. • Incorporates text-to-self or text-to-world connections related to Northeast region Native Americans' use of corn, deer, ceremonial beliefs, ideas of tribe, or other details using knowledge of content and concepts. • Uses consistently accurate data to explain Northeast region Native Americans' use of natural resources to meet their needs and wants (transportation, shelter) with examples from the text. • Develops thorough and full ideas of how the Northeast region Native Americans used natural resources with examples from the text. • Demonstrates a logical plan of organization and flow of information; includes an introductory paragraph, a body, and a conclusion. • Expresses consistently clear ideas about the Northeast region Native Americans' use of natural resources.	Artifacts, History, Native Americans, Meeting Basic Needs and Wants, Early Inhabitants and European Encounter, Culture and History of World Communities